Charles Simeon

Charles Simeon
——— Parish Pastor ———

Zack DiPrima

WIPF & STOCK · Eugene, Oregon

Charles Simeon
Parish Pastor

Copyright © 2025 Zack DiPrima. All rights reserved. Except for brief quotations in critical publications or reviews, no part of this book may be reproduced in any manner without prior written permission from the publisher. Write: Permissions, Wipf and Stock Publishers, 199 W. 8th Ave., Suite 3, Eugene, OR 97401.

Wipf & Stock
An Imprint of Wipf and Stock Publishers
199 W. 8th Ave., Suite 3
Eugene, OR 97401
www.wipfandstock.com

PAPERBACK ISBN: 979-8-3852-5057-8
HARDCOVER ISBN: 979-8-3852-5058-5
EBOOK ISBN: 979-8-3852-5059-2

VERSION NUMBER 09/10/25

Scripture quotations are from the The Authorized (King James) Version. Rights in the Authorized Version in the United Kingdom are vested in the Crown. Reproduced by permission of the Crown's patentee, Cambridge University Press.

To my beloved wife Erin, my light when all else fails,
For the glory of God.

Contents

Preface | vii

1 Introduction | 1
2 Ministerial Mentor | 15
3 Anglican Archetype | 57
4 Personal Piety | 92
5 Parish Pastor | 129
6 Preaching Paragon | 155
7 Conclusion | 192

Bibliography | 199

Preface

As an heir to the Reformed tradition, I find myself in constant debt to evangelicals of the eighteenth and nineteenth centuries. And even though I was reared in the heritage of the *Second London Baptist Confession*—a statement of faith to which I remain loyal—my spirituality has been mostly shaped by evangelical Anglicans. Besides living mentors, I have learned most from the ministries of Richard Sibbes (1577–1635), John Newton (1725–1807), Charles Bridges (1794–1869), J. C. Ryle (1816–1900), and of course, Charles Simeon (1759–1836). These men were not only exemplary exegetes, but they were also bright and shining models of pastoral faithfulness. As a young pastor, I am in constant need of mentors, both dead and living. I am deeply indebted to my faithful wife Erin for her tireless support over the years dedicated to this project. I also am profoundly grateful for the churches that have encouraged my studies, particularly Mount Vernon Baptist Church in Sandy Springs and Trinity Church Kennesaw.

My hope is that this project on the pastoral theology of Charles Simeon will cast a spotlight on the zealous, warm, evangelical character of his ministry. I desire that pastors recognize not only the truth of his theology, but also the beauty of his character. The broader evangelical movement today aches for a generation of pastors whose ministries are infused with the savor of Christ. Therefore, I wish to see a recovery of the tenor of Simeon's ministry.

Zack DiPrima
Atlanta, Georgia
June 2025

CHAPTER 1

Introduction

ON SEPTEMBER 18, 1836, Charles Simeon (1759–1836) descended from the pulpit of Holy Trinity Church in Cambridge for the last time. The "leading evangelical clergyman"[1] preached his final sermon on 2 Kgs 10:16, "Come with me and see my zeal for the Lord," a fitting text for a ministry marked by unbridled devotion to God and his church.[2] After more than a half-century in the pastorate, the aged and illustrious Simeon reaped the rewards of his extensive ministry. By this point, hundreds filled the church, flocking to hear the seasoned preacher in his golden years. Many of his hearers were young ordinands who would go on to fill Anglican pulpits across the British Empire. Simeon died on November 13, 1836, with thousands in Cambridge mourning his passing.[3]

One might assume Simeon was warmly received by his congregation when ordained vicar at the age of twenty-three. This was not so. Though in a former period, Holy Trinity benefited from an extraordinary heritage of celebrated preachers such as Richard Sibbes (1577–1635), John Preston (1587–1628), and Thomas Goodwin (1600–1680), the circumstances of Simeon's appointment were controversial, resulting in the congregation's bitter opposition toward him for many years.[4] The parishioners despised his evangelical convictions. Their dislike of their

---

1. Atherstone, *Charles Simeon*, 4.
2. Hopkins, *Charles Simeon of Cambridge*, 210.
3. Hopkins, *Charles Simeon of Cambridge*, 212.
4. Carus, *Memoirs*, 40–43.

new vicar was such that they made every effort to impede his ability to preach. Regularly, the churchwardens would lock the building to prevent the hearing of Simeon's sermons. Not only would members boycott his preaching, but some also went as far as to lock their pews to prevent others from hearing him.[5] Such antics were the norm for Simeon during the first several years of his ministry. Even when these more extreme measures subsided, many of Simeon's parishioners remained cold toward him and the gospel he preached. Such was the environment of his early days in Cambridge in the 1780s and 1790s.

Yet opposition failed to remain the dominant theme of Simeon's life. Rather, his tenure at Holy Trinity was marked by triumph through perseverance, leading a ministry which spanned the reign of three kings. Moreover, evangelicalism in Cambridge—and the Church of England more broadly—experienced meteoric growth over the course of his lifetime. When Simeon arrived at Cambridge in the late 1770s, the evangelical movement had limited institutional influence on the Church of England.[6] By his death in 1836, it is estimated that a third of Anglican pulpits were evangelical.[7] Such a massive shift in the established church is partly attributable to the influence of Simeon's pulpit, an eminent element of a larger philosophy of ministry.[8] Thus, Lord Macaulay (1800–1859)—nearly a decade after Simeon's death—testified of Simeon's titanic impact on the nation and her church. "As to Simeon, if you knew what his authority and influence were, and how they extended from Cambridge to the most remote corners of England, you would allow that his real sway in the church was far greater than that of any primate [i.e., Archbishop]."[9] Historian Charles Smyth attests that Simeon "more than any other inspired and promoted the evangelical revival in the second and third generation of its course."[10] From his post at Holy Trinity, Simeon revitalized a local church, raised a new generation of pastors, and refined a burgeoning global movement.[11]

---

5. Carus, *Memoirs*, 43–45.
6. Prime, *Charles Simeon*, 239.
7. Prime, *Charles Simeon*, 239.
8. Bebbington, *Evangelicalism in Modern Britain*, 31–32.
9. Hopkins, *Charles Simeon of Cambridge*, 118.
10. Smyth, *Simeon and Church Order*, 18.
11. Hindmarsh, *Life and Spirituality*, 326.

Charles Simeon's Life and Ministry

Simeon was born the fourth and youngest son of Richard Simeon (d. 1784), a gentleman who afforded Charles an education at Eton College. Subsequent to his childhood, Simeon spent his entire adult life in Cambridge. Shortly after his matriculation at King's College, he experienced an evangelical conversion in the context of the Anglican communion service. Despite the lukewarm tone and presentation common in his day among Cambridge ministers, the rich words of the liturgy, assisted by a devotional work titled *Instruction for the Lord's Supper*,[12] haunted Simeon's conscience in the weeks leading up to taking communion. Simeon recounted his conversion in the following way.

> But in Easter week . . . I met with an expression to this effect: "That the Jews knew what they did when they transferred their sin to the head of their offering." The thought rushed into my mind, What! May I transfer my guilt to another? Has God provided an offering for me, that I may lay my sins on his head? Then, God willing, I will not bear them on my own soul one moment longer. Accordingly I sought to lay my sins upon the sacred head of Jesus . . . and on the Sunday morning (Easter-day, April 4) I awoke early with those words upon my heart and lips, "Jesus Christ is risen today! Hallelujah! Hallelujah!" From that hour peace flowed in rich abundance into my soul; and at the Lord's table in our chapel I had the sweetest access to God through my blessed Saviour.[13]

Soon after his conversion, Simeon earned the attention of Henry Venn (1725–1797), the experienced, evangelical vicar of Yelling. Under Venn's close guidance, he blossomed into an earnest, powerful preacher. At the Bishop of Ely's appointment, partly through his father's influence, Simeon assumed the role of priest at Holy Trinity Church in 1783. He would be despised for over a decade. In this prolonged season, Simeon found comfort in the apostle Paul's words to Timothy: "The servant of the Lord must not strive; but be gentle unto all men, apt to teach, patient" (2 Tim 2:24). Though bruised by the opposition of his flock, Simeon emerged through years of trials with a steadfast commitment to the spiritual good of his parish. Year by year, Simeon's congregation grew—warmed to and won over by his way of conducting ministry. Gradually, yet definitively,

---

12. Wilson, *Short and Plain Instruction*.
13. Carus, *Memoirs*, 9.

his pulpit became a mainstay in the middle of Cambridge, granting him influence over both the town and gown.

As a fellow of King's College, and eventual dean, Simeon made a steady habit of mentoring young men. These relationships were not primarily academic, but spiritual in nature. Simeon gave most of his time to men who aspired to ministerial service. Perhaps the most famous of these men was Henry Martyn (1781–1812), who served as Simeon's curate before pursuing missionary work in India.[14]

Simeon made concerted efforts to mentor young men through various means. He hosted regular tea meetings for anyone interested in asking questions about the Bible.[15] These "conversation parties" normally took place on Friday nights with up to eighty students crammed into a sitting room. There they probed the mind of the veteran preacher regarding Scripture, theology, and pastoral ministry. At these meetings, Simeon made a point of personally acquainting himself with each of his guests. When young men attended a conversation party for the first time, they seldom left without Simeon greeting them and recording their names in a journal.

Simeon also hosted sermon classes for men called to preach.[16] These smaller gatherings were by invite only. In each session, Simeon would offer a text for consideration. Men would then be charged to produce a sermon outline for the text. After they presented, feedback would follow. Thus, Simeon slowly transmitted his particular brand of evangelical preaching to an entire generation of Anglican ministers.

The pulpit of Holy Trinity was of course the primary means by which Simeon exerted his influence. To this day, his preaching arguably remains his most enduring legacy. The twenty-one volumes of *Horae Homileticae* capture well Simeon's method of expository preaching. These sermon skeletons (as he called them) have served preachers for generations, including a young Charles Spurgeon (1834–1892) who read Simeon's sermons as a teenager. Simeon was renowned for his regular verse by verse exposition of biblical texts. He always asserted, "My endeavor is to bring out of Scripture what is there, and not to thrust in what I think might be there."[17] According to Simeon, true preaching

---

14. For a short treatment of the life of Henry Martyn, see Rhea, *Life of Henry Martyn*.

15. Brown, *Recollections*.

16. Brown, *Recollections*, 51.

17. Moule, *Charles Simeon*, 97.

must ultimately possess three chief aims: to humble the sinner, exalt the Savior, and promote holiness.[18] For over five decades, Simeon gave himself to this kind of preaching in the pulpit of Holy Trinity. Thousands gathered to hear Simeon preach over the years, including hundreds of future ministers who embraced Simeon's evangelical faith. Even some fifteen years after his death, budding preachers like Charles Spurgeon were using Simeon's manuscripts, a testament to the latter's enduring, cross-denominational influence.[19]

In addition to training ministers, Simeon gave himself intermittently to a robust itinerancy in Scotland. He also participated in the evangelical Clapham Sect, a London-based activist society which rarely permitted the involvement of non-Londoners. This detail bears witness to Simeon's massive profile within evangelical, Anglican circles. He kept close correspondence with other prominent figures such as John Newton (1725–1807), William Wilberforce (1759–1833), Thomas Chalmers (1780–1847), and Henry Venn.

In his groundbreaking study *Evangelicalism in Modern Britain*, David Bebbington historically surveys the diverse evangelical world, identifying four unifying characteristics of the movement: biblicism, crucicentrism, conversionism, and activism.[20] Invariably, Simeon modeled each of these characteristics, epitomizing the heart of evangelicalism in Anglican mode. Though friendly with Nonconformity, Simeon was a son of England's church. As an Anglican archetype, his great project was to steel the evangelical wing of his denomination. But what gave Simeon such decisive, lasting influence, enough to earn him the accolade of "Evangelicalism's most shining vessel"?[21]

Summary of Research

Though Simeon's written legacy might be described as monolithic, it was nonetheless prolific. He published twenty-one volumes of sermon expositions which covered the range of the entire Bible.[22] The project began in the 1790s after he had discovered a short work on preaching titled

18. Simeon, *Expository Outlines*, 1:xxi.
19. Spurgeon, *Lost Sermons*, 1:258, 1:295.
20. Bebbington, *Evangelicalism in Modern Britain*, 3.
21. Brown, *Fathers of the Victorians*, 271.
22. Simeon, *Expository Outlines*.

An Essay on the Composition of a Sermon by Jean Claude (1619–1687), a French Calvinist Divine.[23] Simeon found Claude to confirm his own developing pulpit philosophy. As a result, he zealously circulated the essay in 1796 along with a hundred of his own sermons. This collection constituted the first edition of Simeon's twenty-one volume magnum opus titled *Horae Homileticae*, which, having been completed in 1832, comprised over 2,500 of his sermon outlines. Though out of print today, these sermons, or "skeletons" as he liked to call them, were widely read in his lifetime and the years thereafter, providing the clearest window into his heart, mind, and ministry philosophy. Besides *Horae Homileticae*, he penned no other major works. Arthur Pollard (1922–2002) has well-preserved Simeon's preaching legacy in an edited volume titled *Let Wisdom Judge*, published by Inter-Varsity Press in 1959.

Simeon died in 1836 at the ripe age of seventy-seven. The following decades were flooded with a steady stream of Simeon memoranda. Within the nineteenth century, three works emerged as most influential. First, Simeon's last curate and successor at Holy Trinity, William Carus (1804–1891) published *Memoirs of the Life of the Rev. Charles Simeon, M.A.* in 1837. Though hagiographical by intent, the work provides the starting point for all Simeon historiography and scholarship. The first section of the work includes a few hundred pages of biography which toggle between Carus's narrative and Simeon's own autobiographical reflections. The second part presents roughly four hundred pages of Simeon's personal correspondences. The final and briefest section records the narrative of Simeon's death and funeral, followed by a tribute from Daniel Wilson (1778–1858), the Bishop of Calcutta. Though a thorough memoir, Carus refrains from a detailed focus on how Simeon developed his specific philosophy of ministry and the impact that philosophy had on his followers.

The second significant Simeon biography of the nineteenth century was *Charles Simeon* by Handley Carr Glynn Moule (1841–1920), published in 1892. Moule studied at Trinity College Cambridge in the 1860s, a time when Simeon's posthumous presence still loomed large. His account of Simeon relies heavily on Carus and other memoirs, tracing an orderly cradle-to-grave narrative of Simeon's life. Notably, Moule heavily draws on *Recollections of the Conversation Parties of the Rev. Charles Simeon, M.A.* by Abner Brown (1800–1872), published in 1863. Similar

---

23. Claude, *Composition of a Sermon*.

to Carus's narrative, Moule foregoes a rigorous examination of Simeon's pastoral theology, though his fulsome use of Brown reveals more of the heart behind Simeon's ministry than previous accounts.

Brown's *Recollections* was undoubtedly the third most significant nineteenth century resource on Simeon. As noted above, Simeon's conversation parties—or "Colloquial Lectures" as Brown referred to them—were a highly strategic means of influencing his followers.[24] What he could not accomplish in the pulpit he achieved in personal discourse with his pupils. Dozens upon dozens crammed into a crowded parlor to hear from Simeon. There from the confines of his own home, he knew and was known. *Recollections* offers a fresh and fascinating glimpse into the mind of Simeon. Brown reflected on the motivation for his work,

> To the literary world, Simeon is chiefly known as the compiler of twenty-one volumes of very dry sermons, mainly useful for assisting young Clergymen in Sermon writing. The popular idea depicts him as an amiable and somewhat eccentric Preacher of the last generation, an enthusiastic promoter of strictness in religion, and an active leader of the Evangelical Party. These estimates are sufficiently accurate; yet who that knew Simeon would accept either or both as a satisfactory delineation of him? As a speaker in public or in private, he was never dry; his eccentricity was not what usually bears the name; and he belonged much more to a *via media* position than to the ranks of a party. A volume which, though not literally so, should be something in the nature of "Simeon's Table Talk," appears to be still a *desideratum*, both to the religious world at large, and to those individual Clergy and others with whose undergraduate life his memory is associated.[25]

Indeed, as Martin Luther (1483–1546) had his *Table Talk* and Charles Spurgeon delivered his *Lectures*, Simeon's thought and personality are well preserved in *Recollections*.[26] Abner Brown—who pursued undergraduate studies at Cambridge from 1827 to 1830—was one of Simeon's many close pupils. He sought to record nearly every interaction with his mentor by diligently taking notes. However, while commending his process and impartiality, Brown quickly acknowledged the limitations of his project. He wrote,

---

24. Brown, *Recollections*, xiii.
25. Brown, *Recollections*, x.
26. Spurgeon, *Lectures to My Students*.

> Although not aware of inaccuracies, the writer cannot hope that his notes would be always free from mistakes; and, however desirous to write down exactly the impression left on his mind, he may probably at times have misunderstood Simeon's meaning, or have failed to record some explanatory remarks. If there be found discrepancies between these notes and Mr. Simeon's published writings, they have arisen either from those causes, or from Mr. Simeon's having, as sometimes happened, slightly modified an opinion or qualified some of its bearings. The work is not designed as a eulogy on the venerable man to whom it refers, but as an honest record of recollections of him, occasionally containing opinions with which the writer may happen to disagree, or anecdotes which, perhaps, he may regret.[27]

Recollections is arguably the greatest window into Simeon's pastoral theology. However, it does not systemize Simeon's thought, nor does it examine the influence of Simeon's ministry philosophy on his pupils.

Over the course of the twentieth century, three works significantly advanced Simeon historiography. First, Cambridge Press published Charles Smyth's *Simeon and Church Order* in 1940.[28] Smyth's work was a product of lectures delivered in 1937. In extraordinary detail, the author examines the academic and religious climate of Cambridge, noting how Simeon advanced an enduring brand of evangelicalism within the Church of England.

> Evangelicals would sooner or later have left the Church of England even as the Methodists had done. And that would have been a great disaster both for the Evangelical Party and for the Church of England. It was Simeon who, more than any other single individual, taught the younger Evangelicals to love the Church of England and enabled them to feel that they belonged within her body.[29]

Smyth shows how Simeon secured the continuity of his convictions without breaking from church order.[30] Simeon followed the regular pattern of Henry Venn of Yelling over the more eccentric John Berridge of Everton (1716–1793). Smyth offers the most substantive study on Simeon's ecclesiology, a subset of his broader pastoral theology. Through focusing on

---

27. Brown, *Recollections*, xii.
28. Smyth, *Simeon and Church Order*.
29. Smyth, *Simeon and Church Order*, 311.
30. Smyth, *Simeon and Church Order*, 310.

Simeon's churchmanship, Smyth's project expounds one of the features that marked Simeon's evangelical Anglican followers.

Second, marking the bicentennial of Simeon's birth, Michael Hennell and Arthur Pollard published an edited volume of essays with the SPCK titled *Charles Simeon (1759–1836)*.[31] Within it, Douglas Webster pens a worthwhile chapter on "Simeon's Pastoral Theology."[32]

Hugh Evan Hopkins produced the third significant Simeon resource of the twentieth century: *Charles Simeon of Cambridge*, published by Hodder & Stoughton in 1977. Hopkins complements the standard source material on Simeon's life with fulsome records from the King's College Library, Simeon Trust, Church Missionary Society, and Ridley Hall.[33] Hopkins's research and prose has preserved the legacy of Charles Simeon. To this day, his work offers twenty-first century readers the greatest introduction to Simeon. Though not indifferent to Simeon's view of the pastorate, Hopkins makes no scholarly attempt to appraise Simeon's pastoral theology and its sustained impact on his followers.

In addition to Smyth and Hopkins, four more narrow academic studies have cast a light on Simeon's life in recent decades. Wesley Balda's "Spheres of Influence" examines the implications of Simeon's patronage of livings for evangelicals, an ecclesiastical project that illumines the nature of evangelical ministry in a post-Simeon Anglican context.[34] John Bennett's dissertation "Charles Simeon and the Evangelical Anglican Missionary Movement" presents an in-depth look at the genesis of the Church Missionary Society and Simeon's broader impact on Christian missiology.[35] Meanwhile, Barbara Becht's thesis "Charles Simeon: Evangelical or Churchman" gives significant attention to Simeon's contribution to historical Anglican disputes over baptism.[36] Despite the title of her work, Becht's central aim is to relay Simeon's view of Christian baptism. Finally, the Oxford historian Andrew Atherstone rounds out Simeon's profile with a short work on his relationship to Anglican worship titled

---

31. Hennell and Pollard, *Charles Simeon (1759–1836)*.

32. Webster, "Simeon's Pastoral Theology," 73–119. Webster's work is mostly focused on the way that Simeon's theology was pastorally applied, rather than providing a comprehensive presentation of his view of the pastorate. Neither does he review the extent of Simeon's influence on his pupils. That said, he notably considers Simeon as a "spiritual director, concerned with helping people to live the Christian life" (101).

33. Hopkins, *Charles Simeon of Cambridge*, 7.

34. Balda, "Spheres of Influence."

35. Bennett, "Charles Simeon."

36. Becht, "Charles Simeon."

Charles Simeon on the Excellency of the Liturgy.[37] This will not be Atherstone's only contribution. Evangelical historians await his forthcoming collection of Charles Simeon's letters. This survey of scholarship reveals a need for a careful study of that feature of Simeon's ministry which gave him his impact: pastoral theology.

Thesis

This book argues that the driving force behind Charles Simeon's storied ministry was a robust pastoral theology. While due attention has been given to Simeon's preaching, his pulpit formed only one feature of a broader perspective of the pastorate. I believe this perspective is worthy of further study. Simeon held a well-orbed view of the pastorate that included distinct approaches to churchmanship, personal piety, local parish ministry, and preaching.[38] Simeon tirelessly gave his life to training young ordinands in a period when the vast majority of England's ministers were educated in Cambridge and Oxford.[39] The unquenchable flame of his gospel convictions inspired an army of pastors who advanced his view of ministry to every corner of the British Empire. As a mammoth figure in evangelicalism, the breadth of Simeon's impact was not only profound, but also distinct in quality from fellow peers in the long eighteenth century. George Whitefield (1714–1770) and John Wesley (1703–1791) well earned their reputation as the great evangelists of early evangelicalism. Yet it should be noted: the pair unapologetically led *outward-facing* ministries. The extent of their global exploits was nothing short of staggering. Wesley was accurate when he famously quipped, "I look upon all the world as my parish."[40] John Newton, for his part, left a legacy of letters that deeply shaped the spirituality of evangelicals across England. Though a dedicated parish priest, he maintained close correspondence with a wide array of contacts across the country, giving

---

37. Atherstone, *Charles Simeon*.

38. By "pastoral theology," I refer to the subset of practical theology that comprises one's philosophy of ministry. For Simeon, this comprised four distinct emphases: churchmanship, pastoral character, parish ministry, and preaching.

39. For more on Anglican education in the later Georgian Period, see Slinn, *Education*. Slinn has presented compelling research to prove a significant portion of Anglican clergy did not go to Oxford or Cambridge, though the vast majority did, indeed, attend these institutions.

40. Wesley, *Works*, 1:190.

constant attention to needs *outside* his locale. Meanwhile, Simeon had a different strategy for impacting global Christianity. As Historian Michael Hennell asserts, "He himself kept to his parish boundaries and he taught his ordinands to do the same."[41] By staying local and exemplifying an extraordinary commitment to ordinary ministry, he marshalled a multitude of zealous men ready to follow his model. Thus, he indelibly marked the Church of England and the world.

This book highlights Simeon's chosen means of influencing others: pastoral theology. In order to reach people *outside* his parish, he molded pastors—and in order to train pastors, he cared for the people *within* his parish.[42] He developed his philosophy of ministry through the crucible of trials early in his tenure. Over time, he demonstrated his pastoral theology to eager onlookers, explicitly educating them in his way of thought. With profound devotion to the Church of England, he knew his denomination was only as strong as her pastors. From his post at Holy Trinity and King's College, he infused young ordinands with his evangelical doctrine and priorities. Simeon understood every pastorate ("livings" as they were often referred to in his time) in the established church to be a sphere of influence.[43] In his particular sphere, he had a plentiful harvest of both needy members and future ministers.

Methodology

Because my book will examine the pastoral theology of Charles Simeon, I will seek to discern his vision for the Christian ministry, including those parts that were inherited and those that were wholly original. My project will endeavor to uncover what he viewed to be the role of a pastor. I shall accomplish this by examining what he thought, taught, practiced, and preached. My project will also highlight how his pastoral theology manifested itself in his followers.

The greatest window into the mind of a man is the man himself. Thus, I will make liberal use of Simeon's *Horae Homileticae*.[44] Millions

---

41. Hennell, *Sons of the Prophets*, 2.

42. "He succeeded beyond Cambridge because he succeeded in Cambridge." Pollard, "Influence and Significance," 181.

43. Carus, *Memoirs*, 780–81.

44. This work will use the same version of *Horae Homileticae* throughout. See Simeon, *Expository Outlines*. Parenthetical texts of Scripture will be included in as they appear in this version of *Horae Homileticae*.

of words comprise Simeon's expositions of the Bible. For Simeon, the Scriptures formed the only authority for life and doctrine. While he cared little for the thoughts of dead theologians, the Bible was the very word of God. Therefore, Simeon's expositions must dominate my study. His pastoral theology cannot be understood apart from the pervasive citation of his commentaries, especially highlighting his work on the Pastoral Epistles.

As for what Simeon taught, Brown's *Recollections* provides extensive material on his pastoral theology. Every week—whether through conversation parties or sermon classes—he taught students how to shepherd sheep. The greatest challenge of my project will be uncovering Simeon's specific approach to shepherding his parish. However, I expect to sketch a vivid portrait of his parochial practice from the content in Brown's *Recollections*, Carus's work, Simeon's hundreds of letters, local parish records, and the memoirs of his curates, peers, and pupils.[45]

Summary of Content

Chapter 2 ("Ministerial Mentor") will show how Simeon endowed a generation of evangelical ministers with his particular pastoral theology. I will describe the nature of his relationships with pupils, and the values he chose to emphasize. Based on the historical evidence, I will assert the breadth of Simeon's influence on the Church of England, and thus, global Christianity. This chapter will highlight lives and ministries of several of Simeon's prominent followers, including John Sumner (1780–1862), Patrick Brontë (1777–1861), Henry Martyn, Francis Close (1797–1882), Thomas Thomason (1774–1809), William Carus, and Charles Bridges (1794–1869).

In order to treat Simeon's pastoral theology, he must be appreciated in the context of his relationship to Anglicanism. Though Simeon held fiercely to his evangelical convictions, chapter 3 ("Anglican Archetype") will present Simeon as a devoted son of England's established

---

45. Scotland, *Evangelical Anglicans*, 362. On Simeon's letters in particular, Scotland remarks that he was "a prolific letter writer and stated that he had seven thousand copies of his letters, which he retained in case anyone should attempt to misrepresent him. For Simeon as for many Evangelicals, letter writing was not merely an art; it was a very real part of his spirituality. In correspondence he encouraged those on the mission field, congratulated people on their appointments, consoled the bereaved, advised younger and misguided clergy, and gave advice on anything from domestic to doctrinal matters."

church. Throughout his life, he evidenced an unwavering devotion to the Anglican Way.[46] In fact, perhaps the two words that best encapsulate his ministry are "evangelical churchman." At least one scholar has identified Simeon as the most influential Anglican evangelical, "who in many respects was the shaper, if not the founder, of the movement within the Church of England."[47]

Chapter 4 ("Personal Piety"), will describe the character of Simeon's spirituality, and how his brand of piety shaped his pastoral theology. I intend to demonstrate how the view he inherited—and advanced through his countless pupils—became a prime concern to the evangelicalism which blossomed in the nineteenth century. For example, a similar emphasis on piety can be seen in the evangelical classic *The Christian Ministry* by Charles Bridges, who, while educated at Cambridge, encountered Simeon at the height of his powers.[48]

Chapter 5 ("Parish Pastor") will examine Simeon's approach to parochial ministry. This chapter will survey his ecclesiology, relationship to Nonconformity, and general strategy of caring for his flock. Though doggedly committed to the established church, Simeon dabbled in some irregular practices, though nowhere near to the degree of some of his evangelical Anglican peers.

Chapter 6 ("Preaching Paragon") will treat Simeon's pulpit philosophy, locating it in his broader pastoral theology. Simeon viewed preaching as divine communication and communion—an event in which God spoke to his people through appointed ambassadors. I will first place Simeon in his religious context, and then examine Simeon's view of preachers, preaching, and those who hear preaching, namely, the congregation. Historian Philip Thomas argues that Charles Simeon "and especially those who learnt from him, ensured that biblical and pastoral preaching found its proper place in parochial ministry."[49] According to the "Old Apostle" of Cambridge, true preaching was God's word delivered through God's man directed toward God's people. The final chapter will restate my thesis, reviewing my chapters and major conclusions.[50] In an effort to present Simeon and his peers as they were, all older quotations

---

46. "Standard Divines," in Booty, *Study of Anglicanism*, 181–82.
47. Bray, *Anglicanism*, 28.
48. Bridges, *Christian Ministry*.
49. Thomas, "Doctrine of the Church," 257.
50. "Old Apostle's Legacy," in Hopkins, *Charles Simeon of Cambridge*, 210.

have retained the idiosyncratic spellings and italicized emphases of the original authors unless otherwise noted.

CHAPTER 2

Ministerial Mentor

NEAR THE END OF the twentieth century, John Stott (1921–2011)—one of the world's leading figures in evangelicalism—published *Evangelical Preaching: An Anthology of Sermons by Charles Simeon*.[1] There he attested how in the early 1940s, "Simeon's uncompromising commitment to Scripture captured my imagination and has held it ever since."[2] Stott acquainted himself with the legacy of Simeon during his undergraduate years at Cambridge University. To Stott, Simeon ranked as "one of the greatest and most persuasive preachers the Church of England has ever known."[3] With a century and a half between them, Simeon exerted a vast influence on Stott from the grave. Indeed, the Australian archbishop Sir Marcus Loane (1911–2009) commented on the connection between the two men, "John Stott was for our generation all that Charles Simeon had been for his generation. Stott at All Souls in London, like Simeon at Holy Trinity at Cambridge—each for more than fifty years, reaching out to touch the ends of the earth for God."[4] The profundity of Simeon's posthumous impact grew from the seeds he sowed his entire life. Stott, along with many modern evangelicals who have followed, numbers among the teeming host of men mentored by Simeon before and after his death.

---

1. Stott, *Evangelical Preaching*.
2. Stott, *Evangelical Preaching*, xxvii.
3. Dudley-Smith, *John Stott*, 258.
4. Loane, *John Stott*, 91.

It is estimated that Simeon trained 1,100 ministers during his lifetime, well-supplying England with an evangelical clergy committed to his brand of pastoral theology.[5] This chapter will cover the *how* and *who* of Charles Simeon's strategy of mentorship. In other words, it will survey the various methods Simeon employed to train men as well as the legacies of several of his most prominent pupils. Yet before Simeon can be appreciated as a ministerial mentor, I must first highlight his earliest influences.

Early Influences

Though originality marked Simeon's ministry, he was not without models. Three men emerge as most significant: John Berridge (1716–1793), John Thornton (1720–1790), and Henry Venn (1725–1797). Each of these figures applied a distinct and varying degree of impact on Simeon.

John Berridge

The eccentric John Berridge of Everton proved to be one of his earliest helps in ministry.[6] Berridge is remembered for his decades of evangelical itinerancy throughout the counties of Bedford, Cambridge, Essex, Hertford, and Huntingdon. In Berridge's twilight years, Simeon dined with him weekly. These occasions provided the young Cambridge pastor a plethora of anecdotes.[7] Notably, Simeon embraced many aspects of Berridge's ministry while rejecting others. For example, while Simeon thoroughly opposed itinerancy, he inherited Berridge's evangelical

---

5. Fitzgerald, *Quiet Worker for Good*, 62–63, quoted in Jenkins, *Tale of Two Preachers*, 4. John Charlesworth came under the influence of Simeon in the 1820s. Fitzgerald asserted, "Eleven hundred Clergyman are said to have learned the living Gospel's power—the majesty and glory of a Saviour's atonement as the one central object of a minister's preaching—from Simeon's lips. He, by the mercy of God, had reached a height which might be well called an Episcopate or Primacy through England, by no smooth or compromising process."

6. For more on John Berridge, see Pibworth, *Gospel Pedlar*. The small rural village of Everton, Bedfordshire, which was home to Berridge, should not be confused with the more populous Everton, Liverpool. Depending on the route, Everton, Bedfordshire, is only fifteen to twenty miles from the heart of Cambridge.

7. Brown, *Recollections*, 202. Simeon told of one occasion when Berridge accidentally took the coat of a guest who was a smaller man, supposing it to be his. After wearing the coat for some time, Berridge concluded that he had swollen over the course of the evening and could no longer fit in the coat. Such bizarre antics were common for Berridge.

Calvinism. Simeon also followed Berridge's example of singleness, a feature of their respective pastorates which maximized their investment in others.[8] On the topic of marriage, Berridge remarked to the Countess of Huntingdon (1707–1791),

> There is no trap so mischievous to the field-preacher as wedlock; and it is laid for him at every hedge corner. Matrimony has quite maimed poor Charles Wesley, and might have spoiled John Wesley and George Whitefield, if a wise Master had not graciously sent them a brace of ferrets. Dear George has now got his liberty again; and he will escape well if he is not caught by another hook. Eight or nine years ago, having been grievously tormented with house-keeping, I truly had thought of looking out for a Jezebel myself. But it seemed highly needful to ask advice of the Lord. So, kneeling down on my knees before a table, with a Bible between my hands, I besought the Lord to give me a direction.[9]

Though Simeon may not have shared as unfavorable a view of marriage as Berridge, he certainly viewed the institution as an impediment to his ministry in Cambridge. He reflected in 1807, "What has been my language at *all times* and to *all persons?* Has it not been this?—I should hate the University above all places as a married man; but the singular way in which I have been called to my present post, and its almost incalculable importance, forbid the thought of my now leaving it:—therefore I think I shall never marry."[10] Regardless of their similarities and differences, Simeon and Berridge were so close that Simeon preached the latter's funeral in 1793.

John Thornton

Another mentor worth brief mention is John Thornton, the famous evangelical philanthropist. It was Thornton who, in 1780, placed John Newton in the influential station of rector of St. Mary Woolnoth in London.[11] Thornton furnished Simeon with an ambition to see evangelical doctrine spread throughout England. By 1813, Simeon had become an

---

8. Smyth, *Simeon and Church Order*, 269–70.
9. Whittingham, *Whole Works*, 508.
10. Carus, *Memoirs*, 230.
11. For more on John Thornton, see Klein, *Amazing Grace*.

active trustee to the livings acquired by Thornton.[12] The nature of this trust will be expounded below. For the purposes of this study, the most important point of Thornton's influence on Simeon came in the arena of pastoral character. When a young Charles was distressed by the obstinance of his congregation, it was Thornton who gave the following advice: "Watch continually over your own spirit, and do all in love; we must grow downwards in humility to soar heavenward. I should recommend your having a watchful eye over yourself, for generally speaking as is the ministry so are the people."[13] Elsewhere, he wrote to a young Simeon in the 1780s of three lessons every minister must learn: "1. Humility—2. Humility—3. Humility." Through various trials, including a lifelong battle with pride, Simeon regularly reflected on the great worth of meekness in ministry.[14] More could be said of Simeon's relationship to Berridge and Thornton. Yet in terms of deepest impact, most attention must be given to the man Berridge referred to in a letter to Thornton as the "Archdeacon of Yelling": Henry Venn.[15]

Henry Venn

It is difficult to overstate Henry Venn's influence on Simeon. One evening in his home, thronged by dozens of disciples, Simeon declared, "I love everyone who has a drop of Henry Venn's blood in his veins."[16] Venn—who finished his ministry as the rector of Yelling, Huntingdonshire—indelibly marked Simeon's ministry from early on in his tenure at Holy Trinity. Throughout his life, Simeon warmly acknowledged his debt of gratitude for Venn's spirituality and model of ministry.

The best biographical resource for Henry Venn comes from his son John (1759–1813), who offered an account of his father's life, along with a collection of his letters.[17] J. C. Ryle (1816–1900) also penned a lengthy sketch of Venn in his work *The Christian Leaders of the Last Century*. Ryle esteemed Venn as one of the leading lights of early evangelicalism. He counted him among giants like George Whitefield, John Wesley, William

---

12. Carus, *Memoirs*, 368.
13. Hopkins, *Charles Simeon of Cambridge*, 43–44.
14. Brown, *Recollections*, 160.
15. Whittingham, *Whole Works*, 414.
16. Brown, *Recollections*, 139.
17. Venn, *Life and Letters*.

Grimshaw (1708–1763), and John Berridge. By way of influence, Ryle viewed Venn in distinction from lesser-known evangelical Anglicans like Samuel Walker (1714–1761) and Augustus Toplady (1740–1778).

Venn was born at Barnes, in Surrey, on March 2, 1724, to a long line of ministers ranging back to 1621.[18] Throughout his adolescence, he had the advantage of attending a number of rigorous schools before matriculating at St. John's College, Cambridge in 1742 at the age of seventeen.[19] He went on to be ordained as a deacon in 1745.

The first significant development in his ministerial life transpired in 1749 with his appointment to the curacy of Barton, near Cambridge. In 1750, he moved south to assist Adam Langley (1723–1789), the rector of St. Matthew, Friday Street in London and West Horsley, outside the city. Until his Clapham curacy in 1754, Venn resided in London during the summer months and in Horsley the rest of the year. For those studying Venn's life in the 1750s, some of the dynamics of his spiritual life remain unclear. For example, it is difficult to nail down the precise date or season of his evangelical conversion. Ryle, for his part, attributes Venn's spiritual awakening to a letter he received from Selina Hastings, Countess of Huntingdon (1707–1791), in which she criticized his preaching. She wrote,

> The Lord Jesus Christ is the Lord our righteousness. Cling not to such beggarly elements, such filthy rags, mere cobwebs of Pharisaical pride; but look to him who has wrought out a perfect righteousness for his people. You find it a hard task to come naked and miserable to Christ; to come divested of every recommendation but that of abject wretchedness and misery, and receive from the outstretched hand of our Immanuel, the riches of redeeming grace.[20]

Regardless of the exact details of his conversion, the year 1756 marks a distinct turning point in Venn's ministry. John Venn records the shift in his father's ministry after a debilitating illness.

> He had time to reflect upon his principles and his conduct; and he used to observe, that after that period he was no longer able to preach the sermons which he had previously composed. His views of eternal things had now become clearer—his

---

18. Ryle, *Last Century*, 256.
19. Venn, *Life and Letters*, 9.
20. Ryle, *Last Century*, 265.

meditations on the attributes of God more profound—his views of the greatness of the salvation of Christ more distinct; and the whole of his religion had received the tincture of more elevated devotion, which rendered his conversation and his preaching doubly instructive.[21]

It appears Venn emerged from his London years in an entirely different state of heart and mind than that of the beginning of his ministry.

After marrying his wife Eling in 1757, he was appointed vicar of Huddersfield, in Yorkshire, in 1759—the same year as Simeon's birth. Venn arrived in northern England during the waning years of William Grimshaw of Haworth, the great evangelist of Yorkshire. From his post in Huddersfield, Venn led a diligent parish ministry. This included a rigorous schedule of pastoral visitation and preaching, which customarily had Venn delivering eight to ten sermons per week in Huddersfield.[22] Ryle notes the significance of Venn's Yorkshire years, namely, he was the "first clergyman in England who fairly proved the power of evangelical aggression on a manufacturing parish."[23]

Evidently, Venn's preaching had a massive impact on his people. From the year 1759 to 1771, he estimated that he had led nine hundred souls to faith in Huddersfield.[24] One parishioner recalled of Venn, "I never heard a minister like him. He was most powerful in unfolding the terrors of the law. When doing so, he had a stern look that would make you tremble. Then he would turn off to the offers of grace, and begin to smile, and go on entreating until his eyes filled with tears."[25] John Venn recounts a time when a certain Socinian attended a gathering in Huddersfield for the sole purpose of ridiculing the vicar. After witnessing Venn's solemnity in the pulpit, the mocker later sought the preacher for counsel. John Venn writes how the gentleman "earnestly begged [Mr. Venn] for forgiveness . . . and from that time to the hour of his death he became one of Mr. Venn's most faithful and affectionate friends."[26] Such was the character of his Huddersfield ministry. Yet despite all his local activity, Venn did not confine his labors to his parish. Records from Lady Huntingdon's *Life and Times* reveal that he was a frequent itinerant minister in Yorkshire and

21. Venn, *Life and Letters*, 23.
22. Ryle, *Last Century*, 271.
23. Ryle, *Last Century*, 269.
24. Bull, *Memorials*, 248.
25. Venn, *Life and Letters*, 41.
26. Venn, *Life and Letters*, 27.

beyond.[27] Venn often partnered with the Wesleys and other Methodists in field preaching, though he later gravitated away from such irregularity.[28] Perhaps his most significant friendship among the Methodists was with William Grimshaw, whose funeral he preached in 1763.

During Venn's tenure in Huddersfield, he fulsomely embraced Calvinism. John Venn highlights how this doctrinal shift for Henry was formed in the furnace of suffering and poverty.

> During the severe trials with which he was exercised, a change took place in his sentiments respecting some particular points in Divinity. He had hitherto been a zealous Arminian, hostile to the principles of Calvinism, which he thought equally repugnant to reason and to Scripture; but the experience he now had of the corruption of his nature, of the frailty and weakness of man, of the insufficiency even of his best endeavours led him gradually to ascribe more to the grace of God, and less to the power and free-will of man.[29]

Venn's Calvinist convictions—which would later be described as moderate—became a hallmark of his ministry. From Huddersfield, he also published his most significant written work, *The Complete Duty of Man*.[30]

In 1771, Venn retired from Huddersfield to a rectory in Yelling, a small rural village outside of Cambridge. While John Venn attributes his departure from Yorkshire to the decline of Henry's health, others cite the loss of his wife in 1767 as a decisive factor in his move.[31] Eling's death left Henry with four young children to raise. Regardless of his main reason for leaving Yorkshire, Venn served the church in Yelling until his death in 1797. From this station near Cambridge, Venn had easy access to influence young ordinands. This sphere of ministry was zealously facilitated by Charles Simeon, who became acquainted with Venn in 1782. By the end of his life—and thereafter through Simeon—Venn imbued the ministries of hundreds of young men with his evangelical ideals.

---

27. Seymour, *Selina Countess of Huntingdon*, 224.
28. Bebbington, *Evangelicalism in Modern Britain*, 31.
29. Venn, *Life and Letters*, 28–29.
30. Venn, *Complete Duty of Man*.
31. Ryle, *Last Century*, 280.

Venn's Practical and Pastoral Theology

When examining Henry Venn's life, several features of his practical and pastoral theology starkly emerge, a few of which clearly impacted a young Charles Simeon.

Law and Gospel

With regards to Venn's practical theology, his understanding of law and gospel, along with his moderate Calvinism forged an archetype for evangelicals that followed. To appreciate Venn's relationship to God's moral law, one must first consider his view of faith. Venn defined saving faith in *The Complete Duty of Man* as "a dependence upon the righteousness and death of Christ, as a full satisfaction to the justice of God for the sin of the world, in the breach of his law; and the sole ground of our acceptance to the reward of eternal life."[32] Though this view dominated evangelical circles, there was not always full consensus. For example, William Romaine (1714–1795), John Hervey (1714–1758), and William Grimshaw (1708–1763) all emphasized that assurance must accompany faith in order for it to be *true* faith.[33] Nevertheless, Venn's view prevailed among evangelicals. Bebbington summarizes Venn, "Faith, he taught, must not be based on inward feeling only. Yet real faith produces a clear and permanent sense of dependence on Christ."[34] Venn contended, "The sensible comforts of a Christian, it is true, are in their nature fluctuating, but his dependence does not vary as his consolations do.'"[35] He thus concluded, "Hence, he that is oppressed with gloom, and tormented with fear lest he should have no part in Christ, merely because he feels no transporting hope in his heart, may be able, when his judgment is better instructed in the nature of faith, to prove himself a believer by proving his whole dependence to be upon Christ."[36]

Crucial to Venn's perspective of the law was that one's soul must be won to Christ before the believer can meaningfully obey the law. "Christ the lawgiver," said Venn, "will always speak in vain, unless Christ the

---

32. Venn, *Complete Duty of Man*, 35.
33. Bebbington, *Evangelicalism in Modern Britain*, 45.
34. Bebbington, *Evangelicalism in Modern Britain*, 45.
35. Venn, *Complete Duty of Man*, 124.
36. Venn, *Complete Duty of Man*, 124.

Saviour is first known."[37] Elsewhere he wrote, "All treatises . . . written to promote holiness of life must be deplorably defective, unless the cross of Christ be laid as the foundation."[38] After the believer was united to Christ in faith—far from setting aside God's moral commands—he or she held a solemn duty to pursue positive righteousness. He believed Christians were to be marked by a quality of holiness that could only be attributed to the work of the Holy Spirit. He asserted, "faith is not understood, much less possessed, if it is not productive of more holiness, than could possibly be attained in any other."[39] Historian Bruce Hindmarsh explains how Venn's view of anthropology and conversion informed his ethics.

> For the most part, evangelicals did not question the rule of law and its administration, but they saw the human condition most clearly reflected in the condition of the condemned felon. This was, as Henry Venn said, a levelling doctrine. More profoundly, as evangelicals considered the basis for moral law generally, they articulated an evangelical ethics that stood in marked contrast to the whole tenor of British moral philosophy. In the moral thought of Henry Venn, John Wesley, and Jonathan Edwards, for example, it is clear how conversion was central to their ethics, for it was only as the human person was saved by Christ, indwelt by the Spirit of God, renewed inwardly, and assimilated to the divine nature that it was possible to rise to "true virtue" and to bear witness to what Edwards described as a primary, general, and spiritual beauty.[40]

For Simeon, he clearly understood faith and conversion to produce a natural pursuit of holiness in the Christian, along with high regard for God's law. In a sermon addressed to the University of Cambridge, he commented on the apostle Paul's doctrine.

> Strongly as he enforced the necessity of relying on Christ, and founding our hopes of salvation solely on his obedience unto death, he was no less earnest in promoting the interests of holiness. Whilst he represented the believers "dead to the law" and "without law," he still insisted that they were "under the law to Christ," and as much bound to obey every tittle of it as ever.[41]

---

37. Venn, *Complete Duty of Man*, 44.
38. Venn, *Complete Duty of Man*, 45.
39. Venn, *Complete Duty of Man*, 42.
40. Hindmarsh, *Spirit of Early Evangelicalism*, 274.
41. Simeon, *Evangelical Religion*, 12.

It is clear from Simeon's expositions, he adopted Venn's view of the evangelical relationship between law and gospel.

Moderate Calvinism

As highlighted above, Venn gravitated toward Calvinism during his Huddersfield vicarship. Notably, having once been an Arminian, he never reflected a reactionary commitment to Calvinism. Rather, he always sought to apply the doctrines of grace warmly, affectionately, and experientially. He wrote to a friend in 1772,

> As to Calvinism, you know I am moderate. Those who exalt the Lord Jesus Christ as all their salvation, and abase man, I rejoice in; and would not have them advance farther, till they see more of the plan of sovereign grace, so connected with what is indisputable, that they cannot refuse their assent. . . . If any man think that he knoweth any thing yet as he ought to know, that man knoweth nothing.[42]

What Venn strove for in his application of Calvinism, he admired in others. Commenting on the doctrine of John Berridge, he said, "He is a blessed man, a true Calvinist; not hot in doctrine, nor wise above what is written, but practical and experimental."[43] Charles Simeon clearly followed Venn on this point. The former charged his pupils not "to be wise above what is written" in matters of Reformed soteriology.[44] Simeon's view of Calvinism will be expounded in subsequent chapters. Suffice it to say, both Venn and Simeon decried ministers who forced any theological system over the natural interpretation of Scripture.

Letters

Venn's greatest written legacy was his letters. Ryle comments on this aspect of his ministry, "He lived in the good old time when letters were really well thought over and worth reading, and the letters that left Yelling parsonage are a proof to this day how wisely and well he used his pen."[45] John Venn preserved over five hundred pages of his father's letters,

---

42. Venn, *Life and Letters*, 31–32.
43. Smyth, *Simeon and Church Order*, 194.
44. Brown, *Conversation Parties*, 273.
45. Ryle, *Last Century*, 283–84.

a catalog rivaling that of John Newton. This correspondence ranges in topics and recipients. It appears Venn gave as much attention to women in his letters as men. It is also striking how much he wrote to his children. Though few remember Simeon for his letters, his memoirs include over three hundred and fifty pages of personal correspondence, representing a noteworthy part of his pastoral ministry.

Family Life

The quality of Venn's devotion to his family distinguishes him from many of his evangelical peers. Despite the rigor of his ministerial schedule, he maintained warm ties with each of his children. Ryle highlights the *"singular prudence and tenderness in the management of his children."*[46] Each letter to his children is tinctured with the wisdom and sweetness of a loving father. They are rich with reflection on his relationship with God. Writing to his daughter Jane in 1785, he said,

> A great part of our warfare is to overcome our natural propensity to seek happiness in food and drink, in dress and show; which only nourish our disease, and keep us from communion with God as our chief good. More than thirty-seven years ago he was pleased, in his adorable mercy, to give me a demonstration that all was vanity and vexation of spirit, but himself. From that hour (such is the energy of divine teaching), rising up and lying down, going out and coming in, I have felt this truth. I began and continued to seek the Lord and his strength and his face evermore. *I was then led to know how the poverty and emptiness of all terrestrial good could be well supplied from the fullness of an adorable Jesus.*[47]

Evidently, Venn had a vivid way of instructing his children. One of Simeon's biographers, Henry Moule, records that one day after a young Simeon had visited the Venn family, one of Henry's daughters complained of Simeon's angular character. Henry took the opportunity to teach his children a lesson in patience and Christian conduct.

> "Come into the garden, children," their father said, and led them out into that favourite school-room. "now, pick me one of those peaches." But it was early summer, and "the time of peaches was

---

46. Ryle, *Last Century*, 298.
47. Venn, *Life and Letters*, 417–18.

not yet"; how could their father ask for the green fruit? "Well, my dears, it is green now, and we must wait; but a little more sun, and a few more showers, and the peach will be ripe and sweet. So it is with Mr. Simeon."[48]

Simeon certainly imbibed something of the character of Venn's value of family. Though he remained single his entire life, Simeon sought the good of the family lives of his parishioners and other pastors. For example, he understood wives to be so indispensable to their husbands that he hosted an annual retreat for ministers and their wives.[49]

Mentorship

The final decades of Venn's life propelled him to a large sphere of influence among Cambridge ordinands.[50] Far and away, his most significant pupil was Charles Simeon. Simeon became acquainted with Venn right before the former's appointment to Holy Trinity. By 1782, Simeon had found himself starved for spiritual mentors. He recounted his first encounter with Venn. "He, Mr J. Venn, soon took me over to Yelling, and introduced me to a man of no ordinary character, his own dear and honoured Father. O what an acquisition was this! In this aged minister I found a father, an instructor, and a most bright example: and I shall have reason to adore my God to all eternity for the benefit of his acquaintance."[51] The record shows that Venn reciprocated Simeon's appreciation, praising the young man's zeal for the Lord. "My soul is always the better for his visits. Oh to flame, as he does, with zeal, and yet be beautified with his meekness!"[52]

Venn equipped his followers with a high view of the Christian ministry. He spoke of the parson's life as "the best service that men or angels can be called to work in."[53] Historian Charles Smyth notes how Simeon—when faced with the ministerial paradigms of the highly irregular John Berridge and Henry Venn—chose the way of Venn.[54] This was no small thing considering Berridge's massive profile in evangelical

---

48. Moule, *Charles Simeon*, 45.
49. Carus, *Memoirs*, 268–71.
50. Smyth, *Simeon and Church Order*, 272.
51. Carus, *Memoirs*, 23.
52. Venn, *Life and Letters*, 345.
53. Hopkins, *Charles Simeon of Cambridge*, 85.
54. Smyth, *Simeon and Church Order*, 195.

circles. One of Simeon's greatest tributes to Venn can be found in the latter's biography, in which he remarked,

> Scarcely ever did I visit him, but he prayed with me, at noon-day, as well as at the common seasons of family worship: scarcely ever did I dine with him, but his ardour in returning thanks, sometimes in an appropriate hymn, and sometimes in a thanksgiving prayer, has inflamed the souls of all present, so as to give us a foretaste of Heaven itself: and in all the twenty-four years that I knew him, I never remember him to have spoken unkindly of any one, but once; and I was particularly struck with the humiliation which he expressed for it, in his prayer the next day.[55]

Simeon understood himself to owe an incalculable debt to Venn as his spiritual father. Later in life, he remarked to Venn's grandson, "Though in the efforts of a thousand years I never can repay my obligation to him for all his labours of love."[56]

Despite Simeon's great indebtedness to his mentor, it was Venn's delight to invest in young pastors. Indeed, caring for developing ministers nourished his soul. His grandson once remarked, "I have understood that nothing so powerfully excited his spirits as the presence of young ministers whose hearts he believed to be devoted to Christ."[57]

For all his influence in the evangelical movement, Henry Venn is profoundly deserving of greater study. His life forms a bridge between evangelicalism's roots in revival in Georgian England to its massive cultural influence in the Victorian period. As a pastor, his preaching shook Yorkshire. As a father, he warmly promoted the Christian life and ministry. As an evangelical sage, he influenced juggernauts like Simeon, who not only imbibed his doctrine, but shared his priority of ministerial mentorship. An agèd Simeon wrote to one of Venn's grandsons, "I wish you had known your grandfather, the only end for which he lived was to make all men see the glory of God in the face of Jesus Christ."[58] Having considered Simeon's fathers in the faith, the means of his own influence on his followers will now be considered.

---

55. Venn, *Life and Letters*, 53–54.
56. Hopkins, *Charles Simeon of Cambridge*, 101.
57. Ryle, *Last Century*, 285.
58. Balleine, *Evangelical Party*, 58.

Evangelical Influence in an Eminent Place

As early as 1782, Simeon evidenced a strategic perspective on pastoral ministry in Cambridge. Long before he was the rector of Holy Trinity, he had developed ambitions for the church.

> I had often, when passing Trinity Church, which stands in the heart of Cambridge, and is one of the largest churches in the town, said within myself, "How should I rejoice if God were to give me that church, that I might preach his Gospel there, and be a herald for him in the midst of the University!" But as to the actual possession of it, I had no more prospect of attaining it, than of being exalted to the See of Canterbury.[59]

At a time when the vast majority of Anglican clergy were trained at either Cambridge or Oxford Universities, Simeon understood the tactical significance of such a position.[60] Ministry in Cambridge afforded him the opportunity for sustained influence on his nation's Church. This priority constantly held his attention. In 1780, Simeon attended the church for the Lord's Supper, a service in which he found himself to be one of only three communicants.[61] By the end of his life, he could boast, "Yesterday I preached to a Church as full as it could hold, and partook of the Lord's Supper in concert with a larger number than has been convened together, on such an occasion, in any Church in Cambridge since the place existed upon earth."[62] At this point, the building had been enlarged to seat 1,100 congregants.[63]

Notably, Simeon was not merely interested in total attendance. He also paid special attention to the number of students in his congregation. In 1795, he referred to "multitudes of gownsmen" coming to his services.[64] He shared with his former curate Thomas Thomason in 1817, "The gownsmen are sometimes almost one half of my congregation."[65] The following year he wrote to Thomason, "As for the Gownsmen, never was anything like what they are at this day. I am forced to let them go up into the galleries, which I never suffered before; and notwithstanding

---

59. Carus, *Memoirs*, 40–41.
60. Slinn, *Education*, 1.
61. Hopkins, *Charles Simeon of Cambridge*, 30.
62. Carus, *Memoirs*, 787.
63. Carus, *Memoirs*, 729.
64. Carus, *Memoirs*, 104.
65. Carus, *Memoirs*, 445.

that, multitudes of them are forced to stand in the aisles for want of a place to sit down. What thanks can I render to the Lord for a sight of these things!"[66] Throughout his tenure at Trinity, he kept a close eye on the number of future ministers attending his church.[67] Daniel Wilson, the Bishop of Calcutta, paid this tribute to Simeon: "Thus he drew around him a constant succession of pious youth, whose minds he imbued with his own sound and laborious views of Ministerial diligence."[68] By the end of his life, Simeon had employed various means of raising and training up leaders, and thereby streamlined his pastoral theology into the Church of England.

"Not My Curate, My Brother"

One of the ways Simeon raised up leaders was through the curacy of Holy Trinity.[69] Simeon employed his first assistant in 1796. By that point, he had labored for over a decade at Trinity and had weathered the conflict of his formerly embittered congregation. It was not until 1794 that Simeon had become the chosen lecturer of Holy Trinity. Two years later, Thomas Thomason was selected as his first curate. In 1803, Simeon brought on Henry Martyn as a second curate, a testament to the size and activity of Trinity during the early nineteenth century. William Carus, Simeon's last curate, warmly reflected on Simeon's treatment of his co-laborers.

> The generous and affectionate feeling he habitually cherished, and on suitable occasions manifested, towards those who have successively stood to him in the relation of Curates, is gratefully remembered by every one of them. Considering that the term Curate—honourable as it is, and elsewhere attached to the office of the principal—is commonly regarded in this country as implying inferiority of rank, he was disposed to discard it. "Not my *curate*," he would say, "my *brother*."[70]

---

66. Carus, *Memoirs*, 496.

67. Michael Hennell writes of the focus that Simeon gave to students in his preaching. "In term time Simeon said that he hardly ever prepared a sermon without the students in view, especially on a Sunday evening when there was a large student congregation." See Hennell, *Sons of the Prophets*, 1–2.

68. Carus, *Memoirs*, 843.

69. "Location."

70. Carus, *Memoirs*, 243.

One of the curates' favorite pastimes was the supper they enjoyed with Simeon at the close of every Lord's Day. In the deeply hierarchical context of the Church of England, Simeon viewed the men laboring in his parish as his peers. As will be highlighted more below, his relationships with his curates were attended with great affection, friendship, and mutual commitment. This is especially borne out in his post-curacy correspondence with Thomas Thomason and Henry Martyn. Though the curacy was a significant feature of Simeon's ministry, and a means of raising up a few notable disciples, it represented only one weapon in his training arsenal.

"One Might Style Them Colloquial Lectures"

Though Simeon had a high view of his calling as a local church pastor, he attested in an 1820 letter, "My chief usefulness is amongst my academic hearers."[71] Simeon understood the sheer number of future pastors present in his parish was a profound stewardship, and by 1812, he discovered one of his most effective means of mentoring ministers: conversation parties.[72] In these gatherings, dozens of men and some women would assemble in a sitting room to learn at the feet of the sagely Simeon. Each Friday night, England's future ordinands would press the vicar on various issues in ministry. Abner Brown described how these occasions took on different modes. "Mr. Simeon's Conversation Parties—one might style them Colloquial Lectures, for they bring to mind the modes of teaching used by the great Greek moralists—were of four kinds: Clerical Meetings, Sermon Classes, Undergraduates' Friday Evening Parties, and ordinary Social Parties."[73] The majority of Brown's reflections came from the latter two. The content of conversation ranged from fine points of exegesis to the character of pastoral ministry. In many of the parties, he cautioned against the peculiar besetting weaknesses of young pastors. For example, at one party in 1828 he said, "Young Ministers should inquire, not what can I teach my people, but what can they receive. Jesus did not tell His disciples that which they could not bear, but spake to them as they were able to bear it; and St.

---

71. Carus, *Memoirs*, 536.
72. Brown, *Recollections*.
73. Brown, *Recollections*, xiii.

Paul fed his people with milk when they could not bear strong meat."[74] Simeon's conversation parties provided him an opportunity to address precise points of pastoral theology in an unhurried environment.

"His Directions on the Composition of Sermons Were Invaluable"

As an offshoot to his famous conversation parties, Simeon hosted sermon and theology classes for gownsmen.[75] These smaller gatherings were by invite only. In each session, Simeon would offer a text for consideration and charged the men to produce a sermon outline for the text during the meeting. After they presented their outlines, Simeon would offer feedback. Thomas Thomason was an early beneficiary of this type of instruction from Simeon. He wrote jubilantly to his mother in the 1790s, "God has heaped upon me more favours than ever. Mr. Simeon has invited me to his Sunday evening lectures. This I consider one of the greatest advantages I ever received. The subject of his lectures is natural and revealed religion. These he studies and puts together with much pains and attention."[76] In John Sargent's biography of Thomas Thomason, he recorded Thomason's mature appreciation of Simeon's homiletical instruction.

> I cannot pass over this opportunity of acknowledging my debt of obligation to this truly estimable friend. We were admitted often to his rooms, and enjoyed regular lectures from him on various topics connected with the ministry to which we were looking forward; and I cannot help ascribing to these occasions much of the little good that has resulted from my official labours. His directions on the composition of sermons were invaluable, and I owe to him whatever I have obtained of ease in preparing many hundreds of discourses for the pulpit.[77]

Simeon made use of a panoply of methods—organic and formal—to embed within young men his evangelical values.

---

74. Brown, *Recollections*, 95.
75. Brown, *Recollections*, 51–53.
76. Carus, *Memoirs*, 97.
77. Sargent, *Rev. T. T. Thomason*, 41.

"They Purchase Income—I Purchase Spheres"

Though other evangelical Anglicans before Simeon may have placed a priority on training preachers, few were effective at placing young men in prominent posts throughout the British Empire. At the turn of the nineteenth century, the problem in evangelicalism lay not in its appeal to the common man, but its continuity in churches. Simeon not only excelled in training pastors, but he also had great success in securing the perpetual influence of evangelicalism in a variety of parishes throughout the Church of England.[78] As will be noted in the next chapter, part of what ensured Simeon's ability to sway the established church was his dogged commitment to her. In distinction from many of his evangelical peers, Simeon evidenced a sincere dedication and affection for the doctrine and practices of the Church of England.[79] Simeon secured livings through a range of means, both formal and informal. By 1813, he had become an active trustee to the livings acquired by John Thornton, the famous evangelical philanthropist and, as noted earlier, a notable influence of Simeon.[80]

To Simeon, his aim in purchasing livings was clear: "That in them may be preached those doctrines which have produced so happy an effect on my own soul."[81] He desired to see evangelical doctrine flourish in more churches. Distinguishing himself from other patrons, Simeon summarized his philosophy in this assertion, "there is a difference between myself and others: they purchase *income*—I purchase *spheres*, wherein the prosperity of the Established Church, and the kingdom of our blessed Lord, may be advanced; and not for a season only, but if it please God, in perpetuity also."[82] In an 1814 letter to a certain Mr. Richardson of York, Simeon relayed the strategy of his patronage:

> 1st, To consider truly, as before God, who is, all thing considered, fittest for the particular sphere. 2d, To enquire carefully, whose removal to a new sphere will be least injurious to any

---

78. Gareth Atkins writes, "The footholds Evangelicals carved out at the ancient universities served their purpose: to secure their place in the Church of England by producing pious gentlemen with a broad education, sufficient social polish and—crucially—the right sort of connections." *Converting Britannia*, 47.

79. Smyth, *Simeon and Church Order*. See also "Standard Divines," in Booty, *Study of Anglicanism*, 181–82.

80. Carus, *Memoirs*, 368.

81. Carus, *Memoirs*, 590.

82. Carus, *Memoirs*, 780.

other place; because, if I take a person from a large sphere, which will not be well supplied afterwards, I do an injury, rather than a service, to the Church at large. 3d, On a supposition things be equal in these two respects, *but not otherwise*, to prefer the person whose circumstances are most straitened. It is for the *people* and for the *Church of God* that we are to provide, and not for any individual, whatever be his necessities, his virtues, or his attainments.[83]

Historian Wesley Balda expounds Simeon's philosophy, "For Simeon, a 'sphere of influence' particularly defined a living in terms of its potential usefulness; this factor might include the population size, the spiritual needs, and the physical facilities, but not the income."[84] Elsewhere, Balda comments on what distinguished the nature of Simeon's patronage. He writes, "Yet his innovative approach to parish patronage contrasted sharply with the spirit of his age and presaged rising ecclesiastical standards throughout the country."[85] David Bebbington concurs with Balda when he comments on the effect the Simeon Trust had on the progress of evangelicalism in modern Britain:

> It was Simeon who dealt most effectively with the problem of continuity. In order to achieve a succession of Evangelical clergy in strategic parishes such as Cheltenham, he created, in 1817, a trust to purchase rights of patronage. It expanded and was also imitated by other trusts. In this, as in many other ways, Simeon gave an assured place to what was becoming an Evangelical party in the Church of England.[86]

One of Balda's most useful contributions to Simeon scholarship is his documentation of the strategic parishes secured by the Simeon Trust. By the end of his life in 1836, he had secured twenty-one advowsons—the right to appoint clergyman to particular parishes subject to the presiding bishop's consent.[87] By 1865, the trust administered forty-four livings, and by 1896, it owned one hundred and fifty.[88]

---

83. Carus, *Memoirs*, 382.
84. Balda, "Spheres of Influence," 6–7.
85. Balda, "'Spheres of Influence," 8.
86. Bebbington, *Evangelicalism in Modern Britain*, 32.
87. Scotland, *Evangelical Anglicans*, 393.
88. Balda, "Spheres of Influence," 130–31. See also Scotland, *Evangelical Anglicans*, 393.

But purchasing livings was not Simeon's only means of placing evangelical ordinands in strategic pulpits. As an elder Anglican statesman, his counsel was regularly sought for by influential men in the established church. For example, William Gladstone's (1809–1898) father Sir John Gladstone (1764–1851) once visited Simeon in order to recruit a minister. The elder Gladstone was a Scottish merchant responsible for erecting church buildings in Liverpool and Litherland. In 1815, he requested that Simeon supply one of his churches with a minister. Simeon gladly obliged. William recorded the encounter, remembering Simeon as "a venerable man, and although only a fellow of a college, was more ecclesiastically got up than many a dean, or even here and there, perhaps, a bishop of the present less costumed if more ritualistic period."[89] On another occasion, Sir John selected another one of Simeon's disciples, William Rawson (1788–1872), to be his own local minister at St. Thomas Church in Seaforth. In addition to the vicarage, Rawson ran a preparatory school, educating the future Prime Minister William Gladstone until he enrolled at Eton in 1821.[90] Indeed, Simeon's position in Cambridge allowed him to double as both ministerial mentor and minister-maker.

Prominent Pupils

The remainder of this chapter will survey the legacies of notable followers of Simeon. To be such often came with social and professional disadvantages. Gareth Atkins notes how Thomas Kerrich (1748–1828), who served as president of Magdalene in the 1790s, "was not favourable to serious religion, having the 'impudence' to interrogate undergraduates as to which of them attended 'Simeon's Church.'"[91] During Simeon's life and thereafter, his pupils were known as "Simeonites" or "Sims," terms which at times had pejorative connotations. For example, they are portrayed unappreciatively in Samuel Butler's (1835–1902) novel *The Way of All Flesh*.[92] Regardless of Butler's impression of Simeon and his followers, the evangelicalism that the Cambridge minister championed reached its zenith in the Church of England during the nineteenth century.

---

89. Morley, *William Ewart Gladstone*, 1:11.
90. Bebbington, *William Ewart Gladstone*, 26.
91. Atkins, *Converting Britannia*, 41.
92. Butler, *Way of All Flesh*, 231–34.

Bishops

Simeon interacted with a number of bishops and future-bishops in his lifetime. Though eighteenth-century evangelicalism saw little institutional capture of the established church, the climate changed significantly in Simeon's lifetime and the following generation. By the turn of the nineteenth century, there were no bishops who would have identified as or considered themselves evangelical. In fact, many opposed evangelicals with animus. Simeon described his own rocky relationship with Thomas Dampier (1748–1812), the bishop of Ely.

> Bishop [Dampier]—had now succeeded to the See of Ely; and in his first Charge he had spoken in no very favourable terms of those who maintain what I believe to be the Gospel of Christ. Aware, from the moment he was appointed, what were his dispositions towards persons of my sentiments, and towards myself in particular, I had used the most prudent means in my power to conciliate him.[93]

John Sargent (1780–1833) commented on the dynamic between Ely and Holy Trinity, asserting, "no young man, who had been an attendant at Trinity Church, could escape suspicion at Ely."[94] Despite these challenges, the evangelical vicar of Holy Trinity influenced a number of distinguished bishops.

Henry Ryder (1777–1836).

The year 1815 witnessed the groundbreaking appointment of Henry Ryder (1777–1836) to the see of Gloucester, making him the first evangelical Anglican bishop.[95] He would later be promoted to Lichfield in 1824. Ryder probably did not come to evangelical convictions until 1811 when he was vicar of Lutterworth.[96] Nevertheless, he was a dear friend and confidant of Simeon's.[97] In 1813, Simeon and Ryder preached in each other's pulpits, the latter preaching twice at Holy Trinity.[98] Upon Ryder's

---

93. Carus, *Memoirs*, 326.
94. Sargent, *Rev. T. T. Thomason*, 74.
95. Harris, *Evangelicals and Education*, 346.
96. Davies, *First Evangelical Bishop*, 4–5.
97. Carus, *Memoirs*, 406.
98. Carus, *Memoirs*, 372.

appointment to Gloucestershire in 1815, Simeon counseled him on how to conduct himself in his new role. Ryder replied, "I hope and desire to undertake the awful office, about probably to be committed to my charge, with the exact views which you recommend, and with the expectations which your unusual degree of experience in these matters enables you to lay before me."[99] He concluded his correspondence with Simeon, "I shall treasure up your written counsel, and hope to have it often confirmed by personal intercourse." Ryder—who had such obvious regard for Simeon's character and convictions—blazed the trail for later evangelical episcopates like J. C. Ryle and Handley Carr Glynn Moule (1841–1920).

The Sumner Brothers

Though Simeon had an impact on Ryder, his influence did not stem from the latter's years at Cambridge. This was not so for John and Charles Sumner. John Sumner (1780–1862)—"that excellent man" according to King George IV—served as Bishop of Chester for twenty years (1828–1848).[100] In 1848, he was elevated to the highest position in the established church, the Archbishop of Canterbury. Charles (1790–1874) served as Bishop of Llandaff and Winchester respectively in his lifetime. Though this chapter gives more attention to John Sumner, Simeon's relationship with the younger brother Charles was not insignificant. For example, the letters between Charles Sumner and Simeon reveal the lasting impression Holy Trinity's pastor had upon Sumner.[101] Indubitably, the traces of Simeon's profound impact on these brothers could be seen throughout both their ministries.

John Sumner matriculated at King's College, Cambridge, in 1798 after Simeon had assumed his role as dean of Divinity.[102] John quickly became an evangelical under the tutelage of Simeon.[103] Over his subsequent ministry, his literary output was substantial, publishing over forty works in his lifetime.[104] E. R. Moore has demonstrated a significant and tight

---

99. Carus, *Memoirs*, 411.
100. Atkins, *Converting Britannia*, 139.
101. Moule, *Charles Simeon*, 97.
102. Scotland, "John Bird Sumner," 60.
103. Scotland, "John Bird Sumner," 60.
104. Scotland, "John Bird Sumner," 60.

link between the writings of John Sumner and Simeon.[105] But the depth of Simeon's influence stretched far beyond similarities in their writing.

For starters, John Sumner evidenced a profound commitment to evangelical doctrine and values. Nigel Scotland argues Sumner followed the train of the more moderate Claphamite evangelicals, in distinction from a "progressively introverted" strand of evangelicals emergent in the 1820s. Scotland says this period is normally dated from "the time when Robert Haldane took up the editorship of the newly founded periodical, the *Record*. During the 1830s, the 'Recordites' moved increasingly into a narrow and withdrawn posture towards contemporary culture."[106] Meanwhile, the Clapham Sect, whose members were referred to as Claphamites, was a London-based society that evidenced a more optimist view of the culture and societal action. As mentioned in the previous chapter, Simeon gained notable access to the society, despite his distance from the capital city.[107] Like his mentor, Sumner committed himself to the doctrinal and philosophical hallmarks that gave evangelicalism its ascendency in the nineteenth century. For example, in an 1829 address, he reminded the clergy of Chester that their hearers "need to be convinced . . . of the sinfulness of sin: to be taught that 'the wages of sin is death,' eternal death. And the atonement made by the Son of God, the sacrifice of the cross, is the great instrument of working this conviction."[108] Such evangelical emphases on display in Sumner were robustly challenged throughout the latter half of the nineteenth century in denominations throughout England.[109] By 1858, J. C. Ryle could identify at least two streams of opposition to the evangelical cause, the first being the Tractarians of the Oxford Movement.[110] He described the second stream in the following way:

> [Those] who are called Church-of-England men, who publicly and privately put forward strange and unscriptural views about the atonement, about the vicarious sacrifice of Christ, and about His substitution for us on the cross. There are clergymen

---

105. Moore, "John Bird Sumner," 30.

106. Scotland, "John Bird Sumner," 58.

107. For more on the Clapham Sect—and Simeon's involvement in it—see Pratt, *Evangelical Leaders*.

108. Sumner, *Charge Delivered*, 11.

109. Murray, *J. C. Ryle*, 177–96. See also Iain Murray on the Downgrade Controversy in *Forgotten Spurgeon*, 139–65.

110. A treatment of the Oxford Movement cannot adequately be given here. For more, see Brown et al., *Oxford Movement*; and Chadwick, *Victorian Church*, 167–231.

> in England, who hold strange views about inspiration, and the eternity of punishment which Scripture speaks of as being the desert of unbelief. These men go on unrebuked, No effort is made to put them out of the Church.[111]

Against Rome and the rising tide of theological liberalism, Sumner proved himself a reliable bulwark.

Sumner also followed Simeon in his aversion to Calvinism as a system.[112] Simeon is rightly remembered as a moderate Calvinist, but his general distaste for systematic theology modeled a biblicism readily received and replicated by his disciples. John Sumner, for his part, displayed an allegiance to the evangelical doctrine of his ministerial mentor.

Beyond doctrinal similarities, Sumner dedicated himself to the priorities of the evangelical movement, particularly in what Bebbington has described as activism.[113] Scotland highlights many of his achievements during his episcopacy in Chester.

> During Sumner's period in office 233 new districts and new district churches were formed giving added accommodation for 194,745 persons. The number of clergy increased by 361. Some 671 new day-schools were erected and a great many Sunday schools were improved and strengthened. The result of this growth was seen in a steady increase in those attending church services and rising numbers at Holy Communion Services.[114]

Simeon's concern and care for the poor in Cambridge inspired Sumner with a similar interest in mercy ministry. He further demonstrated his evangelical activism by his vigorous engagement with the Church Missionary Society (CMS). Founded by Simeon and others in the late 1790s, this organization helped galvanize the modern missionary movement, a charge which had been initiated by William Carey (1761–1834) and the Baptist Missionary Society in 1792.[115] Eugene Stock recorded that Sumner spoke at the national anniversary of the CMS twelve times

---

111. Ryle, *Home Truths, Seventh Series*, 256–67.
112. Scotland, "John Bird Sumner," 61.
113. Bebbington, *Evangelicalism in Modern Britain*, 10.
114. Scotland, *John Bird Sumner*, 61.
115. Bebbington, *Evangelicalism in Modern Britain*, 42.

throughout his ministry.[116] Such an honor was later described as the "blue ribbon of the evangelical pulpit."[117]

One of the most powerful leadership principles Sumner learned from Simeon was the power of delegation. Chapter 5 will treat Simeon's extensive use of the laity in his ministry. Similar to his mentor, Sumner charged his clergy to use layman in "visiting and examining the schools, by reading and praying with the infirm and aged, by consoling the fatherless and widows in their affliction."[118] Sumner's delegation skill was not limited to his use of the laity. Scotland also comments on Sumner's shrewd management of various offices, which earned the commendation of Simeon himself.

> Sumner's nineteen years at Chester were widely acclaimed as a model of leadership, pastoral care and clear-sighted strategy. He began his task by appointing Henry Raikes as his chaplain. Two years later, in 1830, Henry, who was the brother of Robert Raikes, the Sunday school pioneer, was made chancellor of the diocese. Many of the projects which Sumner initiated, were done in concert with Raikes, causing Charles Simeon to remark: "The great diocese of Chester enjoys a sort of double episcopacy in the coadjutorship of the Chancellor with the Bishop of the See."[119]

Through the perspectives, priorities, and practices of Bishop Sumner, the pastoral theology of Simeon shined brightly.

Sumner also proved his evangelical bona fides through a number of controversies that rattled the Church of England in the nineteenth century. This period was rife with fierce divisions, especially around the issue of baptismal regeneration. Though Sumner articulated a nuanced position on baptism in his work *Apostolic Preaching*, he argued that the doctrine of conversion must be clearly preached to nominal members of the church.[120] Like Simeon, Sumner understood baptism and membership in the established church brought no *inherent* saving benefits.[121] In other words, citizenship in England was no proof of citizenship in heaven. As Archbishop of Canterbury, Sumner presided over the famous

---

116. Stock, *Church Missionary Society*, 1:258.
117. Toon and Smout, *John Charles Ryle*, 67.
118. Sumner, *Charge Delivered*, 23.
119. Scotland, "John Bird Sumner," 66.
120. Sumner, *Apostolic Preaching Considered*, 29.
121. For more on Simeon's view of baptism, see Becht, "Charles Simeon."

Gorham Judgement in 1850. George Gorham (1787–1857) was a priest who—when examined for a living in Exeter—expressed an evangelical view of baptism. The Bishop of Exeter, Henry Phillpotts (1778–1869), refused Gorham the appointment due to the latter's denial of baptismal regeneration. As a venerated high churchman, Phillpotts was sympathetic to the Oxford Movement, a theological retrieval project which gained steam in the middle of the 1800s. Gorham's appeal of Phillpott's decision eventually reached the Judicial Committee of the Privy Council, where it was reversed in 1850. Sumner reinforced his approval of Gorham by appointing him to the living of Brampford Speke.[122] Anglican historian Gerald Bray asserts the magnitude of the controversy. "In the Gorham case, the widespread belief that Anglicans held to 'baptismal regeneration' on the basis of words in the Prayer Book . . . was rejected on the ground that the Articles of Religion do not support such a view."[123] The Gorham judgement not only hastened the conversion of several high churchmen to Roman Catholicism, but according to Bray, it solidified the rejection of baptismal regeneration as the uncontested position of the Church of England to this day.[124] Arguably, had Sumner the Simeonite not been elevated to the see of Canterbury, the evangelical cause in the established church could have been significantly stymied.

Missionaries

The fact that some of Simeon's followers advanced to episcopates evidenced the depth of his impact. Simeon did not merely influence men—he influenced influencers. He trained pastors who trained other pastors, thus spreading his philosophy of ministry throughout England. He also mentored men who gave themselves to missionary enterprise, which forwarded his pastoral theology throughout the globe. To this day at Trinity Church, Cambridge, two tablets commemorate the legacies of Thomas Thomason and Henry Martyn—eminent mentees of Simeon who zealously spread the gospel to foreign nations.

---

122. Scotland, "John Bird Sumner," 72.
123. Bray, *Anglicanism*, 38.
124. Bray, *Anglicanism*, 113.

Thomas Thomason

The legacy of Thomas Thomason remains best preserved in the work of John Sargent, another notable disciple of Simeon's. By the time of Thomason's death, Sargent had already gained acclaim for his account of the life of Henry Martyn. Thomason, Martyn, and Sargent were unified in their high regard for their mentor. In fact, Sargent dedicated his biography of Thomason to Simeon: "To you above all, under God, it is mainly to be attributed, that I am able to appreciate the exalted principles which were the pole-star of the characters I have endeavored to delineate [referring to Martyn and Thomason]."[125]

Born in the southwest port town of Plymouth in 1774, Thomas Thomason matriculated at Magdalene College, Cambridge, in 1792. He soon became acquainted with Simeon, who had yet to finish his first ten years as vicar of Holy Trinity. "In him," wrote Sargent, "Mr. Thomason found the fidelity of a devoted pastor; the affection of a father and a friend."[126] After four years under Simeon's tutelage, he took holy orders in 1796 at Holy Trinity and Stapleford, about five miles from Cambridge.[127] By 1798, he had taken on a tutorship at Queen's College. This required four daily lectures, adding to his preaching duties, which at times, required Thomason to preach five times per week.[128] In January of 1799, he married Elizabeth Jane Fawcett (d. 1826). Remarking on the peaceful character of their marriage, Simeon said, "[I]n all the ten years I lived under their roof, I never heard on any occasion an angry word from either of them; nor ever saw a different countenance in either of them towards the other, or in either of them towards me."[129] Avidly assisted by Elizabeth, Thomas labored for nearly ten years in his parish assignments. Simeon later reflected on the fruitfulness of this season: "The name of Thomason in Shelford and Stapleford is remembered like that of Swartz[130] in Tanjore

---

125. Sargent, *Rev. T. T. Thomason*, vi.
126. Sargent, *Rev. T. T. Thomason*, 40.
127. Sargent, *Rev. T. T. Thomason*, 75.
128. Sargent, *Rev. T. T. Thomason*, 83.

129. Sargent, *Rev. T. T. Thomason*, 90. Elsewhere, Thomason commented on the nature of his living arrangement with Simeon, which spanned ten years. "Mr. Simeon has a room on the ground floor, which opens into a delightful pleasure garden, surrounded by a wall, where he can walk privately, in which he so much delights. One door of his room opens into my study, so that we are as near each other as possible." (Sargent, *Rev. T. T. Thomason*, 102–3).

130. Christian Frederick Swartz (1726–1798) was German Lutheran missionary to

and Trichinopoly, and I doubt not but to all eternity many will have reason to bless God for his affectionate ministrations."[131]

Though Thomason was indispensable to Simeon's ministry at Holy Trinity, the latter passionately supported the missionary cause. Thus, when Thomason expressed a desire to go overseas, Simeon labored for a number of years to help him secure a post abroad. Thomason was appointed chaplain of the East India Company in 1808 on Simeon's recommendation and nomination. Simeon himself accompanied Thomas and Elizabeth on part of their departure journey from England.[132] Carus wrote of their extended farewell, "Mr. Simeon remained with him to the very last: and not only went on board the vessel, but actually proceeded with him on his voyage as long as it was practicable to return."[133] In a subsequent letter to Thomason, Simeon reflected on his sorrow at Thomas's departure.

> Adored be the name of God for so uniting our hearts in love. For a long time I could not even look up—but at last I cast an eye of grief and affection towards your ship, and repeated it at intervals till you were about fifteen miles off; then finding you were almost out of sight, I went down into the cabin. I arrived at home at twelve o'clock, thankful that I had been permitted to enjoy in our separation a pledge that we should meet again at the right hand of God. Our love will be there the same—it is the expression of it only that will be different.[134]

Extended passages like this reveal the quality of affection that deepened Simeon's disciples in their commitment to evangelical values.[135] Men like Thomason did not imbibe Simeon's pastoral theology merely through information transfer, but through personal experience with a living, breathing exemplar.

Thomas Thomason served as chaplain at the Mission Church in Calcutta, a congregation that included both expatriates and natives. He founded the Calcutta Bible Society in 1810 for the dispersion of the Scriptures throughout India.[136] In addition to the ministry of the Word,

---

India. For more, see Pearson, *Reverend Christian Frederick Swartz*.
  131. Sargent, *Rev. T. T. Thomason*, 110.
  132. Sargent, *Rev. T. T. Thomason*, 135.
  133. Carus, *Memoirs*, 258.
  134. Carus, *Memoirs*, 258–59.
  135. Sargent, *Rev. T. T. Thomason*, 162.
  136. Sargent, *Rev. T. T. Thomason*, 178.

Thomason tirelessly labored to translate the Bible to Urdu, finishing the Old Testament in his lifetime.[137] Thomason also established various schools and societies for ministry to the poor.

In the course of all of these missionary ventures, he sought the approval of his mentor, rejoicing whenever their wills aligned. Sargent said of Simeon's influence, "By him [Simeon] he [Thomason] was thus animated to persist in his course."[138] Thomason relied on commendations from Simeon like the following: "Every work in which you engage is so much to my heart and mind, that my soul appears to be cast into the very same mould with yours."[139] Simeon admired the calculated way in which Thomason patiently sought the spiritual progress of his hearers.

> Could not Jehovah have revealed every thing as plainly by Moses, as by the Lord Jesus? Could not our blessed Lord have spoken more intelligibly than by parables, and Paul have gone at once to perfection, instead of dwelling so much on the first principles of the oracles of God? But the object was to give that, which in existing circumstances, was fittest for the recipients. With such examples before us, let us not be grieved, if we be blamed for treading in their steps. The Christian community amongst you, as well as the native population, needed caution and sobriety to be exercised towards them. . . . I trust the time is not far distant, when multitudes of the natives will "drink water with joy out of the wells of salvation."[140]

A vast number of letters reveals the reciprocal affection between Simeon and the Thomasons. So great was the Thomasons' love and trust of Simeon that they made him the godfather and unofficial guardian of their eldest son James (1804–1853), who came to live in England for schooling in 1814.[141] Simeon made various arrangements for James's living and education as his parents gave their lives to service in India, a debt for which Thomas remained grateful. James went on to be a British administrator of the East India Company and Lieutenant-Governor of the North-Western Provinces of India.

Thomas Thomason died on June 21, 1829, finishing the life course of a dedicated missionary. As he faced his approaching death, he had

137. Sargent, *Rev. T. T. Thomason*, 274.
138. Sargent, *Rev. T. T. Thomason*, 275.
139. Sargent, *Rev. T. T. Thomason*, 275.
140. Sargent, *Rev. T. T. Thomason*, 275–76.
141. Hopkins, *Charles Simeon of Cambridge*, 169.

an opportunity to share some final words regarding his mentor. "To my very dear Mr. Simeon say, I feel unworthy of the great love he has at all times honoured me with. Oh may his bow abide in strength, and may he be, if possible, still more useful in his age."[142] In the chancel of Holy Trinity Church, a tablet was erected in honor of Thomason. It can be found next to another commemorating the legacy of a fellow distinguished curate, Henry Martyn.

Henry Martyn

Though Martyn was younger than Thomason, his life was shorter, and his influence on evangelicalism was far wider. Martyn's tablet at Holy Trinity reads thus:

> This Tablet
> is erected to the Memory of
> The Rev. HENRY MARTYN, B.D.,
> Fellow of St. John's College,
> and two years Curate of this Parish,
> He gained by his talents the highest Academical honours;
> But counting all loss for CHRIST,
> he left his Native Country, and went into the East,
> as a Chaplain of the Hon. East India Company.
> There, having faithfully done the work of an Evangelist,
> in preaching the Gospel of a Crucified Redeemer,
> in translating the Holy Scriptures into the Oriental Languages,
> and in defending the Christian Faith in the heart of Persia
> against the united talents of the most learned Mahometans,
> he died at Tokat on 16th of October, 1812,
> in the 31st year of his age.
> The chief monuments which he left of his piety and talents are
> Translations of the New Testament
> Into the Hindostanee and Persian Languages;
> And "by these he, being dead, yet speaketh."

---

142. Sargent, *Rev. T. T. Thomason*, 334.

"Pray ye the Lord of the harvest,
that He will send forth labourers into His harvest."[143]

Martyn was born in Truro, Cornwall, in 1781. His promising intellect led him to matriculate at St. John's College, Cambridge, in 1797, where he distinguished himself as senior wrangler, a staggering achievement reserved for the top mathematics undergraduate in Cambridge.[144] In the year 1800, Martyn experienced an evangelical conversion, which eventually led him to seek the guidance of Simeon.[145] Martyn enjoyed "the happiness of an admission to the most friendly and unreserved intercourse with him [Simeon], and was in the habit of soliciting and receiving, on all important occasions, his counsel and encouragement."[146] Sarah Rhea recounts the impact Simeon sustained on Martyn in this season.

> At this time he also received great benefit from attendance on the faithful ministry of Rev. Charles Simeon, under whose pastoral instructions he himself declares that he "gradually acquired more knowledge in divine things." With this excellent man he had the most friendly and unreserved intercourse. Mr. Martyn received his first impressions of the transcendent excellence of the Christian ministry of Mr. Simeon, from which it was but a short step to choose this calling for his own, for until now he had intended to devote himself to the law "chiefly," he confesses, "because he could not consent to be poor for Christ's sake."[147]

Forsaking a career in law, Martyn diligently pursued a life of vocational service to God, receiving holy orders on October 22, 1803.[148] For the next two years, he served alongside Thomason and Simeon as a curate at Holy Trinity, the three forming a "happy triumvirate."[149] During these years, Martyn grew in his missionary ambitions. Rhea records the circumstances of his call.

> Henry Martyn's attention was called to the great cause of Foreign Missions by some remarks of Rev. Mr. Simeon on the work

---

143. Carus, *Memoirs*, 363.
144. Sargent, *Rev. Henry Martyn*, 15.
145. Sargent, *Rev. Henry Martyn*, 9–15.
146. Sargent, *Rev. Henry Martyn*, 18.
147. Rhea, *Life of Henry Martyn*, 8.
148. Carus, *Memoirs*, 198.
149. Carus, *Memoirs*, 198.

> of Carey in India, but more particularly by reading the memoir of David Brainerd, who preached with apostolic zeal and success to the North American Indians, and who finished a course of self-denying labors for his Redeemer with unspeakable joy. ... Henry Martyn's soul was filled with holy emulation, and after deep consideration and fervent prayer he was at length fixed in a resolution to imitate his example. Nor let it be conceived that he could adopt this resolution without the severest conflict in his mind, for he was endued with the truest sensibility of heart, and was susceptible of the warmest and tenderest attachments.[150]

By 1805, he left for India as chaplain for the East India Company. This afforded him the opportunity to preach in Dinapur and Cawnpore. Between the years of 1806 and 1810, Martyn translated the New Testament into Urdu, Arabic, and Persian.[151] A similar current ran through his life as his hero David Brainerd (1718–1747): namely, an acute awareness of eternity and the urgency of life. For example, on Martyn's thirtieth birthday, he wrote in his journal after years of missionary service and translating the New Testament into different languages,

> This day I finished the thirtieth year of my unprofitable life, the age at which David Brainerd finished his course. I am now at the age at which the Savior of men began his ministry, and at which John the Baptist called a nation to repentance. Hitherto I have made my youth and insignificance an excuse for sloth and imbecility, now let me have a character and act boldly for God.[152]

Such a tenacious commitment to missionary enterprise blazed within Martyn his entire life. He passed away on October 16, 1812, after his journey to the Ottoman Empire (modern day Turkey), receiving a Christian burial by Armenian Clergy.

Simeon's influence on Martyn cannot be overstated. He not only inspired Henry with what Rhea refers to as the "transcendent excellence of the Christian ministry," but he also supplied Martyn with his original inspiration to pursue a missionary calling. Sargent recorded how "the immediate cause of his [Martyn's] determination to undertake this office, was hearing a remark from Mr. Simeon on the benefit which had resulted from the services of a *single* Missionary* in India; his attention was thus arrested, and his thoughts occupied with the vast importance of

---

150. Rhea, *Life of Henry Martyn*, 9.
151. Sargent, *Rev. Henry Martyn*, 396. See also Bennett, "Martyn, Henry," 438–39.
152. Rhea, *Life of Henry Martyn*, 29.

the subject."[153] The missionary referenced here was the Baptist William Carey. With over two centuries having elapsed since the dawn of the modern missionary movement, such an anecdote might seem insignificant. However, by early nineteenth century standards, for a local parish pastor to have such an interest in frontier Christian missions is noteworthy.[154] Simeon traced his own influence in India when, in 1814, he regarded Abdul Masih (1776-1827)—an Indian native who converted from Islam to Christianity under the preaching of Martyn—as "'a descendant of mine' through our beloved Martyn, who is my son in the faith."[155]

As mentioned above, Martyn's memoirs, prepared by John Sargent, gained a wide readership in the nineteenth century and beyond. It was this volume that seized the attention of a recently converted Robert Murray M'Cheyne (1813-1843), who would go on to become the famous Presbyterian pastor whose ministry shook Scotland.[156] He wrote in his journal, "Reading H. Martyn's Memoirs. Would I could imitate him, giving up father, mother, country, house, health, life, all—for Christ. And yet, what hinders? Lord, purify me, and give me strength to dedicate myself, my all, to Thee!"[157] M'Cheyne's words exemplify the effect Martyn's legacy had on countless evangelicals, motivating them to urgent labor for the sake of the gospel. Simeon himself mirrored the same sentiment. Carus wrote how he often gazed at a portrait of Martyn that hung over his fireplace,

> Mr. Simeon used to observe of Martyn's picture, whilst looking up at it with affectionate earnestness, as it hung over his fireplace: "There!—see that blessed man! What an expression of countenance! No one looks at me as he does—he never takes his eyes off me; and seems always to be saying, Be serious—Be in earnest—Don't trifle—don't trifle." Then smiling at the picture, and gently bowing, he added: "And I won't trifle—I won't trifle."[158]

---

153. Sargent, *Rev. Henry Martyn*, 25.

154. Three followers of Simeon—Richard Johnson (1756-1827), Samuel Marsden (1765-1838), and John Crowther (1792-n.d.)—were notably appointed to ministries in newly settled Australia, though their profiles are beyond the scope of this book. Hardwick, "Australia and New Zealand," 238.

155. Carus, *Memoirs*, 390.

156. The best biographical resource on M'Cheyne is Bonar, *Rev. Robert Murray M'Cheyne*.

157. Bonar, *Rev. Robert Murray M'Cheyne*, 13.

158. Carus, *Memoirs*, 391.

In the case of Martyn, this devoted disciple reversed the relationship dynamic between mentor and pupil, deeply influencing his father in the faith from the grave.

Ordinary Pastors

Thus far, this chapter has examined the legacies of men who served the established church in elevated and extraordinary spheres. Yet the vast majority of Simeon's disciples lived out his pastoral theology in the context of simple callings. In other words, the extent of Simeon's impact needs to be measured in the multiplicity of ordinary ministers made in the image of their mentor. I shall conclude with three such ministers.[159]

Patrick Brontë (1777–1861)

Primarily remembered as the father of literary genius, Patrick Brontë had a fruitful pastorate in West Yorkshire. Though born into an impoverished working-class family in North Ireland, he earned an opportunity to enter St. John's College, Cambridge, in 1802 as a sizar.[160] He quickly came under the influence of Charles Simeon. In particular, Henry Martyn took Patrick under his wing, writing to William Wilberforce: "There is reason to hope that he will be an instrument of good in the church, as a desire of usefulness in the ministry seems to have influenced him hitherto in no small degree."[161] Wilberforce and Thornton went on to sponsor Patrick through university.[162] Brontë historian Dudley Green asserts the high likelihood that Patrick attended Simeon's conversation parties with regularity during his Cambridge years.[163] This is evidenced by his significant interest in Simeon's biography later in life. Patrick's daughter Emily (1818–1848) wrote to Ellen Nussey (1817–1897), "Your offer of Simeon's

---

159. Another notable pastor of ordinary placement that is beyond the scope of this survey was Thomas Jones of Creaton, an evangelical clergyman for whom Simeon secured a living in a small Northamptonshire village. See Balleine, *Evangelical Party*, 122–23.

160. Sizars were lower-class students who were offered subsidized education and lodging often in exchange for certain menial duties. William Grimshaw attended Cambridge as a Sizar. George Whitefield enrolled at Oxford in a similar role.

161. Hopkins, *Charles Simeon of Cambridge*, 114.

162. Atkins, *Converting Britannia*, 55.

163. Green, *Patrick Brontë: Father of Genius*, 35.

'Life' is a very kind one, and I thank you for it. I dare say papa would like to see the work very much, as he knew Mr Simeon."[164] Three months later she wrote again, "Papa has been very much interested in reading the book. There is frequent mention made in it of persons and places formerly well known to him; he thanks you for lending it." After graduating in 1806, he served as a minister in Essex alongside Simeon's close friend Joseph Jowett (1752–1813), a leading evangelical of the time.[165] By 1809, he had moved to West Yorkshire, ultimately taking a living at St Michael and All Angels' Church in Haworth in 1820. From his post in Haworth, Patrick gave himself to a robust visitation circuit and preaching the evangelical doctrine that captured his attention in Cambridge. There, he outlived his wife and six children, including celebrated authors Charlotte (1816–1855), Emily, and Anne (1820–1849).

Though aptly claimed as a Simeonite, Patrick was not without differences from his Cambridge mentor. For example, he forthrightly despised Calvinism. In a letter to James Franks (1793–1867), the Vicar of Huddersfield, he shared his preferences for what he wanted in a curate.

> Yet, I could not feel comfortable with a Coadjutor who would deem it his duty to preach the appalling [sic] doctrines of personal Election and Reprobation. As I should consider these, decidedly derogatory to the Attributes of God—so, also I should be fearful of evil consequences to the hearers, from the enforcement of final perseverance as an essential Article of belief. . . . I want, for this region, a plain rather than an Able preacher; a zealous, but at the same time a judicious man—One, not fond of innovation, but desirous of proceeding on the Good Old plan—which, alas! Has often been mar'd but never improved.[166]

While Simeon freely criticized Calvinism as a system, he was himself an avowed moderate Calvinist, and valued signature Calvinist doctrines. Hopkins also highlights how Simeon would "have strongly disapproved of his [Patrick's] free and easy way in the pulpit." Yet Simeon's imprint can clearly be seen in Patrick's statement in his novelette *The Maid of Killarney*. "I do believe that no preaching is good or calculated to profit except that which is truly apostolical. . . . Let the minister hold up Christ and he will draw all men after him. Let him preach the doctrines of the gospel

---

164. Green, *Patrick Brontë: Father of Genius*, 35–36.
165. Green, *Patrick Brontë: Father of Genius*, 38.
166. Green, *Patrick Brontë: Father of Genius*, 165.

faithfully and plainly, and his church will be crowded."[167] Hopkins concludes that the Haworth minister "was in fact a worthy son of Simeon, and his daughters owed a great deal indirectly to the ideals of Christian family life and worship which were so faithfully being taught to young ordinands like Patrick Brontë."[168]

Francis Close (1797–1882)

Francis Close was born into a ministerial family in Somerset on July 11, 1797. His matriculation at St. John's, Cambridge, occasioned his acquaintance with Simeon. Reminiscing on their relationship, Francis wrote, "In October, 1816, I presented my introduction to him [Simeon]. From that day till his death he was my affectionate father, and my wise and helpful counselor. There were few like him; a perfect gentleman, a deeply taught Christian."[169] In 1820, Francis received his Bachelor of Arts and was ordained a deacon. By 1822, he assumed the role of curate of Willesden and Kingsbury in the London area.[170] He was elevated in 1826 to rector of St. Mary's, Cheltenham, a highly influential parish in the heart of Gloucestershire. For thirty years Francis pastored in Cheltenham before receiving the appointment as the Dean of Carlisle from Prime Minster Henry John Temple (1784–1865), known as Lord Palmerston. This nomination came with the approval of Queen Victoria (1819–1901).[171] Francis Close finished his course in 1882 at the ripe age of eighty-five years old, and was buried in the town to which he gave his golden years. From his posts in Cheltenham and Carlisle, Francis led a ministry of an unapologetic evangelical, a reputation well-earned by his fierce opposition to the Oxford Movement.[172] Doubtlessly, Francis confronted the Tractarians in the spirit of his mentor, though Simeon did not live to see the movement grow into full fruition.[173] In addition to his evangelical convictions, Francis's preaching clearly imbibed the style of Simeon. This element will be more thoroughly examined in chapter 6. Perhaps the highest commendation

---

167. Brontë, *Maid of Killarney*, 13.
168. Hopkins, *Charles Simeon of Cambridge*, 114.
169. Moule, *Charles Simeon*, 45.
170. "Late Dean of Carlisle."
171. *London Gazette*, 3919.
172. Close, *Apology*. William Gresley (1801–1876) was a noteworthy Tractarian and leader in the Oxford Movement.
173. Hopkins, *Charles Simeon of Cambridge*, 117.

Francis received was from Simeon himself, who visited Francis in Cheltenham months before his death in Cambridge. Commenting on the spiritual health of the region, the elderly Simeon wrote,

> Here at Cheltenham, I have almost had a heaven upon earth. The churches so capacious and so filled; the schools so large; so numerous, so beneficial; the people so full of love; the ministers such laborious and energetic men; and God himself so graciously with me in my exertions; in truth I can scarcely conceive any higher happiness on earth than I am now privileged to enjoy.[174]

Simeon's reference to a plurality of "laborious and energetic men" perhaps speaks of Francis's influence on the area, given that this was written over a decade after the latter's arrival in Cheltenham.

Of the numerous disciples of Simeon, Francis Close provided some of the most vivid insights into his mentor's character. Moreover, it is this Cambridge ordinand who may have been closest to Simeon in personality and constitution, aptly described by Hopkins as "a man of like temperament."[175] In the final year of his life, Francis recounted a fascinating anecdote about Simeon that shows something of the magnetism which granted him success as a ministerial mentor.

> His knowledge of men and things was wonderful, and his conversation about them original and unique. There was a racy wit about him, and a natural playfulness perfectly captivating. He had a surprising faculty for reproving persons for their faults with great fidelity, yet without offending them. "How do you manage to do this?" said I one day to him. "I will tell you the secret," said he; "observation has taught me that men's faults and failings generally lie immediately above their excellencies; so I first always give them full credit for their good qualities, and then they are more disposed to listen to their delinquencies. For instance, there is an evangelist whom I much admire; he gets into the pulpit, opens his Bible, and looks round on his large congregation with a somewhat defiant aspect; and then he fully declares both judgment and mercy. But perhaps there is a little want of love, and gentleness, and consideration for the weak and timid." And looking upon his great arched eyebrows, I instantly perceived that his illustration was intended for myself![176]

---

174. Carus, *Memoirs*, 783.
175. Hopkins, *Charles Simeon of Cambridge*, 170.
176. Moule, *Charles Simeon*, 179.

It is noteworthy that Francis could bear such eloquent witness to Simeon's playful charm roughly sixty years after the encounter. But wit and humor were not the only things admired by the Dean of Carlisle. Francis learned pastoral endurance from Simeon, who always maintained a tenacious commitment to his convictions, unhindered by any fear of man.[177] Thus, Francis preached to his congregation in his Cheltenham years, "In the discharge of duty to be indifferent alike to the frowns and smiles of his fellow-creatures, what courage, firmness, wisdom and love are needful."[178]

Francis Close maintained a manifestly intimate friendship with Simeon until the latter's death in 1836. The rector of Cheltenham was numbered among the few men who were invited to Cambridge to celebrate Simeon's Jubilee in 1832.[179] Francis found himself privy to Simeon's deepest moments of introspection. In an 1827 letter, Simeon wrote to Francis, "You perhaps see much amiss in me which my own self-love has hidden from my view. But this I can say, I desire to mortify sin so far as I can discover it; though, alas, my desire is miserably thwarted through my own unwatchfulness."[180] Chapter 4 will expound more of the personal piety Simeon promoted in ministry. Suffice it to say, Francis—along with a great host of fellow Simeonites—was deeply affected by Simeon's humility.

Francis Close ended up providing the most enlightening commentary on the funeral of Simeon. As an "astonished spectator,"[181] he recounted,

> The like of it was never seen, nor ever will be seen again. More than 1500 gownsmen attended to honour a man who had been greatly despised. When his venerable remains were deposited in that glorious building, every bell of the College Chapels tolled for him, and the Vice-Chancellor (Ainslie, Master of Pembroke,) regretted that the great bell of St Mary's could not, as its use was confined to the Royal Family, or to a Vice-Chancellor dying in office. Such was the honour the great King was pleased to bestow upon his servant.... "And they glorified God in him."[182]

---

177. Hopkins, *Charles Simeon of Cambridge*, 170.
178. Close, *Occasional Sermons*, 183.
179. Moule, *Charles Simeon*, 248.
180. Close, *Occasional Sermons*, 204–5.
181. Moule, *Charles Simeon*, 179.
182. Moule, *Charles Simeon*, 275–76.

In the mind of Francis, such was the influence of Simeon that he traced a "parallel between Pusey[183] at Oxford and Simeon at Cambridge."[184]

Charles Bridges (1794–1869)

Though there exists scant biographical material on Charles Bridges, he left behind a phenomenal literary legacy. When Robert Murray M'Cheyne journeyed to the Holy Land in 1838, he brought with him only three books: a Hebrew Bible, a Greek New Testament, and Charles Bridges's *The Christian Ministry*.[185] To M'Cheyne, Bridges was the only uninspired author able to keep him and others "in mind for [their] ministerial work." This commendation certainly served Bridges's posthumous profile, for it is estimated that by 1910, over half a million copies of M'Cheyne's memoirs were in circulation.[186] Within twenty years of its first publishing, *The Christian Ministry* went through nine editions, earning significant acclaim in evangelical circles. In addition to this work, Bridge's commentaries were also widely read. For example, in 1827, he wrote his first work: *Exposition of Psalm 119*. Thirty years later, he penned a preface to the twenty-second edition of the same work.[187] With such achievements in writing, one might have expected Bridges to have a large and influential parish ministry. In reality, he did not.

Born in 1794, Bridges matriculated at Queen's College, Cambridge, in 1812. This was the same year Simeon began his famous conversation parties. By that point, over a decade had transpired since the vicar of Holy Trinity was despised by his people. He had earned tremendous esteem in the halls of Cambridge and the wider evangelical world. Throughout the 1810s and onward, hundreds of Cambridge students worshiped at Simeon's church and dozens gathered weekly in his home for colloquial lectures. Bridges reflected Simeon's influence in his subsequent writings. After his ordination in 1817, he served as vicar of Old Newton, Suffolk from 1823 to 1849. The last twenty years of his life he ministered in two parishes in Dorset.[188] Despite Bridges's literary accolades, his ministry

---

183. Edward Pusey (1800–1882) was a leading figure in the Oxford Movement. For more on Pusey, see Liddon, *Edward Bouverie Pusey*.

184. Moule, *Charles Simeon*, 179.

185. Bonar, *Rev. Robert Murray M'Cheyne*, 87.

186. Bridges, *Christian Ministry*.

187. Bridges, *Psalm 119*, xvi.

188. "Bridges, Charles."

was that of quiet service in relatively small parishes. Yet the character of his pastorate did not escape the attention of some prominent men. For example, the Scottish Presbyterian Thomas Chalmers (1780–1847) developed a close friendship with Bridges. In a visit to Suffolk in 1833, Chalmers wrote of Bridges's tender care for his flock, evidenced by a robust visitation schedule, "I never witnessed such closeness and efficiency of pastoral work as he exemplified in his addresses to the mothers of families."[189] In a subsequent treatise titled *The Right Ecclesiastical Economy of a Large Town*, Chalmers attested of Bridges,

> My excellent friend, the Rev. Charles Bridges, of Old Newton, Suffolk, finds, I am sure, most ample occupation among those six hundred people whom he may be said to have domesticated into one parochial family; and, were it not for his still more important services to the Christian church at large, would show, by his incessant labours, how possible it were to make out a most beneficial expenditure of all his strength and all his time amongst them.[190]

Bridges is remembered for a life that epitomized pastoral care.

The pastoral theology of Charles Bridges most clearly manifested itself in his magnum opus *The Christian Ministry*, a volume that became a ministry manual for generations of evangelicals, Anglican and Nonconformist. Simeon's fingertips can be seen throughout the book, particularly in the sections on preaching, where he is extensively referenced. Notably, Bridges applauded Simeon's preface to *Horae Homileticae* "as a full, clear, and unfettered display of Evangelical truth."[191] Elsewhere, Bridges wrote, "Perhaps the highest commendation of the work [*Horae Homileticae*] is that a mere copyist would exhibit the Skeletons like the bones in the prophetic vision: very dry. Whereas a thoughtful mind would find ample and profitable employment in clothing them with solid matter, in the form of symmetry and strength."[192] It is significant at this point, for example, to highlight how Charles Spurgeon interacted with Bridges on the work of Simeon. In a lecture to his students, Spurgeon—who read Bridges frequently—commended Simeon's work with Bridges's words in mind. He issued the following comment on *Horae*

---

189. Hanna, *Writings of Thomas Chalmers*, 396–97.
190. Chalmers, *Right Ecclesiastical Economy*, 24.
191. Bridges, *Christian Ministry*, 304.
192. Bridges, *Christian Ministry*, 199.

Homileticae, "Not commentaries, but we could not exclude them. They have been called 'a valley of dry bones': be a prophet and they will live."[193] As shall be shown in chapter 6, Simeon's expositions were best used as helps rather than manuscripts. For now, the salient point is to show how the remarkable breadth of Simeon's influence reached England's most celebrated Victorian preacher through the work of Bridges.

One of the greatest ways Simeon influenced Bridges was in the former's death. Carus's memoirs offer a narrative of Simeon's final days in which the Cambridge pastor expressed profound peace and contentment in Christ as he lay dying. In his final published work *An Exposition of the Book of Ecclesiastes*, Bridges remembered Simeon's last words as he charged his readers to find satisfaction in God.

> Looking then to him—anxious soul—stretch your expectation to the uttermost. The world has left you dissatisfied, restless, and unhappy. Now let God's remedy be fairly tried. If this does not fill up the void, ease the disquietude, and sustain the heart in the conflict—let it be cast away. The testimonies to its efficacy are undoubted. "It is all that is valuable"—said the dying Scott. "You may think that it does little for me now. But it is all. I have found more in Christ, than I ever expected to want." Another witness we have in the last exercise of the venerated Simeon—"I am in a dear Father's hand. All is secure. I see nothing but faithfulness—and immutability—and truth. I have not a doubt or a fear, but the sweetest peace." . . . So fully does the precious remedy unfold its entire satisfaction and triumph in the moment of nature's extremity![194]

Once again, Simeon's evangelical spirituality and pastoral theology reverberated through another notable disciple.

Conclusion

This chapter has shown the staggering impact Simeon had on evangelicalism. In particular, it highlighted the legacies of prominent pastoral pupils in a variety of spheres: episcopate, missionary, and ordinary. It remains important to reiterate that the figures sketched here form a mere fraction of the followers Simeon led in his lifetime. Historian G. R. Balleine aptly describes the character that lent breadth to his influence:

193. Spurgeon, *Commenting and Commentaries*, 42.
194. Bridges, *Exposition*, 94.

"A teacher so wise, so genial, so spiritual, moulding the lives of the men from whom the bulk of the clergy were drawn, acquired a position almost unique in the English Church."[195] Daniel Wilson, the Bishop of Calcutta also summarized this point well:

> And the result, be it observed, was, that by these and similar causes, that is, the mere force of evangelical truth and holiness thus exhibited during fifty or sixty years, and not by great talents, or extraordinary powers of judgment, or particular attainments in academical learning, God gave him this wide and blessed influence over the age in which he lived. So far from being the man whom we should at first abstractedly have selected for the delicate and difficult post of an University, we should have perhaps considered him peculiarly unfitted for it.[196]

Indeed, through an extraordinary commitment to ordinary pastoral ministry, Simeon exerted a "wide and blessed influence" on his age and far beyond.

---

195. Balleine, *Evangelical Party*, 130.
196. Carus, *Memoirs*, 846.

CHAPTER 3

Anglican Archetype

IN THE YEAR 1869, J. C. Ryle published *The Christian Leaders of the Last Century*, a four hundred page collection of historical sketches on various leading lights of early evangelicalism.[1] As then Rural Dean of Hoxne, Ryle asserted his aim in writing the book: "My object in drawing up these papers was to bring before the public in a comprehensive form the lives, characters, and work of the leading ministers by whose agency God was pleased to revive Christianity in England a hundred years ago."[2] Ryle esteemed men like Whitefield, Wesley, Grimshaw, Berridge, and Venn as eminent servants of God who, in varying degrees, maintained an admirable devotion to the Church of England. As a distinguished evangelical churchman himself, Ryle had a vested interest in proving the viability of evangelicalism within the walls of Anglicanism. Thus, throughout his biographies, he sought to prove that evangelicalism was not merely consistent with the forms and doctrine of the established church, but was her greatest source of health. For example, commenting on the legacy of William Romaine, he wrote,

> Romaine had a very deep sense of the value of the Church of England. He loved her Articles and Prayer-Book with no common love. Whatever her defects in administration, and however ill she treated her best children, he believed that the occupant of her pulpits had peculiar advantages; and he

1. Ryle, *Last Century*.
2. Ryle, *Last Century*, iii.

steadfastly refused to leave her. He was catholic, and kind, and liberal to those who were not churchmen, and lived in habits of friendly communion with many of them.³

According to Ryle, the early evangelicals fostered an attitude of enthusiasm toward the Church of England.⁴ Likewise, Ryle understood himself to be carrying the same banner as his forebears: namely, he earnestly promoted evangelical ideals that would produce a more vibrant Church of England, without sacrificing an ounce of affection for her. In doing so, he followed a pattern perfected and popularized by Charles Simeon. This leads historian Kenneth Hylson-Smith to argue that by 1880, Ryle emerged "as the first undisputed leader in [evangelical] ranks since the days of Charles Simeon."⁵ Ryle represented evangelical commitment to the established church—a hallmark of Simeon's ministry, if not its crowning feature. This chapter will explore Simeon's relationship to the Church of England, revealing it to be a distinct element of his pastoral theology, and thus, an eminent part of his indelible influence.

For over a half century, Simeon embodied the spirit of evangelicalism, which reached full fruition in his lifetime.⁶ Indeed, he left a legacy of unparalleled commitment to the movement. While his interest in missions, expository preaching, and ministerial training has been well documented, his relationship to the Church of England, on the other hand, remains less emphasized in Simeon scholarship. Throughout his life, he evidenced an unwavering devotion to the Anglican Way. In fact, perhaps the two words that best encapsulate his ministry are "evangelical churchman." At least one scholar has identified Simeon as the most influential of Anglican evangelicals, "who in many respects was the shaper, if not the founder, of the movement within the Church of England."⁷ George Russell, for his part, asserted, "Simeon was fundamentally and essentially an Evangelical of the Evangelicals, but not less distinctly a loyal son of the Church of England. He exalted the Christian ministry."⁸

For much of its history, the established Church of England has consisted of several informal constituencies. Gerald Bray offers brief

---

3. Ryle, *Last Century*, 164.

4. Ryle pervasively makes this assertion throughout his writing. On Whitefield, Wesley, Grimshaw, and Venn respectively, see Ryle, *Last Century*, 39, 103, 128–29, 258.

5. Hylson-Smith, *Evangelicals*.

6. Bebbington, *Evangelicalism in Modern Britain*, 3.

7. Bray, *Anglicanism*, 28.

8. Russell, *Short History*, 53.

descriptions of various traditions: low church, high church, latitudinarianism, evangelicalism, Anglo-Catholicism, liberalism, and broad church—none of them representing a monolith.[9] For example, "evangelical" and "low church" have often been used synonymously.[10] At the beginning of Simeon's Cambridge ministry in the 1770s, low church evangelicalism had negligible institutional sway in the Church of England. By his death in 1836, it is estimated that a third of Anglican pulpits were evangelical.[11] John Walsh and Stephen Taylor write, "Estimates of Evangelical clerical numbers for the early nineteenth century vary considerably, but by 1830 they were clearly a formidable phalanx. One Dissenting estimate puts their strength in 1839 as possibly, 3,000 clergymen."[12] Regardless of the precise figures, such a massive shift in the established church would have been unthinkable apart from the sustained influence of men like Simeon. Yet before examining Simeon as an archetypal Anglican, one must first survey the state of evangelicalism in the eighteenth century, noting the relationship between several prominent evangelical ministers and the Church of England.

Evangelicals and the Church of England

As previously stated, Simeon's life saw the status of evangelicalism in the established church move from that of a barely tolerated radical fringe to a thriving, forceful influence. Various factors explain the institutional resistance to evangelicalism in the first several decades of the eighteenth century. Though some have identified limitations to Bebbington's work on evangelicalism, he has helpfully summarized the movement as one committed to biblicism, crucicentrism, conversionism, and activism.[13] Such a movement with profound doctrinal, ethical, and missional implications could not evade opposition. Bebbington summarizes.

> To be told that sincerity in the performance of the religious duties of one's station did not command the blessing of God was startling, if not insulting. To be assured that good works were as filthy rags seemed subversive of all morality. To hear faith lauded

9. Bray, *Anglicanism*, 25–33.
10. "Charles Simeon," Britannica.
11. Prime, *Charles Simeon*, 239.
12. Walsh and Taylor, "Introduction," 44.
13. Haykin and Stewart, *Emergence of Evangelicalism*.

to the skies aroused suspicions of fanaticism, the "enthusiasm" that the eighteenth century shunned because its seventeenth-century version had killed a king. Polite society was alarmed. It is true that Frederick, Prince of Wales, was so impressed that he was rumoured to be intending to use his powers as monarch to make Whitefield a bishop. But Frederick was on bad terms with his father, George II, and in any case predeceased him in 1751. Evangelical penetration of high society, with the notable exceptions of the Countess of Huntingdon and the Earl of Dartmouth, was deferred until the aftermath of the French Revolution, when a high religious profile began to have welcome anti-revolutionary connotations. So the Evangelical movement laboured under severe disadvantages. Undergraduates were expelled from Oxford for Methodist practices in 1768; young men suspected of Evangelical views were denied ordination in certain dioceses of the Church of England; and unwelcome ministers of more sober outlook were imposed on parishes with Evangelical preferences in the Church of Scotland.[14]

Perry Butler concurs with Bebbington when he asserts that evangelical views "provoked hostility: bishops were disinclined to ordain them and livings were difficult to procure."[15]

Opposition to evangelicalism never ultimately waned in England. For example, later Victorian literature sharply criticized the movement. In George Eliot's (1819–1880) tale, *Janet's Repentance*, the evangelical curate Mr. Tryan is portrayed as preaching against good works, reflecting the ongoing accusation that evangelical commitment to a gospel of grace would produce societal decline.[16] In Charles Dickens's (1812–1870) *The Pickwick Papers*, Mr. Stiggins is presented as a hypocritical minister who drinks excessively despite his church's opposition to drunkenness.[17] Meanwhile, Jane Austen (1775–1817) serves as a fascinating case study, as her own opinion on evangelicalism exhibited the shifting sentiment in the nineteenth century among many members of the Church of England. At one point, she explicitly declared to her sister Cassandra (1773–1845) in 1809, "I do not like the Evangelicals."[18] This she wrote in reference to

14. Bebbington, *Evangelicalism in Modern Britain*, 22–23.
15. Butler, "Early Eighteenth Century," 34.
16. Eliot, *Janet's Repentance*, 4.
17. Dickens, *Pickwick Papers*, 359.
18. Austen, *Jane Austen's Letters*, 177. On the influence of Hannah More at this period of time, see Collins, *Jane Austen*, 145–47. On Jane's dislike of evangelical preaching, see Collins, *Jane Austen*, 216–17. For other areas where Jane disagreed with

the fierce convictions of Hannah More (1745–1833) manifested in the latter's writings.[19] Yet, it appears her posture eventually softened, for by 1814, she told her niece Fanny Knight (1793–1882), "I am by no means convinced that we ought not all to be Evangelicals, & am persuaded that they who are so from reason & feeling, must be happiest & safest."[20] This letter to Fanny was written in the same year that she published *Mansfield Park*. Within that novel, she promoted a brand of ministry tinctured by evangelical values. She also subtly critiqued the low ebb of spiritual vitality in the Church of England. Thus, while Austen criticized a deficient view of the clergy in her satirical depiction of Mr. Collins in *Pride and Prejudice*,[21] she promoted a robust parish ministry through Edmund Bertram in *Mansfield Park*.[22]

Despite multiple forms of antipathy, the turn of the nineteenth century saw the formation of a well-defined evangelical party in the Church of England, with somewhere around three hundred to five hundred ministers.[23] Moreover, the first three decades of the eighteenth century—the peak of Simeon's influence in Cambridge—has aptly been described as Evangelicals' "golden age."[24] For the purposes of this chapter, it is worth highlighting how various evangelicals operated in the shifting landscape of conformity. In most discussions on early evangelicals, much attention must be devoted to Whitefield and Wesley. However, due to the highly revivalistic, outward-facing nature of their ministries, they are not useful case studies for discerning the relationship between the average evangelical vicar and the established church.[25] Therefore, this chapter will survey the ecclesiological convictions of John Newton, John Berridge, William Romaine, and Henry Venn—four men who exerted varying degrees of commitment to the Church of England and influence on Simeon.

---

evangelicalism, see Collins, *Jane Austen*, 186–88.

19. Hannah More was an influential writer, philanthropist, poet, playwright, and esteemed member of the evangelical Clapham Sect. For more on her life, see Prior, *Fierce Convictions*.

20. Austen, *Jane Austen's Letters*, 292.

21. Austen, *Pride and Prejudice*.

22. Austen, *Mansfield Park*, 68.

23. Butler, "Early Eighteenth Century," 34.

24. Butler, "Early Eighteenth Century," 34.

25. Neither Whitefield nor Wesley ever held a living in the Church of England. Ryle, *Last Century*, 107.

John Newton

John Newton's dramatic conversion from an immoral life in the slave trade is well known.[26] His subsequent ministry essentially took place in three stages. First, he gave himself to lay ministry during his time as a surveyor in Liverpool from 1757 to 1764.[27] He prayed and preached in various societies and churches as he patiently waited for a formal call to ministry. During these years, he solidly established his reputation for interdenominational irenicism—entertaining ministries among Independents, Methodists, Presbyterians, and Anglicans.[28] The second stage of his career was his curacy in Olney, where he served as pastor of a bustling parish from 1764 to 1779. His sermons were so deeply evangelistic that by 1775, he could claim one hundred souls had been converted under his oversight.[29] His evangelical fervor was accented by a rigorous visiting schedule, often visiting several families per day. In his third stage of ministry, he was admired as an evangelical statesman in his post at St. Mary Woolnoth in London from 1779 until his death in 1807. On the whole, Newton the evangelical was conformist by convenience. This was demonstrated generally by his lukewarm attitude toward ecclesiology and generous posture toward Methodism and Dissent.

Though maintaining some ecclesiastical convictions, Newton's denominational nonchalance stands out as the most noteworthy part of his ecclesiology, especially in the first half of his ministry. In other words, the most distinctive feature of his ecclesiology was his lack of one. As noted above, he could have happily served in several different denominations. He even nursed an affection for Particular Baptists his entire life. This came at the expense of stoking the ire of his friends and family.[30] Though he would grow in his loyalty to the Church of England, he was thoroughly unattached to any denomination for the first several years of his ministry. He actually once remarked to a friend in a 1762 letter, "I do give preference to that Church order which is generally called Independent."[31]

---

26. For more on John Newton, see Aitken, *John Newton*; Hindmarsh, *John Newton*; Hindmarsh, *Life and Spirituality*.
27. Hindmarsh, *John Newton*, 84.
28. Hindmarsh, *John Newton*, 83–118.
29. Hindmarsh, *John Newton*, 188.
30. Hindmarsh, *John Newton*, 77.
31. Newton, *Twenty-Five Letters*, 52.

Arguably, it is unlikely that Newton would have held that same view by 1779, when he began his London rectorship.

As an Anglican, Newton regularly attested that the Prayer Book was "the most satisfactory writing of its kind, being of a merely human authority."[32] In 1789, after serving for decades in the established church, he commented on some criticism that he had received from Dissenting friends: "A dear Dissenting brother of mine who was hurt by the publication of Apologia,[33] said to me, I am sorry you are much more of a churchman than you were formerly. I answered, I do not think myself more of a churchman, but I am indeed less of a Dissenter."[34] This quote comes from a letter to John Ryland Jr. (1753–1825), one of the many Particular Baptists with whom Newton warmly and regularly corresponded.[35] Thus, while it appears that Newton retained a deep respect and appreciation for Evangelicalism, in each of its denominational expressions, he ultimately found the channel of the established church to be most superior and strategic. However, Newton's place in the Church of England formed no meaningful part of his pastoral theology. Despite his massive profile, he charted no path for sustainable evangelical influence on the state church.

John Berridge

The previous chapter highlighted the personal impact John Berridge had on Simeon. But as shall be shown below, Berridge's influence on Simeon did not extend into the realm of ecclesiology, for Berridge represented an entirely different type of Anglican. Historian Mark Noll describes William Romaine as an *evangelical Anglican*, and John Wesley as an *Anglican evangelical*, with Charles Wesley somewhere in between.[36] On such a spectrum, John Berridge certainly aligned with the elder Wesley. With relatively little interest in denominational life, the chief aim of his life was to arouse the faith of his hearers, often through the means of irregularity. Like Newton, Berridge's indifference toward the Church of England was borne out in his relationship to Methodism and Dissent. But unlike

---

32. Hindmarsh, *John Newton*, 88.
33. Newton, *Apologia*.
34. Hindmarsh, *John Newton*, 318.
35. For more on Newton's relationship to Ryland Jr., see Newton, *Wise Counsel*.
36. Noll, *Rise of Evangelicalism*, 116.

Newton, his disregard for the Church of England manifested itself in his ministerial distinctives, particularly his evangelism style.

Itinerancy

Itinerancy defined the second half of Berridge's life. Though he preached in prestigious pulpits throughout Cambridge,[37] his great pleasure was "to go round the neighbourhood, preaching in the fields, wherever a door is opened, three or four days in every week."[38] While some men may have sought a profit in itinerancy, Ryle notes Berridge's profound generosity in his travels.

> Berridge was a man of singular kindness and self-denial. No man perhaps ever carried on Christ's work with more thoroughly unselfish views. Whether at home or abroad, he was always giving, and never receiving, and went through all his immense labors gratuitously. Houses and barns were rented for preaching, lay-preachers maintained in all directions, and his own traveling expenses defrayed by himself. Whenever he preached in a cottage, he invariably left half-a-crown for the use of it; and, during his itinerancy, he actually spent £500 in this way alone. Cases of distress and suffering always met with munificent help from him. His whole income, both private and professional, was annually spent in doing good, and even his family plate was sold to buy clothes for his itinerant preachers.[39]

Ryle's point not only highlights *where* Berridge preached, but *how* he conducted himself. Though many later evangelical Anglicans rejected Berridge's brand of itinerancy, even Simeon asserted that he "lived when few Ministers cared about the Gospel, and when disorder was almost needful. I don't think he would do now as he did then; for there are so many means of hearing the Gospel, and a much greater spread of it; a much greater call for order, and much less need of disorder."[40] Peter Virgin believes Simeon's aversion to itinerancy emerged from a larger pastoral theology. He asserts, "Simeon was upholding what he saw as a fundamental principle of Establishment—the maintenance of a constant relation between one pastor and one flock. For him, it was a spiritual matter. It

---

37. Smyth, *Simeon and Church Order*, 177.
38. Smyth, *Simeon and Church Order*, 169.
39. Ryle, *Last Century*, 246–47.
40. Brown, *Recollections*, 200.

was his influence that did much to prevent a split within the Evangelical movement on the itinerancy issue."[41]

Methodism and Dissent

Berridge freely owned the title of a Methodist throughout the latter half of the eighteenth century. As soon as he began his preaching circuits, he drew the attention of John Wesley. A certain Methodist named John Walsh wrote to Wesley in 1758, "[Berridge] meets little companies of his Converts from several towns and villages, at his own house. He was once ashamed of the word Methodist, but takes it to himself now as freely as I do. The country seems to kindle round him."[42] Throughout the bustle of Berridge's revivals, he sensed great freedom in his irregularity. He rejoiced to see sinners come to what he believed to be a saving knowledge of God. Notably, Berridge took on a conciliatory posture toward evangelical Dissenters. For example, he warmly approved of Robert Robinson (1735–1790), encouraging him to engage in itinerant ministry.[43] Such an irenic gesture was uncommon between later Cambridge ministers Charles Simeon and Robert Hall Jr. (1764–1831), the pastor who replaced Robinson at St Andrews Street Baptist Church. For the purposes of this study, though Berridge failed to deeply influence Simeon's ecclesiology, he represented a prominent way of being evangelical in the established church during the formative years of Simeon's ministry.

William Romaine

By the middle decades of the eighteenth century, the burgeoning evangelical movement still held little sway in the elite circles of the Church of England, with continued ire directed toward the likes of Whitefield and the Wesleys. Despite this ongoing challenge, the Anglican William Romaine served as a harbinger of the greater evangelical influence exerted in following generations. He was the very first evangelical to attain a post in London, followed by John Newton in 1780. This fact alone merits close

---

41. Virgin, *Age of Negligence*, 143.

42. Smyth, *Simeon and Church Order*, 164.

43. Smyth, *Simeon and Church Order*, 179. Robert Robinson was a Particular Baptist remembered for a variety of eccentricities. He was the pastor of St. Andrews Street Baptist Church, which experienced significant growth under his tenure. For more on Robinson, see Dyer, *Robert Robinson*.

study. Ryle summarized Romaine's London legacy, saying he "*became a rallying point for all in London who loved evangelical truth in the Church of England*. Man after man, and family after family, gathered round his pulpit, until his congregation became the nucleus of a vast amount of good in the metropolis."[44] But Romaine also deserves attention for his brand of evangelicalism that manifested itself within the regular channels of the established church. Noll's moniker of *evangelical Anglican*, in distinction from *Anglican evangelical*, proves to be useful as it helps to explain significant differences between Romaine and his peers.[45] It also provides a paradigm for the type of ministry that Simeon would later popularize.

Born to a French Protestant refugee in the country of Durham, William matriculated at Christ Church, Oxford, in the early 1730s. Though his Oxford years coincided with Whitefield and the Wesleys, he did not come into contact with evangelical emphases in their infancy. Known for his academic brilliance, Romaine gave himself diligently to study. One Oxford instructor described Romaine as "one of the greatest geniuses of the age, and is likely to be one of the greatest men in the kingdom."[46] After his ordination as a deacon at Hereford in 1736, he became priest in 1738. Like many in the eighteenth century, Romaine experienced an evangelical conversion while in ministry. Noll estimates this event to have occurred around 1745, or shortly after.[47] From then on, his preaching was marked by distinctly evangelical fervor. From the years 1748 to 1766, he served in a variety of churches in London. During this period, Romaine experienced persecution from his church wardens similar to what Simeon would endure later in Cambridge.[48] Despite these challenges, he gained special notoriety for his evangelistic preaching during the aftermath of the Lisbon Earthquakes of 1755.[49] Romaine's final calling in 1766 was as

---

44. Ryle, *Last Century*, 168.

45. Noll, *Rise of Evangelicalism*, 116.

46. Cadogan, *Rev. William Romaine*, 6. In 1749, he assumed the lectureship of St. Dunstan's. During these years, Romaine experienced acute persecution. He was permitted by a certain Lord Mansfield to preach, but not until seven on Sunday evenings. Despising Romaine, the church wardens would leave the church doors locked until the exact moment the service began. They also failed to provide adequate lighting for these evening services. Though Romaine's biographer William Bromley Cadogan (1751–1797) provides little rationale for this behavior, it is reasonable to suppose these high churchmen deprecated Romaine's evangelical convictions.

47. Noll, *Rise of Evangelicalism*, 115.

48. Cadogan, *Rev. William Romaine*, 18.

49. Ryle, *Last Century*, 158.

Rector of St. Ann's, Blackfriars, an assembly less than a quarter mile from St. Paul's Cathedral. Though his election to the position was fraught with controversy, the following twenty-nine years of ministry were characterized by quiet service to God. He died on July 26, 1795, one of the most prominent preachers in the world's largest city.

Romaine numbered among the ministers who, like Samuel Walker of Truro and William Grimshaw of Haworth, forwarded a specific brand of evangelicalism in the Church of England.[50] Though they cooperated with Whitefield and the Wesleys, they represented the "vanguard of an evangelical Anglicanism that could not be subsumed neatly into any Methodist movement."[51] Romaine, for his part, saw fantastic growth in the evangelical wing of the established church in his lifetime. In 1757, he published a letter entitled, "An Earnest Invitation to the Friends of the Established Church to join with several of their brethren, clergy and laity, in London, in setting apart an hour of every week for Prayer and Supplication during the present troublesome times."[52] At the time, only a dozen ministers joined him in this task. By the end of his life in 1795, Romaine could boast over three hundred like-minded ministers in England.[53]

Churchmanship

Romaine evidenced an unflagging loyalty to the Church of England all his days. In his popular trilogy *The Life, Walk, and Triumph of Faith*, he promoted a devotional use of scripture to foster greater piety and communion with God. He called Christians to read, meditate, and pray, that "thou mayest have fellowship."[54] To emphasize this point, he employed the Anglican formularies. For example, quoting the *Book of Common Prayer* in *The Triumph of Faith*, he concluded, "From these authorities, it appears to be the doctrine of the scriptures, and of our reformers in harmony with them, that spiritual life, and knowledge, and faith in Christ . . . come from the holy inspiration of God the Spirit."[55] Elsewhere, he expounds the ninth article of the Church of England to explain the nature of sin in the believer

---

50. For summaries, see Hylson-Smith, *Evangelicals*, 17–32; and Elliot-Binns, *Early Evangelicals*.

51. Noll, *Rise of Evangelicalism*, 114.

52. Ryle, *Last Century*, 178,

53. Ryle, *Last Century*, 179,

54. Hindmarsh, *Spirit of Early Evangelicalism*, 73.

55. Romaine, *Life, Walk, and Triumph*, 406.

and unbeliever.[56] The established church's Articles and her Prayer Book provided tremendous sustenance to his ministry.

Characteristic of many evangelicals, Romaine built his career on the foundation of a robust pulpit schedule. Even at the ripe age of eighty-one, he preached at least three times per week.[57] He believed those entrusted to his care needed God's word to thrive. In addition to his evangelical emphases, Romaine's sermons were staunchly Calvinistic. This invited the criticism of Simeon, who as a moderate Calvinist, accused Romaine of an overly static view of grace.[58] Simeon thought Romaine—in his zeal to preach justification—failed to stress the nature of sanctification in the life of the believer.[59] Historian Bebbington notes a similar deficiency in Romaine's ministry. "[He] so exalted faith that he seemed to depreciate the law. Romaine was said to have made many antinomians—that is, to have propagated the view that the believer is not bound by the moral law."[60] Despite the merits of these critiques, they mainly impugn Romaine's lack of balance rather than any explicit teachings. The burden of his public proclamation was to expose the guilt of sinners before a holy God, and render Christ as a sufficient savior for all who would repent.

Prayer for the Established Church

Romaine did not only seek the good of his own congregation. He assiduously served other churches. Beginning in 1756, he made it his practice every Friday to publicly pray for other Anglican clergy by name. To do this effectively, he acquired intimate knowledge of his city's co-laborers.[61] He also gathered weekly with a few ministers to pray for revival in the established church. In the wake of his death, Romaine's biographer Cadogan credited the improved spiritual health of England to his perseverance in prayer.[62]

---

56. Romaine, *Life, Walk, and Triumph*, 425.
57. Ryle, *Last Century*, 174.
58. Brown, *Recollections*, 102.
59. Brown, *Recollections*, 265.
60. Bebbington, *Evangelicalism in Modern Britain*, 63.
61. Cadogan, *Rev. William Romaine*, 43–45.
62. Cadogan, *Rev. William Romaine*, 56.

Support from Evangelical Elite

As the first evangelical Anglican priest in London, Romaine earned the favor of influential supporters. This included figures like Selina Hastings, the Countess of Huntingdon, the philanthropist John Thornton, and the barrister Martin Madan (1726–1790). Lady Huntingdon was said to have left no stone unturned in her effort to secure Romaine a long-term preaching post in London. But not all of his greatest advocates were amongst the social elite. Ryle recounts a nameless publican in the Blackfriars parish who tirelessly canvassed the region to drum up support for Romaine's rectorship. Evidently, the publican's efforts were fueled by thankfulness for his wife's spiritual growth under the minister's fervent preaching. Romaine entered the stream of many evangelicals who garnered support from both high and low society.[63]

Reverence for Worship

Romaine's biographers note the austere tenor of his ministry. Cadogan characterizes him as "irritable to a certain degree, short and quick in his replies, and frequently mistaken as being rude and morose, where he meant nothing of the kind."[64] In his defense of Romaine, Cadogan continues,

> Had he paid more attention than he did to the various distresses of soul and body which were brought before him, he would have had no time left for reading, meditation, and prayer, and, in short, for what every man must attend to in private who would be useful in public. It was not uncommon for him to tell those who came to him with cases of conscience and questions of spiritual concern, that he said all he had to say in the pulpit. Thus people might be hurt for the moment by such a dismissal, but they had only to attend his preaching, and they soon found that their difficulties had impressed him as well as themselves; that they had been submitted to God, and that they had been the subject of his serious and affectionate consideration.[65]

---

63. Ryle, *Last Century*, 166.
64. Cadogan, *Rev. William Romaine*, 74.
65. Cadogan, *Rev. William Romaine*, 74.

Adding to this reputation, Romaine frequently discouraged his parishioners from speaking after church services in order let the seed of God's word take root in their lives.[66]

Modern readers are helped in understanding Romaine's otherwise harsh behavior by appreciating the sheer joy with which he viewed congregational worship. In a letter from 1789, he reflected on his church's gathering,

> It was a pleasant occasion to the true worshippers, who had received the Holy Spirit, by whom they had living faith in Jesus, and thereby believed and enjoyed the Father's love in him. They went up to the festivals to confirm and to increase their joy; for they knew well that the temple was the type of Christ's body, and all the public services there had relation to him.[67]

Romaine longed for his parishioners to approach worship with an otherworldly reverence for God.

William Romaine's legacy was that of sustained faithfulness in the established church throughout the sprawling metropolis of London. His life sketched an evangelical portrait in an Anglican frame—blazing a path which would inspire later evangelical Anglicans. In the words of Cadogan,

> He entered upon his living not only in the faith and patience of Jesus Christ, but also with a decided preference to the church of England, in which he was called to preach his name. He therefore adhered to her discipline, and explained her doctrines, with a view to enforce upon his hearers conformity to both, and a regular continuance in her communion.[68]

One cannot help but notice striking similarities between Romaine and Simeon. Both evidenced unflagging devotion to the established church. Both pursued and achieved a great degree of influence in significant cultural spheres. And both were well-known for the power of their pulpits. Accordingly, Simeon recognized Romaine's great faithfulness in England's greatest city, confessing his own desire to "like Mr. Newton, Mr. Romaine, and Mr. Wesley die in harness."[69]

---

66. Cadogan, *Rev. William Romaine*, 68.
67. Romaine, *Select Letters*, 219.
68. Cadogan, *Rev. William Romaine*, 63.
69. Carus, *Memoirs*, 538.

Henry Venn

Nearly forty years after his death, Simeon asserted his closeness to Henry Venn. "If any person now living, his surviving children alone excepted, is qualified to bear this testimony, it is I; who, from my first entrance into Orders, to his dying hour, had most intimate access to him, and enjoyed most of his company and conversation."[70] Venn's impact on Simeon simply cannot be overstated. Though his life and legacy were briefly sketched in the previous chapter, his churchmanship deserves further examination. Venn's biography was written by his son John, and edited by his grandson Henry (1796–1873). In the preface of the work, the younger Henry sought to present his grandfather as a thoroughgoing evangelical, yet in distinction from prominent Methodists of the time. "I think I have stated enough to prove, that there was a body of Evangelical Labourers, who were independent of the Methodists, and nearly contemporaneous with them, and whose labours had an immediate and remarkable influence upon the Clergy of the Church of England."[71] According to the younger Henry, the labours of his grandfather—along with his evangelical co-travelers—"were chiefly devoted to the revival of true religion in the Church; and that those labours were, under God, the main cause of the revival which followed."[72]

Love of the Liturgy

Venn's own testimony and life proved his devotion to the Church of England and her Prayer Book. He once praised the forms of the Church, writing to a friend, "You, and all the people, know how I love the Liturgy, and would a thousand times prefer it to any other way of worship."[73] Evidently, Venn's admiration of Anglican worship was well known to his people. In a letter written to a certain Mr. Powley, one of his former Huddersfield curates, he further attested of his love for the liturgy.

> How often have I declared my utmost veneration for the Liturgy! How often in your hearing, how often in the church, declared the superior excellency, in my judgement, of the Liturgy to every

---

70. Venn, *Life and Letters*, 53.
71. Venn, *Life and Letters*, xiv.
72. Venn, *Life and Letters*, ix.
73. Venn, *Life and Letters*, 168.

mode of worship, not only amongst the Dissenters, but that had ever been in the Church of Christ, as far as I had knowledge: nay, more than once have I said, I never was present at any meeting where I perceived the power of godliness, as amongst the congregations of our Church, where the Gospel is preached. Now, after all this, I think, in justice, you ought to have supposed me as much a friend to the Church of England as yourself.[74]

Interestingly, Venn continued in his letter to express his commitment to the liturgy in distinction from his non-evangelical bishop:

On Saturday I dined with our Bishop. I find he has no objection to a revisal and alteration of the Liturgy. This change will one day, I fear, take place; and then the measure of our iniquities will be full, when we have cast the doctrine of Christ out of public worship, avowedly as a nation. May we be the most zealous and active, according to the utmost of our strength; encouraging and comforting both each other and our flocks with the certain success of the Gospel, in spite of earth and hell![75]

Dissent and Dissenters

Though Venn had a blemished record when it came to irregularity, his mature perspective betrayed an overwhelming distaste for Dissent and aversion to irregularity. John Venn explained his father's relationship with irregularity as follows:

Influenced by the hope of doing good, my father, in certain instances, preached in unconsecrated places. But having acknowledged this, it becomes my pleasing duty to state, that he was no advocate of irregularity in others; that when he afterwards considered it, in its distant bearings and connections, he lamented that he had given way to it, and restrained several other persons from such acts by the most cogent arguments; and that he lived long enough to observe the evils of schism so strongly, that they far outweighed in his mind the present apparent good.[76]

He lamented whenever someone would depart from the established church for Nonconforming denominations. "We have had, amongst our visitors, a serious young man from Cambridge (who was a month with

---

74. Venn, *Life and Letters*, 169.
75. Venn, *Life and Letters*, 169–70.
76. Venn, *Life and Letters*, 171.

us, two summers ago): he is now quarrelling with our Liturgy and Articles, and going over to the Dissenters. Alas! How subtle are the devices of the enemy!"[77] Yet at the same time, he celebrated evangelical revival in America with his Dissenting friend Benjamin Fawcett (1715–1780).[78] As we shall see, Simeon followed Venn not only in his warmth as an evangelical, but also in his zeal as a churchman.

Simeon and the Church of England

Unlike some evangelicals in the established church observed above, Simeon led an unapologetically Anglican ministry. He was an archetypal churchman, solidly committed to the teaching and tradition of the Church of England, particularly her liturgy. Fellow evangelical giants like Newton and Berridge had nowhere near the same commitment to Anglican tradition and forms. Even later prominent evangelicals like J. C. Ryle would lead ministries more characterized by criticism of the Church. This was not so with Simeon. For over half a century, he evidenced an exceptional allegiance to his denomination—in both public and private.

At the age of twenty-three, Simeon was appointed vicar of Holy Trinity in Cambridge, a church that enjoyed an extraordinary heritage of prominent preachers such as Richard Sibbes, Thomas Goodwin, and John Preston. Though his early decades at Holy Trinity were characterized by extreme hostility for his evangelical convictions, such opposition would fail to remain the dominant theme of Simeon's life. As an evangelical Anglican, his commitment to the Church of England was nothing new, as demonstrated in the legacies of Romaine and Venn. However, Simeon dwarfed these men in the extraordinary influence he was able to exert on the ecclesiology of his followers. It shall be demonstrated below that Simeon did not merely mentor ministers; he created churchmen. Thus, Thomas Babington Macaulay, who attended Cambridge in the 1820s, said of Simeon "If you knew what his authority and influence were, and how they extended from Cambridge to the most remote corners of England, you would allow that his real sway in the Church was far greater than that of any primate."[79] The rest of this chapter will examine the character of his relationship to the Church

---

77. Venn, *Life and Letters*, 253.
78. Venn, *Life and Letters*, 117.
79. Trevelyan, *Lord Macaulay*, 1:68.

of England and how this part of his pastoral theology affected others. After highlighting his relationship with evangelicalism and irregularity, I will examine his ecclesiology, through the lens of his understanding of Scripture, the Church of England, and the liturgy.

Simeon, Evangelicalism, and Irregularity

Simeon, in a manner of speaking, can be said to have hit his head on the ceiling of the low church tradition. Despite his elevated views of the Church, particularly her liturgy, his theology fell squarely with those of the low church. Upon his conversion in early 1779, the young Simeon swiftly laid hold of the evangelical tradition accessible in the Anglican Church. This was in no small part due to the evangelical nature of his conversion in the context of the Anglican liturgy. Simeon often meditated on his conversion experience.

> But in Easter week . . . I met with an expression to this effect: "That the Jews knew what they did when they transferred their sin to the head of their offering." The thought rushed into my mind, What! May I transfer my guilt to another? Has God provided an offering for me, that I may lay my sins on his head? Then, God willing, I will not bear them on my own soul one moment longer. Accordingly, I sought to lay my sins upon the sacred head of Jesus . . . and on the Sunday morning (Easter-day, April 4) I awoke early with those words upon my heart and lips, 'Jesus Christ is risen today! Hallelujah! Hallelujah!' From that hour peace flowed in rich abundance into my soul; and at the Lord's table in our chapel I had the sweetest access to God through my blessed Saviour.[80]

One could hardly imagine a more evangelical conversion account: meditating on Scriptural truth (biblicism), Simeon ponders Christ's death in his place (crucicentrism) and testifies to his experience of new affections and access to God (conversionism). His account even culminates in jubilation with reference to a hymn popularized in the 1740s by Charles Wesley.[81]

These evangelical hallmarks would form much of the tenor of the rest of his ministry. Daniel Wilson highlighted the genius of Simeon's ability to hold these views in the Church of England while avoiding

---

80. Carus, *Memoirs*, 9.
81. Wesley, "Christ the Lord," 205.

common extremes; he "neither verged towards the great error of over-magnifying the ecclesiastical polity and placing it in the stead of Christ and salvation, nor towards the opposite extreme of undervaluing the Sacraments and the authority of an apostolical Episcopacy."[82] Simeon viewed evangelical doctrine as not only compatible with the *Thirty-Nine Articles*, but as essential to them. Abner Brown reflected,

> Mr. Simeon's views were what bear the name of Evangelical; his body of opinions were based upon the doctrines which constitute what are called the "Grace Articles,"[83] but he equally held all the other articles and formularies of the Church of England, and scrupulously adhered to the plain sense of every doctrine which he found in Scripture, however unable he might be to reconcile it with other doctrines. . . . He was a faithful and devoted son of the Church of England.[84]

This "devoted son" did at times defy church order. He was known to have financially aided the irregular preaching of the Baptist Johnny Stittle (1727–1813), a convert of John Berridge.[85] He also preached outdoors at least once in his younger days. Carus recounts,

> On one occasion, a few years before his death, (in the presence of the Editor) he was good-naturedly reminded by an old friend of some of those instances of his early fervour:—"Do you remember, Mr. Simeon, in former times coming very early in the morning to my great barn, to preach to the men before they went to their work?" After a most significant look, instantly turning his face aside, and then with both hands uplifted to hide it, he exclaimed—*O spare me! Spare me! I was a young man then.*[86]

As fascinating as these anecdotes of irregularity are, they represent outliers in Simeon's ministry. Though he would at times deviate from the norms of the established church, he tended to gravitate toward the pattern of churchmen like Henry Venn, rather than less-conforming Anglicans like John Berridge.[87] Hopkins notes how Simeon's decision to conform to established norms "set a precedent and example to other

---

82. Moule, *Charles Simeon*, 109.

83. Brown referred to Articles ix, x, xi, and xvii on Original Sin, Free Will, Justification, and Election respectively.

84. Brown, *Recollections*, 11.

85. Brown, *Recollections*, 13–14.

86. Carus, *Memoirs*, 278.

87. Charles Smyth, *Simeon and Church Order*, 283.

earnest evangelical Anglicans of his day and went a long way to retaining within the established church much of the new enthusiasm."[88]

Simeon, the Bible, and the Prayer Book

Simeon's broader ecclesiology must be appreciated in reference to his view of Scripture and the *Book of Common Prayer*. Simeon submitted to the Reformation principle of *Sola Scriptura*. Central to his thought and practice was an aversion to theological systems and partisanship. This led him to critique the extremities of Calvinism and Arminianism. He once playfully remarked in his introduction to his expository volumes *Horae Homileticae* that "there is not a determined votary of either system who, if he had been in the company of St. Paul, while he was writing his different Epistles, would not have recommended him to alter one or other of his expressions."[89] To Simeon, the task of a Bible teacher was to faithfully present texts in the tone and tenor of the original authors, allowing Scripture to speak for itself. As a preacher's preacher, his expository bias was to avoid bias at all costs. This meant he did not mind on occasion sounding like an Arminian or a High Calvinist.[90] He famously declared, "Calvinism is a system. God has not revealed His truth in a system; the Bible has no system as such. Lay aside system and fly to the Bible; receive its words with simple submission, and without an eye to any system."[91] To Simeon, the great task of God's people was to "Be Bible Christians, and not system Christians."[92] He once insisted to his students,

> Christianity is a system: so it is, but not according to human ideas of system. It is quite sui generis (of its own kind), and often has incomprehensible and to us irreconcilable points, and we are nowhere required to reconcile them. We must "become fools if we would be wise," according to God's wisdom (1 Cor. iii. 18). We must take the Bible plainly and simply as it is.[93]

Nevertheless, to say Simeon was a rigid biblicist would be untrue, for, he did not reject all notions of systematic theology. In particular, he

---

88. Hopkins, *Charles Simeon of Cambridge*, 191.
89. Simeon, *Expository Outlines*, 1:xxiii.
90. Brown, *Recollections*, 221.
91. Brown, *Recollections*, 269.
92. Brown, *Recollections*, 269.
93. Brown, *Recollections*, 212.

drew from the Anglican liturgical complex his entire life, specifically the *Thirty-Nine Articles* and the *Book of Common Prayer*. "The Bible first," said Simeon, "the Prayer Book next, and all other books and doings in subordination to both."[94] Andrew Atherstone thus asserts, "While most evangelical authors insist on being judged on the basis of the Bible alone, *Sola Scriptura*, Simeon was prepared for his teaching also to be measured by the doctrine of the *Book of Common Prayer*. It became, in this sense, his second rule of faith."[95] This claim is substantiated by how Simeon employed Reformed theology in the context of his conversation parties. Abner Brown noted the great stress he laid on the doctrine of God's sovereignty. For example, Simeon once commented on Rev 7, "*To our God which sitteth upon the throne, and unto the Lamb. . . .* The sovereignty and love of God are here conjoined. I have no hope but in the sovereignty of God; for, unless He choose me of His free sovereign grace, I know that the devils themselves have naturally as much in them as I have to induce Him to choose me."[96] Elsewhere, he commented on 1 Cor 1:30, where the apostle Paul says, "Of Him are ye in Christ Jesus, who of God is made unto us wisdom, and righteousness, and sanctification, and redemption." Commenting on the text, Simeon asserted,

> The little words or particles are very significant. It is of God only that we can be in Christ, in the way of actually laying hold of the Saviour. The words of God are repeated again, to show that the First Cause is of God also, who hid all these treasures in Christ, and gave Him for us fallen sinners, and hath chosen us in Him. Christ is made of God to be all this for us; and it is only of God that we can be grafted into Christ, so as to gain this rich supply of sap and vitality.[97]

The total sovereignty of God in salvation was an undeniable first principle of Simeon's evangelical theology.

Simeon's Ecclesiology

To appreciate Simeon's general outlook on the Church of England, readers must appreciate his thoughts on polity, the Church Fathers, Rome,

---

94. Brown, *Recollections*, 12.
95. Atherstone, *Charles Simeon*, 4.
96. Brown, *Recollections*, 171.
97. Brown, *Recollections*, 172.

and Dissent. Though these categories have always been relevant to post-Reformation ecclesiology, they sharpened into focus during the generation after Simeon in the Oxford Movement.

Church Government

Despite his obvious preference for Anglican polity, Simeon's biblicism prevented him from grounding such a system of church government in Scripture.

> There is no precise line in Scripture drawn with respect to Church Government: yet the whole Christian Church is filled with dissensions and animosities, because all will dogmatize for others, instead of conceding to each other a liberty to judge for themselves, and being content with that Apostolic dogma, "Let all things be done decently and in order."[98]

To Simeon, the exact governance of the Church of England as a denomination lay in the realm of prudence rather than divine precept.

Apostolic Succession and the Early Church

As a devoted Anglican, Simeon revered the Church Fathers while eschewing a blind submission to their teachings. He was well aware of the nineteenth article of the Church, which stated, "The visible Church of Christ is a congregation of faithful men, in the which the pure Word of God is preached, and the Sacraments be duly ministered according to Christ's ordinance in all those things that of necessity are requisite to do the same."[99] This view preserved the Reformation perspective that a true church is one which rightly preaches the word and practices the sacraments.[100] The nineteenth article continues, "As the Church of Jerusalem, Alexandria, and Antioch, have erred; so also the Church of Rome hath erred, not only in their living and manner of Ceremonies, but also in matters of Faith."[101] This article seems to reject any view of apostolic succession that held the early Church Fathers as infallible or superior to other generations. Gerald Bray expounds, "The listing of

---

98. Carus, *Memoirs*, 585.
99. Church of England, *Book of Common Prayer*, 619.
100. Van Dixhoorn, *Creeds, Confessions, and Catechisms*, 102.
101. Church of England, *Book of Common Prayer*, 619.

Jerusalem, Alexandria, and Antioch is that of the ancient patriarchates of the East, which were generally regarded as the supreme depositories of orthodox teaching. . . . Most important of all, however, is the insistence that fallibility applies to the Roman Church also, something that Rome has always denied."[102]

Simeon embraced apostolic succession in the sense that God had preserved ministers to proclaim his name throughout every generation. He said, "The Lord Jesus Christ has had, in uninterrupted succession, servants to make known his name to all the different generations from the apostolic age to the present day: and all who have been called by him to the work of the ministry, have had the same message to deliver."[103] Notice how Simeon emphasizes apostolic continuity based on the same message proclaimed, not the ministerial office itself. He would have rejected what John Henry Newman (1801–1890)—a notable leader of the Oxford Movement—later affirmed: namely, that modern bishops stood in place of the apostles.[104] Newman asserted, "The royal dynasty of the Apostles is far older than all the kingly families which are now on the earth. Every Bishop of the Church whom we now behold is a lineal descendant of St. Peter and St. Paul after the order of a spiritual birth."[105]

Simeon understood some New Testament offices to be temporary, and others to be normative for all subsequent generations. Commenting on Eph 4:11–16, he asserted,

> Of the other blessings he had bestowed upon his Church, the Apostle mentions some which were extraordinary and temporary, as apostles, prophets, and evangelists; and some which were ordinary and permanent, as pastors and teachers, whose office was to be continued for the benefit of the Church in all succeeding generations.[106]

Apostles were limited to a certain dispensation, while pastors and teachers continue in succession. It is evident that Simeon refrained from granting absolute authority to pastors independent of their stewardship of apostolic doctrine.

---

102. Bray, *Anglicanism*, 28.
103. Simeon, *Expository Outlines*, 11:619.
104. For more on Newman, see Ker, *John Henry Newman*.
105. Newman, *Parochial and Plain Sermons*, 639.
106. Simeon, *Expository Outlines*, 17:348.

Simeon also eschewed any commitment to the early Church Fathers which held them as uniquely privileged or authoritative. On the contrary, though he appreciated the patristics, he believed expositors of his own generation were more poised to accurately expound the teachings of the Bible. He said in one of his conversation parties,

> The Fathers of the Church are too much overrated. Fathers do not always know more than their children when grown up do. The Fathers were nearer the fountain head. They give us a view of what the Church thought in their days. They give us the passages of Scripture as they stood then. . . . They are commentators who explain passages the precise original meaning of which had allusions to the apostolic times. But they were only men. Many errors were abroad in the Church in their times, and they had imbibed some of them. Disputed points had not as yet been started and discussed; and, therefore, much investigation, research, and study is left on our hands, which they had not the benefit of. We have reason and judgment as well as they; and we have the advantage over them of possessing all they knew, and much that they did not know. They were often in error, and often wanting in Christian spirit. Who would wish to do as Ignatius did? And yet he was the disciple of St. John himself?[107]

Readers can see from all of this that Simeon's view of the early church completely contradicted the likes of Pusey and Newman. The latter asserted, "The Primitive Church is the best expounder of our *Saviour's* will as conveyed through his Apostles."[108] Simeon thoroughly disagreed. As such, the generation of ministers who followed Simeon in the Victorian period held a view of the Anglican communion starkly at odds with the Oxford Movement.

Simeon and Rome

If Simeon viewed the patristics with relative suspicion, he completely rejected Rome. On the whole, Simeon understood Anglicanism to be in keeping with the tradition of the early church. Meanwhile, he viewed Roman Catholics as the instigators of schism, for "by changing, adding to, and taking from the apostolic doctrines, [they] were, in reality, those who

---

107. Brown, *Recollections*, 295–96.
108. Newman, *Tracts for the Times*, 1:43.

first divided the Church of the Apostles, gradually, it is true, but actually."[109] He believed the medieval church had introduced all sorts of superstition and error.[110] Simeon appreciated the fathers as a means of fortifying the evangelical faith, but not as a foundation for Christian doctrine.

Simeon and Dissent

As a committed Anglican, yet irenic evangelical, Simeon assiduously opposed Nonconformity in all its manifestations. Though he supported the advance of the gospel through non-Anglican channels, he desired such growth to remain within the Anglican Church as much as possible. Abner Brown notes, "In 1799, he refused, on ecclesiastical grounds, to let the new Missionary [movement] be thrown into the mixed *London Missionary Society*, but strongly insisted that it should exclusively belong to the Church of England, and be 'The Church Missionary Society.'"[111] He despised brands of theology and movements poised to divide Christians from one another. For example, he sharply criticized aspects of the millennial theology of his day, believing it to fill believers "only with vein conceits, intoxicates the imagination, alienates the brethren from each other, and, *by being unduly urged upon the minds of humble Christians*, is doing the devil's work by wholesale."[112]

Over the course of his life, he came to see Nonconformity and schism to go hand in hand.[113] In 1779, the year of Simeon's conversion, Selina Hastings, the Countess of Huntingdon, led a Methodist departure from the established church, registering sixty-seven chapels as Dissenting meeting places under the Toleration Act.[114] The Wesleyans instigated further departure from the Church of England in 1795.[115] And the final

109. Brown, *Recollections*, 298.
110. Atherstone, *Charles Simeon*, 33.
111. Brown, *Recollections*, 12.
112. Carter, *Anglican Evangelicals*, 189.
113. It is important to note that Nonconformists would not have viewed themselves as schismatics because they generally did not view the Church of England to be a true church.
114. Harding, *Selina, Countess of Huntingdon*, 177.
115. For more on Methodism and Wesleyans, see Hempton, *Methodism*. Gareth Atkins highlights how the Countess of Huntingdon was gradually forsaken in the late eighteenth century by many of her clergyman. "She lost several leading clergymen who had in the 1760s and 70s been only too glad to accept her scarf of office as chaplains. She denounced them as 'plausible leaders for Satan only': 'half hearted interested

years of Simeon's life saw the rise of the Plymouth Brethren.[116] Simeon likely viewed all of these detractions critically. Grayson Carter summarizes the prevailing attitude of most evangelical Anglicans in this period. "Despite the presence of minor imperfections in the Church and its formularies, most Evangelicals remained adamant that secession to Protestant Dissent was unjustified. Although their catholic spirit could readily countenance fellowship with evangelical Dissenters, they regarded the Church as immeasurably superior to Nonconformity."[117]

From his post in Cambridge, Simeon sharply criticized Dissent to his followers. He believed Nonconformist ministers lacked independence because they were beholden to the shifting whims of their congregations. He once remarked at a conversation party,

> Among the poor, we find Dissenters exhibit a more captious spirit than Churchmen. . . . It is said by those who have had means of knowing, that a good Minister among Dissenters will often receive letters on Monday, criticising and censuring his sermon of the day before, and that he not seldom goes into his pulpit nervous and fearful on account of such letters. On the other hand, there is a story told of a London Incumbent who refused to pray for Queen Caroline, and when some of his congregation came and told him they would leave his church if he did not pray for her, as it was his duty, he replied, "Did God place me here to teach you, or for you to teach me?"[118]

Meanwhile, Simeon felt true independence was to be found in the established church. "How much better to be under one master," he declared, "than to have scores on the right hand and on the left, as Dissenting Ministers have! Newton well said that there were no 'Independent Ministers,' except in the Church, for that Dissenting teachers were 'only Ministers of independent congregations.'"[119] According to Simeon, he had freedom to

---

creatures' that sought only to 'eat, drink and be merry' in plump establishment livings. . . . If her comments were overblown, there was truth in them. Many who had flirted with irregularity now set their faces against it. . . . Their protégés, coming men such as Charles Simeon of Cambridge, Thomas Robinson of Leicester and John Venn of Clapham, further distanced themselves from irregularity, loudly proclaiming the excellence of the Anglican formularies and their allegiance to the national Church." Atkins, *Converting Britannia*, 28–29.

116. For more on the Plymouth Brethren, see Introvigne, *Plymouth Brethren*.
117. Carter, *Anglican Evangelicals*, 16.
118. Brown, *Recollections*, 150.
119. Brown, *Recollections*, 221.

preach exactly what and how he wished. "No Dissenter dares to preach as I do, one day Calvinist, another day Arminian, just as the text happens to be, for his people would take offence."[120] His only obligation was to faithfully deliver the main burden of the text.

Dissent was always a pressing concern for Simeon, as Cambridgeshire and East Anglia had been a hotbed for Nonconformity throughout the long eighteenth century. Losing members to Dissenters was an ever-present threat to his ministry. For example, under the leadership of Robert Hall Jr., St Andrew's Street Baptist Church in Cambridge (a stone's throw from Holy Trinity) grew to seat over eight hundred people in the 1790s.[121] Though friends for many years,[122] Simeon and Hall had a rocky relationship, with the latter forcefully criticizing Simeon in a letter published by the *Cambridge Intelligencer* on August 7, 1795.[123] Despite this, Simeon could speak charitably of Hall decades later.[124] Over the years, many parishioners also abandoned Holy Trinity for the Green Street Meeting House.[125] Simeon voiced his fear of losing members to Dissent to Henry Venn in an ironic defense of his irregular practice of renting a private room in town to preach to eager hearers. "What is to be done?" asked Simeon; "If those whose minds were impressed by my preaching had not some opportunity of further instruction, they would infallibly go to the dissenting meetings, and thus be gradually drawn away from the church."[126] It appears that the Nonconformist exodus posed an existential threat to Simeon's pursuit of a robustly parochial, Anglican ministry.

Despite Simeon's principled opposition to Dissent and various forms of schism, he evinced a warm catholicity towards a great number

120. Brown, *Recollections*, 221.

121. St Andrews Street Baptist Church holds an important place in Baptist history. It was home to the ministries of Robert Robinson and Robert Hall Jr. Charles Spurgeon attended the congregation as a teenager, and later visited to preach in the 1850s. For more, see Parsons, *Church Book*.

122. Moule, *Charles Simeon*, 11.

123. Flower, *National Sins Considered*.

124. Brown, *Recollections*, 180. Simeon seemed to compliment Hall while criticizing Dissenters: "How diffusive, and heavy, and overwhelming is the style of Dissenters' preachings! Witness the four volumes of their 'Skeletons,' just published. They endeavour to collect as much as possible together into a sermon. Robert Hall, of Leicester, is reported to have advised a young St. John's man thus: 'Do not imitate our style; you have plenty of good divines in your own Church. Never attempt to aim at our style of wordiness, diffusiveness, declamation.' The advice is good from whomsoever it came."

125. Hopkins, *Charles Simeon of Cambridge*, 191.

126. Smyth, *Simeon and Church Order*, 285.

of ministers outside of the Church of England. He frequently toured Scotland to preach in Presbyterian assemblies. He maintained an enduring friendship with the Quaker Joseph Gurney (1788–1847) throughout his life.[127] And Simeon was unphased whenever his parishioners left Holy Trinity for Johnny Stittle's Dissenting meeting place at Green Street. In fact, he generously provided Stittle a quarterly allowance with the playful quip, "for shepherding my stray sheep."[128] The members of Stittle's congregation would go on to form Eden Baptist Church, a congregation still thriving in Cambridge today. Such gestures fail to present a partisan churchman who confined his heart and ministry to his preferred denominational tribe. Rather, they paint the portrait of an irenic evangelical statesman who celebrated the spread of the gospel through various channels.

Simeon and the Liturgy

Simeon's churchmanship manifested itself most clearly in his devotion to the Anglican liturgy. This theme in his life probably dated back to his evangelical conversion, which took place in the context of a communion service.[129] Throughout his life, the words of the Prayer Book penetrated Simeon with such brilliance that he longed to see greater renewal in the state church. He reserved some of his most affectionate language for the forms of the church. For example, he once lamented, "If only we had our hearts deeply penitent and contrite, I know from my experience at this hour, that no prayers in this world could be better suited to our wants, or more delightful to our souls."[130] Elsewhere, reflecting on the piety of the framers of the liturgy, Simeon described them as those for whom "I pant, and long, and strive to be."[131] Simeon asserted throughout his ministry that if the liturgy was lively administered, it would lead to great good in the church.[132] He declared, "The finest sight short of heaven would be a whole congregation using the prayers of

---

127. Carus, *Memoirs*, 572.
128. Hopkins, *Charles Simeon of Cambridge*, 191.
129. Carus, *Memoirs*, 9.
130. Carus, *Memoirs*, 10.
131. Carus, *Memoirs*, 520.
132. Atherstone, *Charles Simeon*, 9.

the liturgy in the true spirit of them."[133] Thus Simeon's adoration of the *Book of Common Prayer* is rightly remembered as a "dominant motif in Simeon's teaching."[134] His life project of passing on his pastoral theology was an effort to provide England's Church with many devoted sons who shared his love for the liturgy.

Simeon believed the liturgy was invaluable to spiritual formation. The prayer book promoted complete dependence upon Christ in every element of worship. He once praised the Anglican prayer of confession. "I may venture to say that no fine wisdom could suggest words more suited to the feelings or necessities of a penitent, than these."[135] Therefore, it distressed him if Christians entered worship unmoved by a sense of wonder. He encouraged his fellow churchmen to pursue a spirit of anticipation in Christian worship. "We are too apt," he said, "to rush into the Divine presence without any consciousness of the importance of the work in which we are going to be engaged, or any fear of his Majesty, whom we are going to address."[136]

Simeon's commitment to the *Book of Common Prayer* was notable, considering the fact that his evangelical convictions invited fierce attacks on his Anglican bona fides.[137] Nevertheless, Simeon understood evangelical doctrine to be clearly articulated in the prayer book. Andrew Atherstone asserts, "Charles Simeon could reasonably claim at the start of the nineteenth century that it was the evangelical clergy, more than anyone else, who had the habit of writing and preaching expositions on the Church of England's Liturgy."[138] This claim was substantiated when evangelical publications like the *Christian Observer* entreated ministers to expound the merits of the prayer book,[139] or when *The Eclectic Review* esteemed Simeon as "a sincere protestant, and a strict churchman."[140] One had no need to look further than Grimshaw, Newton, Romaine, Scott, or Venn to find a chorus of evangelicals devoted to the liturgy.

But Simeon did not merely defend his fealty to the English liturgy. He also lauded its supremacy over all other forms of Christian worship.

133. Brown, *Recollections*, 221.
134. Atherstone, *Charles Simeon*, 6.
135. Simeon, *Expository Outlines*, 2:267.
136. Simeon, *Expository Outlines*, 2:261.
137. Atherstone, *Charles Simeon*, 18–19.
138. Atherstone, *Charles Simeon*, 10.
139. Anonymous, "Biddulph's Essays," 559.
140. Anonymous, "Churchman's Confession," 237.

Simeon enjoyed several preaching tours in Scotland throughout his life. Though he joyfully participated in Presbyterian worship, he found aspects of their services to be lacking. He once wrote,

> I have on my return to the use of our Liturgy been perfectly astonished at the vast superiority of our mode of worship, and felt it an inestimable privilege that we possess a form of sound words, so adapted in every respect to the wants and desires of all who would worship God in Spirit and in truth.[141]

Moreover, Simeon found the written prayers of the liturgy far more edifying than the spontaneous prayers of Nonconformists. When others criticized the liturgy, he replied, "Those who most loudly decry the use of forms, do themselves use forms, whenever they unite in public worship. What are hymns, but forms of prayer and praise? and if it be lawful to worship God in forms of verse, is it not equally so in forms of prose?"[142] A cursory survey of Simeon's life reveals a churchman unrivalled in his admiration for the liturgy of the established church, well earning him the title of "the complete Anglican."[143]

Simeon's Influence on Churchmanship

Simeon's means of influencing future ordinands has already been surveyed in the previous chapter. He constantly demonstrated to his disciples the importance of churchmanship in the pulpit, the parish, and in private. Yet, Simeon made efforts to serve the Church of England in a variety of ways, some of which outstrip the scope of this study.

Activism Abroad

Simeon worked closely with members of the Clapham Sect, a London-based activist group. It was the tireless campaigning of the Claphamites, under the leadership of William Wilberforce, that hastened the abolition of the slave trade in British dominions in 1807.[144] He also actively

---

141. Carus, *Memoirs*, 113–14.
142. Simeon, *Expository Outlines*, 2:249.
143. Hopkins, *Charles Simeon of Cambridge*, 181.
144. For more on Wilberforce and the abolitionist movement, see Hague, *William Wilberforce*.

participated in the Eclectic Society, founded by John Newton in 1783.[145] Simeon was invited to join the society in the 1790s as a "country member," a testament to his massive profile within Anglican evangelical circles.[146]

On March 18, 1799, fourteen members of the Eclectic Society gathered in London to discuss a plan for world evangelization, a conversation Simeon had instigated in 1796.[147] With Wilberforce and John Venn (1759–1813) in attendance, Simeon memorably posed three urgent questions to the group:

> *What can we do?——When shall we do it?——How shall we do it?——What can we do?* We cannot join the (London) Missionary Society; yet I bless God that they have stood forth. We must now stand forth. We require something more than resolutions—something ostensible—something held up to the public. Many draw back because we do not stand forward.——*When shall we do it?* Directly: not a moment to be lost. We have been dreaming these four years, while all England, all Europe, has been awake.—*How shall we do it?* It is hopeless to wait for Missionaries. Send out Catechists.[148]

This quote highlights two notable aspects of Simeon's churchmanship. First, though originally inspired by William Carey and the Baptist Missionary Society, he channeled his missionary activism within the established church. In other words, he was ecclesiologically narrow in the application of his missionary zeal. Second, Simeon's words proved to be profoundly influential to the Eclectic Society. The March meeting resulted in the formation of the Church Missionary Society (CMS) the following month. By the twenty-first century, the CMS had sent thousands of missionaries "across geographical, cultural and societal boundaries to make disciples of Jesus."[149] For Simeon to serve as an evangelical statesman in London on top of his Cambridge duties reveals not only his massive ministerial capacity, but also shines light on his great commitment to the established church.

---

145. Hopkins, *Charles Simeon of Cambridge*, 121.
146. Pratt, *Evangelical Leaders*, 102.
147. Pratt, *Evangelical Leaders*, 102–3.
148. Carus, *Memoirs*, 169.
149. "Our Story," Church Mission Society.

Ecumenism at Home

In addition to his activity in London, Simeon made every effort to foster fellowship with Anglican ministers in his region. From the years 1796 to 1817, he hosted yearly retreats for parish pastors and their wives. Brown describes the nature of these meetings.

> The meeting was a social assembly from every part of the kingdom of Clergymen personally intimate with Mr. Simeon, together with the wives of such as were married. The attendance ranged from twenty to thirty persons, all of whom were accommodated on the spot, and the gathering lasted two entire days beside the days of arrival and departure. The Clergymen were occupied most of the time in discussing scriptural and parochial subjects; the ladies, by themselves, in comparing their own various schemes of local usefulness, and all spent the evenings together in general conversation upon subjects of wide interest and importance to religion. These gatherings differed in several respects from the ordinary clerical meetings which have since become common, and were greatly valued by those who took part in them.[150]

The sheer existence of these assemblies demonstrates the high premium Simeon placed on pastoral fellowship in the Anglican communion. Moreover, though a lifelong bachelor, he exhibited great appreciation for the role of wives in their husbands' ministries. Regrettably, there were no recorded minutes taken at these meetings. Nevertheless, Carus describes the character of the clerical conferences.

> While the clergy were thus employed, the ladies were in another room, where they read together, and endeavoured to edify one another. At the hours of repast and in the evenings, all met together. After tea there was usually some leading topic of conversation likely to be interesting and profitable to both sexes, letters also, or any religious intelligence, or schemes of usefulness likely to be generally accept able, were then brought forward.[151]

Historically speaking, Simeon was not unique for organizing conferences for local clergy. Yet the joy with which they were received by attendants remains notable. Carus attested in his memoirs,

---

150. Brown, *Recollections*, 47–48.
151. Carus, *Memoirs*, 270.

> Never, probably, will some of them know more than they then experienced of the delight of the communion of saints, till they shall again meet with Martyn, and Jowett, and Lowe, and Thomason, and Sargent, and Simeon, and Parish, and (we name one only of those still on earth, because he is out of the immediate reach of this record) Daniel Wilson, and others whom we could name—men honoured of God, and much esteemed in the Church—at the Supper of the Lamb in heaven.[152]

Simeon himself viewed these meetings with great fondness, writing to a certain Dr. Ring in 1809,

> Such a season God has never yet vouchsafed unto us. For half a day perhaps I have often known times as precious; but never for nearly three days together. The solemnity, the tenderness, the spirituality, and the love were equal to anything I have ever seen. God was truly in "the midst of us." Ladies and gentlemen were both highly favoured in their separate discussions; and the Sermons, especially Mr. Fry's last night, on "Because thine heart was tender," were accompanied with an unction from the Holy One, and a blessing on all who heard them.[153]

As fellow travelers in the Anglican Way, attendees welcomed each meeting and mourned every parting. Simeon highlighted the sweetness of these meetings in distinction from other ecumenical gatherings, declaring again to Ring,

> Our separation this day has been very affecting; everyone seemed as if taking leave of his dearest friend, who was going to India. . . . Our Jubilee was as different from the religious dissipation of the Mission Societies, as a sweet rustic scene differs from Cheapside. O for more of that divine composure, that tender love, that heavenly ardour which animated the whole company![154]

The Anglican Archetype and His Pupils

Simeon's ceaseless commitment to the Church of England produced an undeniable effect on his followers. He infused his pupils with a

---

152. Carus, *Memoirs*, 271.
153. Carus, *Memoirs*, 271.
154. Carus, *Memoirs*, 272.

profound sense of reverence for the liturgy of the established church, as it had formed a bedrock to his spirituality. Due to Simeon's impact, it was asserted shortly after his death, "we cannot but notice here the reverence and devotion which now prevail in this and our other College Chapels."[155] Likewise, Brown speaks to the degree of Simeon's sway on the Church of England.

> His opinions were gradually recognized as a school of Divinity; his undergraduate friends swelled into the dimensions and definiteness of a party, and his religious movement was unconsciously carried forward on all sides, until now it is difficult to ascertain how much or how little of the present religious element which pervades society has been due to Simeon's influence.[156]

Smyth concurs with Carus and Brown when he notes,

> There is every reason to believe, that the observance of order, which has been so judiciously regarded by Mr Simeon and his followers at Cambridge, has tended greatly to promote the influence of numbers of the zealous clergy, who are now so vigilantly and successfully defending the best interests of the church. On one occasion, Mr Rowland Hill, with his usual delicacy of feeling, refused to preach in a dissenting place of worship at Cambridge, lest he should appear in any way to interfere with the course so wisely pursued by Mr Simeon.[157]

It seems Simeon managed to navigate the challenges of being both an ardent evangelical and established church crusader. Thus, he ensured a path toward enduring influence in the Church of England. Nevertheless, throughout his entire ministry, he was still criticized for being both too much *and* too little of a churchman.

> He was a loyal Churchman, staunch and affectionate to the Church of England, at a time when a man's piety was deemed by many eminent religionists, professedly of the Church, to be questionable exactly in proportion as he adhered on principle, and not for convenience only, to the Church. Even Simeon was accused, by some Clergymen who professed to lead public opinion, of "putting the Church before Christ." The writer remembers to have been himself, along with others who thought like Simeon, similarly reproached, and asked even by Ministers

---

155. Carus, *Memoirs*, 10.
156. Brown, *Recollections*, 58.
157. Smyth, *Simeon and Church Order*, 284.

of the Church of England, "What right have you to care about Church rule and order, while you are holding evangelical doctrine? Why trouble yourselves with such indifferent and insignificant matters? Shake off your Churchmanship, and be content to be Christians."[158]

Conclusion

Though he tenaciously held evangelical beliefs, Simeon demonstrated a profound commitment to the Anglican Church—even in her terrific polarity. More work should be done on Simeon's churchmanship and its effect on the Church of England. In distinction from many of his evangelical peers, he not only loved the established church, he forged a path for evangelical influence within her walls. While eminent evangelicals like John Newton could have quite comfortably carried out their ministries in Dissenting circles, Simeon could not. He drank too deeply from the wellspring of his Church's tradition. The established church was hardwired into his DNA. Even the phrase "low church" seems, at times, unfitting for Simeon in light of his high praise and devotion to the Anglican Way.

158. Brown, *Recollections*, 60.

CHAPTER 4

Personal Piety

IN THE SPRING OF 1800, Thomas Thomason's life was at its happiest. The dawn of the nineteenth century brought with it "an accumulation of joys and comforts."[1] His young marriage to Elizabeth was thriving. He welcomed his first child Esther (d. 1880) into the world. He was enjoying a comfortable living situation in Cambridge. All of this was accented by his relationship to Simeon, under whose tutelage, his curacy at Holy Trinity blossomed into full fruition. Thomason commented on the tranquility of this season of life.

> Mr. Simeon has a room on the ground floor, which opens into a delightful pleasure garden, surrounded by a wall, where he can walk privately, in which he so much delights. One door of his room opens into my study, so that we are as near each other as possible. His friendship I must name amongst my chief blessings: he is more and more dear to us, as indeed he ought to be; his kindness to us is wonderful. It quite overpowers me when I think of it. I hope we shall provoke one another more and more to abound in the work of the Lord. O how short is time! I am sure there is no time for idleness: would to God that the preciousness of each passing hour might be more deeply impressed upon my mind.[2]

---

1. Sargent, *Rev. T. T. Thomason*, 101.
2. Sargent, *Rev. T. T. Thomason*, 102–3.

This quote highlights two significant things about Simeon's character and role as a ministerial mentor. First, the magnetism of his character was irresistibly attractive to his followers. Second, there was something in his piety that spurred men on to greater devotion to God and service in his kingdom. Young ministers did not just learn from Simeon, they longed to be like him. Therefore, Simeon's personal piety proved to be a significant part of his pastoral theology.

The Minister as Model

The epistle of Simeon's life and example did more to prepare pastors than any of his sermons or conversation parties. His character gave color to the ministerial model he longed to see replicated in England. In a 1784 letter to Lady Mary Fitzgerald (1725–1815), Henry Venn wrote, "I have good news to send you from Cambridge.—Mr. Simeon is made for great usefulness."[3] Venn, along with many evangelicals in the long eighteenth century, placed a high premium on "usefulness" in the Christian life and ministry. He once wrote to his daughter Kitty,

> Safety and comfort are not the whole I pray unto the Lord to provide for your soul. *Usefulness* is the very excellency of life. No man, in the real Church of Christ, liveth unto himself. Every true Christian is a tree of righteousness, whose fruits are good and profitable unto men. He is glad to help and to comfort others. He is diligent and industrious. He speaks to edification; dwells in peace, and gentleness, and love. He reproves what is wrong, by an excellent example; and recommends, by his own practice, what is pleasing to God.[4]

Venn knew Simeon's usefulness would not merely stem from his skill, for as will be shown below, his earliest impressions of Simeon took stock of his Christian character, as well as his pastoral competency. Venn understood the link between the two. Simeon, for his part, believed that a man's ministry could only prosper when complemented by his own breathing exemplar. In one conversation party, he remarked on 1 Thess 2,

> In the 10th verse he saith, "Ye are witnesses, and God also, how holily, justly, and unblameably we behaved ourselves among you that believe." A Minister's example is often of more consequence

---

3. Venn, *Life and Letters*, 375.
4. Venn, *Life and Letters*, 287.

than his sermons; nor can his sermons ever counteract the effect of a failure in this respect. Not mere excellence, but holiness; nor merely in the eye of them that are without, but especially as a pattern "among those that believe."[5]

Simeon would have heartily affirmed the relationship Robert Murray M'Cheyne noted between the minister's pursuit of personal holiness and his anxiety for the souls entrusted to his care.[6] Indeed, Simeon saw his own growth in piety in connection to his great pastoral task to present his people blameless to God.

> This alone will answer the end of ministerial exertions—Pastors are appointed for the perfecting of the saints: and unless this be accomplished by the word, it is preached in vain: instead of proving to the hearers "a savour of life unto life, it will be to them a savour of death unto death." Till a minister beholds this change wrought in his people, he must of necessity stand in doubt of them: but when it is wrought in them, he may well rejoice over them, seeing that they shall surely be his joy and crown of rejoicing in the last day. Yes, blessed indeed will be the meeting which he will have with them in that day: he will recognize them as his spiritual children, and present them unto God, saying, Here am "I, and the children thou hast given me."[7]

As a minister, Simeon knew his duty to prepare people for the day of Christ was inseparably linked to the increase of holiness in his own life. Elsewhere, in a sermon on 2 Tim 1, he characterized the pastor's role as standard-bearer for the congregation—one who is unhindered by the trials and temptations of the world.

> A minister is a standard-bearer: and if *he* faint, what must be expected of others? He must go with his life in his hand: he must "set his face as a flint" against the whole world (Note: Isaiah 50:7.). No confederacies, whether of men or devils, must appall him (Note: Jer 1:17 and Ezekiel 2:6–7.). His spirit must be that which is described by the prophet: "Truly I am full of power by the Spirit of the Lord; and of judgment, and of might, to declare unto Jacob his transgression, and to Israel his sin (Note: Micah 3:8.)." And, in the midst of all the afflictions that can come upon him, he must say, "None of these things move me, neither count I

---

5. Brown, *Recollections*, 164.
6. Bonar, *Rev. Robert Murray M'Cheyne*, 149.
7. Simeon, *Expository Outlines*, 18:72.

my life dear unto myself, so that I may but finish my course with joy, and the ministry which I have received of the Lord Jesus, to testify the Gospel of the grace of God (Note: Acts 20:24.)."[8]

Simeon's personal piety was a distinct element of his pastoral theology, and thus, an inarguable part of his enduring influence. Though many aspects of his piety can be highlighted, this chapter will examine five things: (1) the evangelical character of his spirituality, (2) the place of suffering in his ministry, (3) the priority of generosity and social concern in his life, (4) his humility and contentment, and (5) his communion with God.

Evangelical Religion

From the moment of his conversion, Simeon steeped himself in the hallmarks of evangelical faith. Throughout his ministry, he emphasized what the Reformers and English Puritans referred to as "experimental" religion.[9] Joel Beeke explains the historical use of the phrase. "John Calvin uses *experimental* (Latin *experimentalis*) and *experiential* (Latin *experientia*) interchangeably to refer to our testing of our experience of God for its reality according to the standards of Holy Scripture."[10] Simeon opened a sermon on the life of Job by contending,

> The deepest lessons of religion are usually taught us in the school of adversity. Affliction draws forth and discovers to us our latent corruptions. These drive us with more abundant earnestness to God. God takes these occasions to manifest his power and grace. Thus we attain to a more enlarged and *experimental knowledge of God*. This advances and improves us in every part of the divine life.[11]

To Simeon, the Christian faith was not an amalgam of theoretical beliefs and assertions—rather, it was life in the soul. He once insisted to a friend on the subject,

> Christianity is a *personal* matter, not to be commended merely to others, but to be experienced in your own soul: and though you may confound your opponents by your arguments, you will

---

8. Simeon, *Expository Outlines*, 19:3–4.
9. Carus, *Memoirs*, 569.
10. Beeke, *Reformed Preaching*, 47.
11. Simeon, *Expository Outlines*, 4:505, emphasis added.

never do any essential good, and much less will you reap any saving benefit to your own soul, till you can say, "what mine eyes have seen, mine ears have heard, and mine hands have handled of the word of life, that same declare I unto you."[12]

The lifeblood of Simeon's ministry flowed from what he experienced as a Christian from the moment of his conversion, and every day after. Bebbington is useful at this point in providing a framework with which to examine Simeon's evangelical piety. The Bible, the cross, conversion, and evangelism together formed crucial parts of his spirituality.[13]

Evangelical Commitment to the Bible

Simeon left a legacy of stalwart commitment to the Scriptures. He affirmed what today is known as the verbal plenary inspiration of the Bible. "In what they [the authors of Scripture] wrote indeed," said Simeon, "they expressed themselves, each in his own peculiar style, as any other writers would have done: but in *the matter* of what they wrote, they were inspired of God; and in *the manner* of expressing it they were preserved by that same Spirit from any error or mistake."[14] The vicar of Holy Trinity affirmed that the Bible did not merely contain the word of God, but that it was the word of God. "The whole Scriptures, both of the Old and New Testament, we may affirm, that God is the Author of them, and that every part of them has been 'given by inspiration from him.'"[15] His views concurred with his Scottish friend Robert Haldane (1764–1842), who published *The Authenticity and Inspiration of the Holy Scriptures*, a work that addressed early attacks on the Bible.[16] Though Simeon's life roughly coincided with Friedrich Schleiermacher (1768–1834), the vaunted father of modern liberal theology, he did not live to see higher criticism or liberal theology take significant hold in the established church. It was not until the mid 1820s that Connop Thirlwall (1797–1875) translated Schleiermacher's *Treatise on St Luke* into English, introducing a generation of British ministers to theological liberalism.[17] This would have downstream

---

12. Carus, *Memoirs*, 570–71.
13. Bebbington, *Evangelicalism in Modern Britain*, 3.
14. Simeon, *Expository Outlines*, 19:72.
15. Simeon, *Expository Outlines*, 19:72.
16. Haldane, *Holy Scriptures*.
17. Butler, "Early Eighteenth Century," in *Study of Anglicanism*, 38.

effects in the generations after Simeon. In 1860, seven broad church authors combined forces to publish *Essays and Reviews*, which represented a fulsome embrace of higher criticism.[18] Benjamin Jowett's (1817–1893) essay *On the Interpretation of Scripture* incited particular scrutiny, as it flatly rejected traditional views of the inspiration and authority of Scripture.[19] Jowett went on to serve as Master of Balliol College in Oxford, representing the liberal threat to orthodoxy that would be combatted by men like Ryle and Moule. That Simeon affirmed Reformation orthodoxy on the doctrine of revelation is unremarkable. However, the evangelical generations that followed stood on his shoulders amidst the rise of theological liberalism. Victorian evangelicals trod the old paths that had been paved by influential pastors like Simeon.[20]

Simeon's relationship to Scripture is notable not so much for his theological position, but for what it reveals about his posture toward the Bible. And it is in this way, that we gain insight into his spirituality. Simeon lived in humble reverence and submission to the word of God. When he charged his disciples to "be Bible Christians, and not system Christians," he asserted more than a hermeneutical principle—it was a way of life.[21] As a Christian, Simeon sought to receive the Scriptures humbly and trustingly as a child relates to a loving father. He noted this in his own grappling of the doctrine of God's sovereignty.

> I soon learned that I must take the Scriptures with the simplicity of a little child, and be content to receive on God's testimony what he has revealed, whether I can unravel all the difficulties that may attend it or not; and from that day to this I have never had a doubt respecting the truth of that doctrine, nor a wish (as

---

18. Jowett, *Essays and Reviews*.
19. Butler, "Early Eighteenth Century," 39.
20. When J. C. Ryle defended the old paths of the evangelical faith, he cited Simeon as a faithful standard-bearer. "Not least it is a *tried way*. Thousands and tens of thousands have walked in it, and not one of all that number has ever missed heaven. Apostles, prophets, patriarchs, martyrs, early fathers, reformers, puritans, men of God in every age, and of every people and tongue, holy men of our own day, men like Simeon, Bickersteth, Havelock, have all walked in this way. They have had their battles to fight and their enemies to contend with. They have had to carry the cross, and have found lions in their path. They have had to walk through the valley of the shadow of death, and to contend with Apollyon. They have had to cross at last the cold dark river; but they have walked safely through to the other side, and entered with joy into the celestial city, and now they are all waiting for us to walk in their steps, to follow them, and to share in their glory." Ryle, *Old Paths*, 411–12.
21. Brown, *Recollections*, 269.

far as I know) to be wise above what is written. I feel that I cannot even explain how it is that I move my finger, and therefore I am content to be ignorant of innumerable things which exceed, not only my wisdom, but the wisdom of the most learned men in the universe. For this disposition of mind I have unbounded reason to be thankful to God; for I have not only avoided many perplexities by means of it, but actually learned much, which I should otherwise have never learned.[22]

Simeon believed humble acceptance of God's word led to greater knowledge of God. It was his constant aim to never elevate himself "above what is written." In fact, he used that phrase "wise above what is written" throughout his ministry to express his submission to the Bible. For example, in his introduction to *Horae Homileticae*, speaking in the third person, he polemically and playfully quipped, "If he speak in exact conformity with the Scriptures, he shall rest the vindication of his conduct simply on the authority and example of the Inspired Writers. He has no desire to be *wise above what is written*, nor any conceit that he can teach the Apostles to speak with more propriety and correctness than they have spoken."[23] In a letter to the future Bishop of Llandaff Edward Copleston, he used the phrase "wise above what is written" to discourage theological controversy.[24] Elsewhere, Simeon challenged his pupils to interpret unclear texts in the light of clearer texts: "Any dubious passage must be interpreted in a way consonant to the other plain statements of God's Word; and if we cannot do so, we must acknowledge that we cannot. God hath not made the point clear, and we have no right to be *wise above what is written*, nor to expect to understand clearly what God hath not revealed clearly."[25] Simeon had no issue acknowledging his ignorance and finitude, yielding to the conviction that the secret things belong to the Lord.

Simeon had little interest for matters that failed to relate directly to Scripture. As a participant in the Eclectic Society, he rarely, if ever, participated in discussions of politics, whether the subject had to do with the implications of the French Revolution, Roman Catholic emancipation, or foreign policy. Hopkins writes, "Simeon himself seems to have taken no part in discussions when such subjects as these were on the

---

22. Carus, *Memoirs*, 25 (emphasis added).
23. Carus, *Memoirs*, 179.
24. Carus, *Memoirs*, 568.
25. Brown, *Recollections*, 273 (emphasis added).

agenda. He was not really at ease unless the theme was clearly related to the exposition of Scripture or the spread of the gospel."[26] The great passion of Simeon's life was the Bible. To the Scriptures, he devoted all his energy. What Spurgeon famously said of John Bunyan (1628–1688) could be said of Simeon: "Prick him anywhere—his blood is Bibline, the very essence of the Bible flows from him. He cannot speak without quoting a text, for his very soul is full of the Word of God."[27]

Evangelical Commitment to the Cross and Conversion

Simeon's evangelical conversion brought with it a liberating sense of forgiveness and trust in the cross of Christ. He recounted his testimony at an evening party in the following way:

> A passage which I found in a book was the means of giving me deliverance from my bondage: I read that the Israelites believed that their iniquities were forgiven and taken away, by being placed upon the head of the victim that was sacrificed according to the ceremonial law. I thought of this, compared their state with my own, saw that Christ was sacrificed for me, took Him as my Saviour, and was determined that the burden should not remain upon my conscience another hour: and I am confident it did not remain another hour.[28]

Simeon's reckoning of Christ's sacrifice for sins did not only form the bedrock of his own standing before God, but became the clarion call of his pulpit ministry. "To preach Christ crucified," Simeon said, "is the one employment of ministers: and our ministry is called 'the ministry of reconciliation' on this very account, because we proclaim to sinners, 'that God was in Christ reconciling the world unto himself, not imputing their trespasses unto them.'"[29]

Along with cross-centeredness, came a deep conviction of the doctrine of conversion. Notably, Simeon experienced an evangelical conversion independent of any extraneous human influences. In other words, his conversion transpired at a time when evangelical forces exerted little influence on Cambridge. Nevertheless, Simeon's transformation

---

26. Hopkins, *Charles Simeon of Cambridge*, 121.
27. Spurgeon, *Charles H. Spurgeon*, 4:268.
28. Carus, *Memoirs*, 654.
29. Simeon, *Expository Outlines*, 18:502.

was thorough and dramatic. This led him to emphasize the doctrine of conversion throughout the rest of his life, though he did not require all personal conversions to look the same. It was not necessary for every Christian to recount a sensational, personal, salvation narrative. The following sermon quote well-summarizes his view on the topic:

> There must be a real conversion of the soul to God. It is not necessary that this conversion be sudden, or that it should be attended with such circumstances as shall enable a person to declare the precise time and manner in which it was accomplished: but it is necessary that every man should have an evidence within himself that he is "translated from the kingdom of darkness into the kingdom of God's dear Son." He must receive Christ into his heart, and build on him as the only foundation of his hope. "Christ must become truly precious to his soul." Christ must be his life, his peace, his strength, his joy, his all. Till this be done, a minister can have no comfort in any man, because he has no ground to believe him truly and savingly converted to God: but when this change is manifest (for no natural man in the universe ever thus gloried in Christ alone,) then does the person in whom it is wrought become the joy and crown of his minister: he then, in the judgment of charity, is brought to the fold of Christ: and his minister, like a faithful shepherd, rejoices over him, as a sheep that was lost, and is found.[30]

At least two things stand out in this quote: (1) the great sense of duty with which Simeon expected ministers to preach conversion, and (2) the joy he expected them to have whenever a hearer experienced regeneration. For Simeon, the joy of seeing others come to Christ stemmed from his deep personal experience of conversion.

Evangelical Commitment to Evangelism

From the moment of his conversion, Simeon evidenced a blazing compassion for unbelievers. He taught the gospel to his father's servants while on vacation.[31] He led his Cambridge servants in private worship.[32] He also earnestly witnessed to his older brothers, which was met

---

30. Simeon, *Expository Outlines*, 18:303.
31. Carus, *Memoirs*, 11.
32. Carus, *Memoirs*, 18.

with accusations of enthusiasm and a loss of common sense.[33] Indeed, Simeon's early zeal for the spread of the gospel earned him an unsavory reputation among many in Cambridge.

But Simeon's passion for evangelism never waned. As discussed earlier, his dynamic leadership ultimately led to the formation of the Church Missionary Society in the late 1790s. Simeon summarized the Christian burden to reach the unreached in the following manner:

> It may be said perhaps, why are we to waste our strength upon the heathen? Is there not scope for the labours of all at home? I answer, it is well for us that the Apostles did not argue thus: for if they had not turned to the Gentiles till there remained no unconverted Jews for them to instruct, the very name of Christ would probably long since have been forgotten among men. We confess there are great multitudes in our own land as ignorant as the heathen: but yet they have the Bible in their hands; and there are in every part of the kingdom, some who are both able and desirous to instruct them. However ignorant therefore, or abandoned, thousands are amongst us, there is hope respecting them, that sooner or later their feet may be guided into the way of peace. But as for the heathen, what hope can there be respecting them? for "How can they believe in him of whom they have not heard? and how can they hear without a preacher?" Besides, the more our love abounds towards the heathen, the more will "the zeal of others be provoked" for the salvation of our neighbours; and the more confidently may we hope for the blessing of God upon their pious endeavours. Let then all such excuses be put away; and let all exert themselves at least in prayer to the great "Lord of the harvest," and entreat him day and night "to send forth labourers into his harvest."[34]

Notice how Simeon's case for world evangelization did not merely emerge from the exposition of biblical commands. Instead, he appealed to the reason and emotions of his hearers to urge them to reach those without access to the gospel. It was instinctive for Simeon to appeal to the affections because he himself brimmed with compassion for unbelievers. Elsewhere, in an exposition of 2 Tim 1:7, he exhorted his congregation to cultivate a spirit of love for the lost.

> Nothing but a love to immortal souls can reconcile them to all the labours and difficulties which they have to sustain. They

33. Carus, *Memoirs*, 30–31.
34. Simeon, *Expository Outlines*, 18:57.

should therefore "have compassion on them that are ignorant and out of the way": they should be able to "call God to witness that they have great heaviness and continual sorrow in their hearts" for their perishing fellow-creatures: and they should be ready to welcome even death itself, if it may but be subservient to the spiritual welfare of their brethren. At the same time, their whole deportment should be regulated by this benign principle. Everything they do should proceed from it; everything which they suffer should call it into exercise: and their whole walk should be, like that of their Divine Master, in a spirit of love.[35]

This "spirit of love"—which informed Simeon's enormous evangelistic endeavors—represented yet another way in which evangelical values shaped his piety. These same evangelical hallmarks would invariably manifest themselves in each of his followers.

Ministerial Suffering

The next significant aspect of Simeon's piety was the role of suffering in ministry.[36] Simeon's endurance through acute trials—especially in the first twenty years of his pastorate—is, for many, the most memorable part of his life. Thus, it is unsurprising that he thought and taught so much on the topic. Simeon's persecution from his congregation has been briefly highlighted. The circumstances of his appointment were controversial, resulting in hostile resentment towards Simeon for many years.[37] The parishioners deprecated his evangelical convictions so much that they made every effort to impede his ability to preach. Regularly, the churchwardens would lock the building to prevent the hearing of Simeon's sermons. Members of the church not only boycotted his preaching, but some of them even went as far as to lock their pews in the church to prevent others from going to hear the young minister.[38] This was no passing gesture of protest. Rather, it continued for at least ten years, forcing Simeon to rent chairs for the aisles at his own expense.[39] Brown recounts how a certain head of college at Cambridge went out of his way to schedule a weekly Greek lecture on Sunday evening to prevent ordinands from

---

35. Simeon, *Expository Outlines*, 19:4.
36. For a popular study of this theme in Simeon's life, see Piper, *Roots of Endurance*.
37. Carus, *Memoirs*, 40–43.
38. Carus, *Memoirs*, 43–45.
39. Moule, *Charles Simeon*, 46.

hearing Simeon preach.[40] Even as late as 1824, Simeon was impeded from the Society of Promoting Christian Knowledge (SPCK) due to his association with evangelicalism.[41] On several occasions, students threw stones through the windows of Trinity Church.[42]

The attempts of the congregation of Holy Trinity to limit their pastor's opportunities to preach were perhaps the most debilitating struggle for Simeon. When he received his living on November 9, 1782, and was formally ordained as a priest on September 28, 1783,[43] his people protested by selecting John Hammond as their lecturer.[44] Hammond would continue in the role for five years, which severely restricted Simeon's ability to preach to his congregation. Even after Hammond's departure, the congregation again overlooked Simeon by appointing Butler Berry (d. 1832) as lecturer.[45] Simeon would not formally assume the lectureship of Trinity until 1795, after shepherding the congregation for over twelve years. One might expect the embattled decades of Simeon's early ministry to produce a callous pastor. The antithesis was the case.

"The Servant of the Lord Must Not Strive"

Simeon resisted the urge to assert his rights when it came to winning the favor of his congregation. In September of 1783, he wrote to John Venn,

> I forgot to tell you that my church wardens have shut my church-doors against me, and prevented my continuing an evening lecture, which I had established, and which was well attended. Their behaviour has been highly displeasing to the whole parish, except two or three enemies to the Gospel. Nor has it been less illegal than uncivil. They gave me no notice; so that a numerous congregation came and were disappointed. May God bless them

---

40. Brown, *Recollections*, 45–46.
41. Balleine, *Evangelical Party*, 181.
42. Carus, *Memoirs*, 89.
43. Hopkins, *Charles Simeon of Cambridge*, 44. One of Simeon's early biographers Matthew Morris Preston dates his first sermon at Holy Trinity to January 4, 1783. See Preston, *Rev. Charles Simeon*, 17.
44. Lectureships were very common in the Church of England in the seventeenth, eighteenth, and nineteenth centuries. Though lecturers were ordinarily chosen by the vestry or chief inhabitants in a parish, they were subject to the approval of the presiding bishop or archbishop. See "Act of Uniformity 1662."
45. Carus, *Memoirs*, 65.

with enlightening, sanctifying, and saving grace: I shall renew the lecture next summer.[46]

That Simeon initially responded gracefully to persecution may seem unremarkable. Yet strikingly, his trials forged within him a rugged perseverance that continued for years after. When after five years in the ministry—his reputation continued to be attacked, his preaching was still thwarted, and the greater part of the pews in Holy Trinity were still locked—he reflected, "I was restrained . . . by that divine declaration, 'the servant of the Lord must not strive.' Many hundreds of times has that one word tied my hands, when a concern for immortal souls, and a sense of the injury done to my ministry, would have prompted me to take off the locks."[47] In the same year, Henry Venn wrote to a certain Mr. Riland after finding a curious note among his protégé's belongings, "As a conspicuous memorandum in his pocketbook for this year, Mr. S. has written in large characters, twice over, on separate pages,—'Talk not about myself. Speak evil of no man.'"[48] Simeon committed himself to blessing those who cursed him, rarely complaining to others about his troubles.

Simeon viewed the minister's endurance of suffering and trials with particular significance. He held pastors to a higher standard than church members. In an 1821 address, he remarked, "the servant of God does not live under the same laws as others; and that if he were to act towards others as they do towards him, the world . . . would be full of indignation against him."[49] In the same message, he illustrated his own posture when treated injuriously.

> Perhaps I ought to take some notice of it; but my rule is—never to hear, or see, or know, what if heard, or seen, or known, would call for animadversion from me. Hence it is that I dwell in peace in the midst of lions. My blessed Lord, "when He was reviled, reviled not again; when He suffered, He threatened not, but committed Himself to Him that judgeth righteously." That seems the right thing for me to do; though some perhaps would think it better for me to stand up for my rights. But to all the accusations that were brought against Him, our Lord made no reply; "*insomuch that the governor marvelled greatly*" I delight in that record: and God helping me, it is the labour of my life so

---

46. Carus, *Memoirs*, 59.
47. Carus, *Memoirs*, 65.
48. Carus, *Memoirs*, 73.
49. Carus, *Memoirs*, 560–61.

to act, that on *my* account also the governor, or spectator, may marvel greatly.[50]

Even after nearly forty years in ministry, Simeon thought daily about the minister's endurance of suffering and persecution, always seeking divine commendation first. "I learn to say, 'Let me be honored of God, and trampled under foot of men.'"[51]

"We Must Suffer for the Good of the Church"

Simeon understood ministers to have a pronounced duty to suffer with Christ for the sake of their flocks. Though all Christians were called to emulate the pattern of Christ, pastors bore peculiar responsibility to endure hardship. He told future ordinands in a Conversation Party, "*We must suffer for the good of the Church.*—'Fill up that which is behind of the afflictions of Christ in my flesh for the Church.'—-(Col. 1:24) A beautiful image. Christ is the Head of the Church; we are the members. If the head suffer, the members also have something to suffer with it."[52] For Simeon, pastoral suffering was a biproduct of his union with Christ and commitment to his bride. In 1831—after shepherding Holy Trinity for nearly half a century—he said to Joseph Gurney, "My dear brother, we must not mind a little suffering. When I am getting through a hedge, if my head and shoulders are safely through, I can bear the pricking of my legs. Let us rejoice in the remembrance that our holy Head has surmounted all His sufferings and triumphed over death. Let us follow Him patiently; we shall soon be partakers of His victory."[53]

One of the more enlightening examples of Simeon's willingness to suffer for the sake of the gospel came in his endurance of his father's reproach. Charles rarely commented on his frigid relationship with Richard Simeon, but it is known that in the five years between Simeon's conversion and his father's death, Richard despised his evangelical convictions. Even his father's disapproval was cause for growth in piety.

> Unhappily my poor father retained his prejudices to the last: but I have never entertained a doubt, but that I did right in obeying God rather than man. Great care must be taken that we act in a

---

50. Carus, *Memoirs*, 561.
51. Carus, *Memoirs*, 576.
52. Brown, *Recollections*, 262.
53. Moule, *Charles Simeon*, 243.

right spirit, and that we "let patience have its perfect work, that we may be perfect and entire, wanting nothing." But if the Cross cannot be removed by mild and gentle means, we must consider it as lying fairly in our way, and must take it up and bear it after our blessed Lord. And if, in this mode of proceeding, we lose father or mother, or house or lands, for Christ's sake, we have His assurance that we shall receive *an hundredfold more in this life*, (and in kind too,) with persecutions, and in the world to come *life everlasting*.[54]

"I Bless God for What He Has Withheld"

In seasons of penetrating trials, Simeon cultivated the ability to trace God's providence in his pain. In December of 1800, he attended a meeting of the Eclectic Society in London, where those in attendance discussed the Book of Job. Simeon asserted, "God made chastisement a subject of *promise*, and that it should be in measure." He continued, "Now we are apt to think God afflicts us *out of measure*. Could Job have seen God measuring out his trials, he would never have been betrayed into impatience. We should endeavour to feel all trial as the subject *of promise*, and *in measure*."[55] Simeon believed God meticulously ordained trials for the purpose of producing eternal prosperity for the Christian. Again, he challenged his disciples,

> In thinking of our afflictions, we may well consider how much evil may have been, by the altered circumstances, prevented from breaking out, which would have broken from our awfully wicked hearts had we been left free. I bless God even more for what He has withheld than for what He has given me. I know how much good I have received by considering what He has withheld.[56]

Considering the outlandish displays of cruelty Simeon endured, it is striking he could see God's goodness in every throe.

Simeon's trust in God's providence evidenced itself in his quiet commitment to employ ordinary means in his ministry even when circumstances looked bleakest. When very few were permitted to hear him preach, Simeon thought, "that if God would only give a double blessing

---

54. Carus, *Memoirs*, 597.
55. Pratt, *Evangelical Leaders*, 208.
56. Brown, *Recollections*, 140.

to the congregation that did attend, there would on the whole be as much good done, as if the congregation were doubled, and the blessing limited to half the amount."[57] He never doubted God's ability to work in ways unseen. Preaching on 2 Tim 2:25–26, he proclaimed the minister's success to only be the work of God.

> [Ministers] know how vain it would be for them to engage in this warfare, if God himself did not interpose to give them the victory. They know, that though "Paul should plant, and Apollos water, God alone can give the increase." Nor are they sure that he will work by them: much less do they know for whose particular benefit they may be sent. They can only "draw their bow at a venture," and leave it to God to direct the shaft. A mere "peradventure," however, is quite sufficient to stimulate their exertions. If they be but the happy instrument of delivering one soul from Satan's yoke, they will account it an ample recompence for a whole life of labour. With their ministrations to men, therefore, they unite their supplications to God; if peradventure he may "give to any a repentance to the acknowledging of the truth." Only let the gifts of repentance and faith be given to any soul, there will be an end of Satan's power over them.[58]

The minister's call was to faithfully proclaim the gospel, not to manufacture results. Charles Bridges later took up Simeon's same agricultural imagery in *The Christian Ministry*.

> The seed may lie under the clods till we lie there, *and then spring up*. "That saying" of the prophets of old "was true; One sows, and another reaps;" they sowed the seed, and the Apostles reaped the harvest. As our Lord reminded them—"Other men laboured, and you have entered into their labours." And is it no ground of comfort that our work may be the seed-time of a future harvest? Or should we neglect to sow because we may not reap the harvest? Shall we not share the joy of the harvest, even though we are not the immediate reapers of the field?[59]

Simeon furnished his followers with a durable reliance on God's sovereignty through various challenges. Though Simeon did live to see great success in his ministry, he continued to suffer in various ways.

---

57. Carus, *Memoirs*, 44.
58. Simeon, *Expository Outlines*, 19:46.
59. Bridges, *Christian Ministry*, 199.

"Whatever My Days Should Be, I Would Die in Harness"

In an 1817 letter to Thomas Thomason, Simeon could attest to gownsmen making up half his congregation. Yet during this same season, his health faltered—often rendering him unable to speak throughout the week.[60] He told Thomason, "I compare myself to bottled small beer: being corked up, and opened only twice a week, I make a good report; but if I were opened every day, I should soon be as ditch-water."[61] Beginning in 1807, he regularly experienced the inability to speak for days at a time. Simeon attributed this illness as God's chastisement for nursing a plan to retire at age sixty. In response Simeon said, "I determined, through grace, that whatever measure of strength God should see fit to allot to me in future life, I would spend it for Him; and that whatever my days should be more or less protracted, I would, like Mr. Newton, Mr. Romaine, and Mr. Wesley, die in Harness."[62] In 1820, at the age of sixty, Simeon attested to the full restoration of his health. His only explanation for this recovery was the comforting rod of God.

> I consider God as saying to me, "I laid you aside, because you entertained with satisfaction the thought of resting from your labour; but now you have arrived at the very period when you had promised yourself that satisfaction, and have determined to spend your strength for me to the latest hour of your life, I have doubled, tripled, quadrupled your strength, that you may execute your desires on a more extended plan."[63]

Readers may draw various conclusions from this anecdote. But for the purposes of this chapter, it should be highlighted how Simeon's experience of suffering, and his understanding of God's providence, propelled him to greater service as a pastor. Thus, the place of suffering in Simeon's piety formed a major part of his pastoral theology. John Sargent, for his part, drew this conclusion from Simeon's example. In his biography of Thomason, he wrote, "In Mr. Simeon he [Thomason] had before him a living example of an elevated description, ever seeming to suggest this is not your rest, you are not come to the land of which the Lord God has

---

60. The precise cause of Simeon's illness is unknown. However, it should be remembered that in the era before modern amplification, preachers had to give great care to the preservation of their voices.

61. Carus, *Memoirs*, 445.

62. Carus, *Memoirs*, 538.

63. Carus, *Memoirs*, 539.

said, 'He will give it you.'"⁶⁴ When Thomason voyaged by sea to foreign lands as a missionary, he carried a picture of Simeon which steeled his confidence through periods of anxiety.⁶⁵ After enduring a heart-wrenching shipwreck, Thomason wrote to his mentor,

> The Lord moves in a mysterious way, but all his doings are in faithfulness and mercy. We were coming to India flushed with hope, full of ardour and sanguine expectations, much animal fervour, and an amazing portion of self-sufficiency. He casts us upon a rock; it was a hard blow and it spoke loudly. . . . Blessed be his name, I say again and again, that he gives us also a heart to think of these things, and to pray for a right improvement of them.⁶⁶

It is reasonable to surmise that Simeon the sufferer endowed his disciples with the ability to process bitter providences—all to the increase of their piety.

Generosity and Social Concern

Simeon's personal piety displayed itself in acts of generosity and social concern, the scope of which outstrips this study. However, it is worth highlighting a couple of features of his care for fellow human beings. Simeon made it his regular practice give at least one-third of his income to charity.⁶⁷ He saw himself as a steward, and endeavored to give his first-fruits to the Lord.

> I have always given at the beginning of the year a proportion of my goods for God. This share is not mine, and all I have to do with it is to use a rigid economy and judgment in distributing it. I feel myself a steward in I all I have, and thus secure a proportion for God. I do not feel that I am giving it. And whatever I can by economy save for God is in addition to that share.⁶⁸

Josiah Pratt (1768–1864) remembered Simeon as a "rigid economist, exact in his accounts to a penny; which was the more remarkable as he always enjoyed a competency, and during many of his later years was in

---

64. Sargent, *Rev. T. T. Thomason*, 101.
65. Sargent, *Rev. T. T. Thomason*, 140–41.
66. Sargent, *Rev. T. T. Thomason*, 160.
67. Carus, *Memoirs*, 18.
68. Brown, *Recollections*, 123.

affluent circumstances: but he considered himself the steward, not the possessor, of this world's goods."[69]

When his riches increased, so did his generosity. Upon his brother Edward's (1755–1812) death, he received a great fortune of fifteen thousand pounds—a figure worth almost two million pounds in today's currency.[70] Though he had gained financial independence, he still kept his fellowship at King's in order to maintain his magnanimous giving schedule. Francis Close recalled,

> He once told me himself that he retained his college fellowship for no other reason than that it enables him to live more economically, and to devote more to the Lord. He was not only true and just in all his dealings, nor merely accurate and punctual to the greatest nicety in all his pecuniary transactions, but he laid down all his property at the foot of the cross, saying, "Lord, behold all that I have is thine, and of thine own have I given thee!"[71]

Thus, Close could say of Simeon, "Nature had bestowed upon him a noble mind and a generous heart."[72]

Simeon followed the path of countless evangelicals in his concern for human rights and flourishing. Bebbington summarizes this particular evangelical emphasis.

> Activism often spilled over beyond simple gospel work. . . . [Lord] Shaftesbury's efforts in such causes as public health provided further outlet for Evangelical energy. Wilberforce's campaign against the slave trade and Nonconformist political crusades around 1900 are but the most famous instances of attempts to enforce the ethics of the gospel. A host of voluntary societies embodied the philanthropic urge. Hannah More, the Evangelical authoress of the turn of the nineteenth century, summed up succinctly the prevailing Evangelical attitude. "Action is the life of virtue," she wrote, "and the world is the theatre of action."[73]

Though generally less interested in political matters, Simeon followed suit in his activism. His heart for the poor of his parish, in

---

69. Pratt, *Evangelical Leaders*, 100.
70. Carus, *Memoirs*, 434.
71. Close, *Occasional Sermons*, 202.
72. Close, *Occasional Sermons*, 201.
73. Bebbington, *Evangelicalism in Modern Britain*, 12.

particular, will be covered in the next chapter. In the meantime, it is worth highlighting his posture toward the slave trade.

Simeon has long been criticized for what was once considered "total silence" on the topic.[74] Hopkins, in particular, asserts that the vicar of Holy Trinity virtually never expressed an opinion on the great issue that burned in the hearts of evangelicals for fifty years.[75] Yet this is untrue. Simeon excoriated the societal scourge of slavery. Several sermons demonstrate his profound vehemence of the practice. Many of these sermon quotes must be marshalled to set the matter straight. For example, in a sermon on 2 Chr 28—likely preached after the abolition of the slave trade—he went out of his way to condemn national sins.

> Doubtless there are great enormities in other lands: the grossest superstitions and the most flagrant impieties testify against the great majority of those who bear the Christian name. But whilst we of this land boast of our superior light and morals, what abominations are found amongst us! Let us not think that because the evils once perpetrated in the slave-trade have been in a measure suppressed, the blood of thousands and tens of thousands does not yet cry to God against us for our insatiable avarice, and our cruel injustice. For centuries yet to come, we need bewail the guilt that has been contracted by our impious traffic in human blood.[76]

Even amidst the perpetuation of slavery in the British Empire, Simeon foresaw corporate judgment from God.[77] In an exposition of Isa 58, he connected the pursuit of love with avoidance of oppression.

> We must put away from us every thing that is contrary to love, and live in the habitual exercise of love in all its branches. There are many things, the offspring of pride and selfishness, sanctioned by the habits of the world, which yet we should be careful not to practise—When addressing you on a day of national humiliation, I may well advert to that great national sin of holding thousands of our fellow-creatures in bondage, and treating them as though they had neither the rights nor feelings of humanity—Whilst this continues, God cannot but have a controversy with us; nor can we expect any thing at his hands

74. Hopkins, *Charles Simeon of Cambridge*, 198.
75. Hopkins, *Charles Simeon of Cambridge*, 198–99.
76. Simeon, *Expository Outlines*, 4:172–73.
77. The British slave trade was abolished by act of Parliament on March 25, 1807. Slavery itself was not outlawed until August 1, 1834, two years before Simeon's death.

> but to be visited with his heaviest displeasure—But there are manifold instances of oppression which obtain amongst ourselves in our daily intercourse with mankind, which, though not of the same flagrant nature with the slave-trade, are most offensive in the sight of God: and against these we should, all of us individually, be on our guard; for God is the avenger of the injured party, whosoever he may be, and will call us to account for all the evils that we inflict upon him.[78]

Simeon understood the slave trade as one of a number of horrors for which God was just to hold Britain into account. Expounding a text in which the priest Ezra extols God for his mercy despite Israel's flagrant sin, Simeon lists slavery among a number of his nation's cultural ills.

> We must confess, however, that our sufferings have by no means equaled our deserts. Take any *one* of our national sins (Note: Our contempt of the Gospel, our open profaneness, our traffic in human blood, &c.), and it might well bring down upon us all that we have endured. If God had proceeded against us according to the tremendous aggregate of our iniquities, we should have been made as Sodom and Gomorrah.[79]

In a sermon on Isa 11, Simeon lamented the barbary of the slave trade, despite some shifting sentiments spurred on by the abolition movement.

> However civilization may have changed the manners of men, it is but too evident that their hearts are the same as ever. In proof of this we need only appeal to the bloody wars which nations wage with each other: to the duels which are fought on account of the most trifling injuries or insults: and to the execrable traffic in slaves, which, to the disgrace of the Christian name, yea, to the disgrace of humanity itself, is justified and carried on amongst us, in spite of all the efforts that have been made for its abolition. If further proof were necessary, we may all find it very abundantly in the various circles in which we move: for there is scarcely a society, or even a single family, in which feuds, dissensions, quarrels, do not frequently arise: yea, the very relatives most interested in cultivating love and harmony, are often most at variance. Does not this shew how untamed we

---

78. Simeon, *Expository Outlines*, 8:505.
79. Simeon, *Expository Outlines*, 4:261.

are, notwithstanding the restraints of wholesome laws, and the instructions given us in the word of God?[80]

Clearly, Simeon abhorred any justification of slavery in the name of Christianity. In yet another example of his opposition to the practice, Simeon includes it among his nation's most heinous crimes against humanity.

> We can see nothing of national reformation. Fasts indeed have been appointed from time to time during the late war, and even on the present occasion: but it will be well if these be not numbered amongst our greatest sins; seeing that they have been little else than an empty form, a hypocritical service, a solemn mockery. As for national repentance, what evidence can be adduced to warrant the hope that it has ever taken place? What national sin has been put away? Have we less pride and arrogance, when speaking of our fleets and armies? Have we ceased from traffic in human blood?[81]

It is notable that Simeon did not merely speak out against the slave trade, but he viewed his pulpit as the proper platform for addressing social injustice. Ever the biblicist, the vicar of Holy Trinity—enflamed by evangelical piety—cultivated a social conscience for the good of his fellow man.

Humility, Patience, and Contentment

Simeon's pastoral piety was forged in the furnace of his earliest days in ministry. Chapter 2 recounted the words of John Thornton to Simeon when the latter faced a defiant congregation. "Watch continually over your own spirit," said Thornton, "and do all in love; we must grow downwards in humility to soar heavenward. I should recommend your having a watchful eye over yourself, for generally speaking as is the ministry so are the people."[82] Humility, patience, and contentment formed enduring features of his pastoral theology. Simeon reflected often on Thornton's immortal counsel of "three lessons which a minister has to learn, 1. Humility—2. Humility—3. Humility."[83] Ministerial meekness proved to be a

---

80. Simeon, *Expository Outlines*, 7:545.
81. Simeon, *Expository Outlines*, 10:211.
82. Hopkins, *Charles Simeon of Cambridge*, 43–44.
83. Carus, *Memoirs*, 74.

dominant theme throughout Simeon's entire life, not just his early career. Simeon understood humility as indispensable to the Christian life, and thus, a non-negotiable for pastoral faithfulness.

Humility in the Christian Life

Forty years after his conversion, he asserted, "Whatever opinions the generality of Christians might form, I confess that this is the religion which I love; I would have conscious unworthiness to pervade every act and habit of my soul; and whether the woof be more or less brilliant, I would have humility to be the warp."[84] This prevailing sense of unworthiness profoundly affected his view of the Christian life and ministry. "It is well," Simeon said, "that our fellow-creatures do not know us as God knows us, or even as we know ourselves; for they could not possibly bear with us: but the patience of God is infinite."[85]

The previous chapter noted Simeon's devotion to the liturgy of the Church of England. Notably, however, it was the humble piety of the prayer book that made it his muse.

> This is the religion that pervades the whole Liturgy, and particularly the Communion Service; and this makes the Liturgy inexpressibly sweet to me. The repeated cries to each Person of the ever-adorable Trinity for mercy, are not at all too frequent or too fervent for me; nor is the confession in the Communion Service[86] too strong for me; nor the "Te Deum," nor the ascriptions of glory after the Lord's Supper, "Glory be to God on high, &c." too exalted for me; the praise all through savours of *adoration*; and the adoration of humility.[87]

---

84. Carus, *Memoirs*, 523.

85. Carus, *Memoirs*, 103.

86. The prayer of confession of the communion service is as follows: "Almighty God, Father of our Lord Jesus Christ, Maker of all things, Judge of all men: We acknowledge and bewail our manifold sins and wickedness, Which we from time to time most grievously have committed, By thought, word, and deed, Against they Divine Majesty, Provoking most justly thy wrath and indignation against us. We do earnestly repent, And are heartily sorry for these our misdoings; The remembrance of them is grievous unto us; The burden of them is intolerable. Have mercy upon us, Have mercy upon us, most merciful Father; For thy Son our Lord Jesus Christ's sake, Forgive us all that is past; And grant that we may ever hereafter Serve and please thee In newness of life, To the honour and glory of thy Name; Through Jesus Christ our Lord. Amen." Church of England, *Book of Common Prayer*, 251.

87. Carus, *Memoirs*, 520.

That Simeon gave particular attention to humility was not unique to evangelical Anglicans, or those of any Christian tradition. Basil of Caesarea (330–379) and Augustine (354–430) gave much attention to this part of character formation. Such an emphasis was as old at the teaching of Jesus himself, who said in Matt 5:5, "Blessed are the meek: for they shall inherit the earth." Strikingly, however, when Simeon expounded this text, he distinguished between learned humility and dispositional humility. The former was that which an individual applied in Christian experience, the latter was possessed by native bent. Simeon elaborated,

> The disposition which distinguishes the persons here spoken of, is not that natural mildness and gentleness with which some are favoured even from the womb: (persons of this description may be as far from true Christian meekness, as others who are of a more violent temper:) but a meekness founded "in poverty of spirit," and in "mourning for sin," a fruit of the operation of the Spirit of God upon the soul.[88]

Simeon, further expounding the text, showed how true Christian meekness manifests itself in certain conduct toward God and men. In his posture towards God, the Christian humbly submits to his precepts and providence. In his posture towards men, the Christian is courteous, patient, and forgiving.[89]

Whether from the pulpit or in the parish, the vicar of Holy Trinity made submission to God's providence a core tenet of the Christian faith. Describing the Christian's posture toward God's sovereign will, he said,

> He no longer, like others, disputes against the word of God, or murmurs on account of the dealings of his Providence. Whatever God requires, appears, in his eyes, to be right (Note: Psalms 119:128): and whatever he does, though for the present it may be dark and inexplicable, is considered as wise and good. He dares not on any account to "reply against God (Note: Romans 9:20)." Instead of objecting to any declaration, command, or threatening, as "an hard saying," he "trembles at it (Note: Isaiah 66:2);" and receives it with meekness as an engrafted word, "able to save his soul (Note: James 1:21)." He may have many and great trials; but instead of "fretting against the Lord," he bows with humble submission, saying, "Not my will, but thine be done."[90]

---

88. Simeon, *Expository Outlines*, 11:52.
89. Simeon, *Expository Outlines*, 11:52–53.
90. Simeon, *Expository Outlines*, 11:52.

To Simeon, trust in the staying hand of God sustained him through the vicissitudes of ministry.

Humility in Ministry

For the purposes of this chapter, it should be appreciated that humility was not merely vital to Simeon's own walk with God—more than this, it was a requirement for the pastorate. In his relentless project to elevate the standards for the Christian ministry, Simeon emphasized to his mentees the monumental worth of meekness. In an 1819 memorandum, reflecting on inward humility, he wrote, "I consider the religion of the day as materially defective in this point; and the preaching of pious Ministers defective also. I do not see, so much as I could wish, an holy reverential awe of God. The confidence that is generally professed does not sufficiently, in my opinion, savour of a creature-like spirit, or a sinner-like spirit."[91] He then illustrated his point by expounding the prophet's call to ministry in Isa 6.

> If ninety-nine out of an hundred, or even good men, were now informed for the first time, that Isaiah in a vision saw the Seraphim before the throne; and that each of the Seraphs had six wings; and then were asked, "How do you think that they employ their wings?" I think their answer would be, "How? Why they fly with them with all their might; and if they had six hundred wings the would do the same, exerting all their powers in the service of their God:" they would never dream of their employing two to veil their faces, as unworthy to behold their God, and two to veil their feet, as unworthy to serve him; and devoting only the remaining two to what might be deemed their more appropriate use. But I doubt much whether the Seraphs do not judge quite as well as they, and serve their God in quite as acceptable a manner as they would, if their energies were less blended with modesty and conscious unworthiness.[92]

Again, Simeon saw "conscious unworthiness" to go hand in hand with Christian ministry.

He especially endeavored to show humility in religious conflict and controversy. Moule writes of Simeon that he was "totally free from

---

91. Carus, *Memoirs*, 522.
92. Carus, *Memoirs*, 522–23.

that easy but fatal mistake of troubled pastors, the scolding accent."[93] In his sermon on Matt 5:5, Simeon first spoke to the general character of patience in the Christian.

> Many in their natural state are so irritable, that it is impossible to please them long together: they are like the sea, tossed and agitated by every breath of wind. Not so the person who has attained the character in the text. We say not, that he *never* speaks unadvisedly with his lips; for even Moses, the meekest of the human race, transgressed in this particular (Note: Psalms 106:33); and, if a man so bridled his tongue, as never in any instance to offend in word, he would be altogether perfect (Note: James 3:2). But the Christian has attained such a measure of self-government, as "not to be easily provoked." . . . Where the offence committed is of such a nature as to require an expression of his displeasure, he endeavours so to guard his anger, so to temper it with love and pity; and so to restrain it both in measure and duration, that he may fulfil the precept, "Be angry, and sin not."[94]

He then moved from discussing patience generally, to illustrating the role of meekness in religious controversy.

> He is particularly on his guard in relation to religious controversy. If his sentiments are represented as erroneous and absurd, instead of yielding immediately to vehemence and invective, he will "give a reason of the hope that is in him with meekness and fear (Note: 1 Peter 3:15);" and will "instruct in meekness them that oppose themselves, if God peradventure may give them repentance to the acknowledging of the truth (Note: 2 Timothy 2:25)." If, on the other hand, it falls to his lot to reprove a fallen brother, he will endeavour to "restore such an one in the spirit of meekness, considering himself, lest he also be tempted (Note: Galatians 6:1)."[95]

Hopkins aptly makes use of William Cowper's description of John Newton in controversy to characterize Simeon's demeanor in the same:

> . . . with a smile
> Gentle and affable, and full of grace,
> As fearful of offending whom he wish'd

---

93. Moule, *Charles Simeon*, 47.
94. Simeon, *Expository Outlines*, 11:53.
95. Simeon, *Expository Outlines*, 11:53.

> Much to persuade, he plied his ear with truths
> Not harshly thunder'd forth or rudely press'd,
> But, like his purpose, gracious, kind and sweet.⁹⁶

When the master of Sidney College, Edward Pearson (1756–1811), openly criticized Simeon in a university sermon entitled *Evangelical and Pharisaic Righteousness Compared*, Simeon chose not to enroll in a protracted, public controversy. Rather, he wrote privately to Pearson,

> I know and feel within myself (as most probably you do also) that controversy is hurtful to the spirit . . . it gratifies some of the worst passions of the heart. Happy shall I be, Sir, to have no occasion ever to resume it. . . . It is my earnest wish that the only strife we may ever know in future may be that which the Apostles recommended, of "contending earnestly for the faith once delivered to the saints," and of "provoking one another to love and good works."⁹⁷

Simeon did not fear controversy when deemed necessary. However, endued with a sense of his own lowliness, he rarely sought the public vindication of men in the context of conflict.

One of his curates, Matthew Preston, noted how Simeon's humility gave him cause to rejoice in the success of other ministers.

> Another of the many interesting traits of Mr. Simeon's character, which may here be properly referred to, was his delight with which he observed the spiritual progress and growing usefulness of other ministers, even when there might seem to be a temptation to the feeling of jealousy, as if another were rising to supersede himself. On such occasions he would say, with evident joy and sincerity, "He must increase; I must decrease."⁹⁸

Preston then recounted how Simeon, after a period of Sabbatical, returned home to find his parish well-cared for by Thomas Thomason. Moreover, many benefited from Thomason's sermons in ways they had not from Simeon's. The vicar of Holy Trinity rejoiced at this discovery. After hearing Thomason preach, he turned to a friend and said, "Now I

---

96. Hopkins, *Charles Simeon of Cambridge*, 66.
97. Hopkins, *Charles Simeon of Cambridge*, 76.
98. Preston, *Rev. Charles Simeon*, 64.

see *why I* have been laid aside: I bless God for it."[99] Simeon celebrated the advance of the gospel through whatever means or servant.

Another point of intersection between personal humility and pastoral ministry was self-sacrifice. Simeon believed that if a minister truly esteemed himself rightly, his love for and devotion to the congregation should never be questioned. In a sermon titled "Ministerial Zeal Depicted," he expounded Phil 2:17–18.

> What then becomes the Christian *minister*, who has consecrated himself to the service of the sanctuary, and bound himself, by the most solemn ties, to live only for his God! The union of love and zeal which the Apostle manifested on this occasion should be visible in the whole of his walk before God; so that at all times he may appeal to his people as the Apostle did; "We were gentle among you, even as a nurse cherisheth her children; so, being affectionately desirous of you, we were willing to have imparted unto you, not the Gospel of God only, but also *our own souls*, because ye were dear unto us (Note: 1 Thessalonians 2:7–8)." O that there were in us such a heart as this! What blessings should we be to the places where our lot is cast![100]

On this point, the relevance of Simeon's personal piety to his pastoral theology proves irrefutable, for, he explicitly drew upon the inward life of the Christian to promote service in the kingdom.

> And how ready should we be to go forth, wherever our God may call us; accounting nothing of the trials that may await us, even though life itself were the sacrifice that we were called to make. Dear brethren, let it not be said of you, "All men seek their own, and not the things of Jesus Christ (Note: ver. 21);" but beg of God that you may rise to your proper character; and be enabled to "follow the Apostle, as he followed Christ."[101]

Humility Applied

Humility as a significant element of Simeon's personal piety—and thus, his pastoral theology—is further demonstrated in the direct instruction he gave his pupils in his conversation parties. On one such occasion, the seasoned pastor asserted, "God is more delighted with your humble

---

99. Preston, *Rev. Charles Simeon*, 65.
100. Simeon, *Expository Outlines*, 18:77.
101. Simeon, *Expository Outlines*, 18:78.

thoughts of Him than with the Preacher's words. The humble and contrite heart God loves—delights in."[102] Simeon found the fight for humility to be a pronounced struggle for young men. Because of this, much of the counsel in his conversation parties was directed to the pitfalls of young ministers. The next chapter will highlight Simeon's repeated criticism of pastors who insisted upon preaching troubling doctrines to their people prematurely. He did not hesitate to cite specific, negative examples of others. For example, he called out Henry Martyn for his lack of patience with his hearers.[103]

> Inflexibility seldom does good on minor points. It is generally useful to comply on points open to Christian liberty; not to yield for self, or for saving trouble or annoyance to ourselves, but for the sake of pleasing all men for their good to edification. Were inflexibility our duty always, why did St. Paul become all things to all men, and circumcise Timothy for good, and refuse to circumcise Titus also for good? Henry Martyn's preaching on hell, after being requested not, was unwise; it was the act of a young man. I preached on board the same ship the morning before he sailed, and they were all offended because I wept over them; and the impression of it has not left the minds of some of them to this day. Henry Martyn should have preached in love and gentleness from some other text, showing that he only desired to do them good.[104]

From the narrative of Martyn's life, he eventually learned humility and patience. Another example came in the impression of Simeon's humility on Francis Close.

> I cannot omit one instance out of many as a mark of his kind nature. It occurred to me when I was almost a freshman. On returning one evening after the Thursday evening service to

---

102. Brown, *Recollections*, 159.

103. One of Martyn's biographers describes Martyn's character on this point. "The time of the delay was spent in zealous service for his divine Master. He was associated with Rev. Mr. Simeon as curate and preached with great zeal and unction, often to very large audiences, and sometimes with such unsparing denunciation of common sins as to awaken opposition. He considered it his duty to rebuke iniquity, and on one occasion severely reproved a student for shocking levity, reading a play with some young ladies while their father lay dying. He feared the result of this might be estrangement from his friend, but prayed earnestly that it might lead to his awakening. This prayer was answered, and afterwards this very friend became his beloved associate in missionary work in India." Rhea, *Life of Henry Martyn*, 10.

104. Brown, *Recollections*, 96.

Mrs Domford's, in Pease Hill, I was asked by a junior member of the family what I thought of Mr Simeon's sermon. I replied, "It was too long by half;" little thinking my questioner would observe to Mr Simeon, "What do you think this boy says of your sermon?" Mr Simeon did not affect to hear the remark; but on its being repeated replied, "The boy is right; I felt it so myself." He was not in the least offended.[105]

Here again, it should be noted that the greatest lesson Simeon ever taught was the example of his own life.

Communion with God

Arguably the most pronounced facet of Simeon's piety was his personal walk with God. What his soul cultivated privately manifested to all who met his acquaintance. Remarking on his faith, Henry Venn wrote to his son-in-law Charles Elliott (1752–1826) in a 1790 letter, "On Monday, my affectionate friend Simeon walked over here and slept. Oh! How refreshing were his prayers! How profitable his conversation! We were all revived: he left a blessing behind him."[106] Venn wrote again to Elliott in the same year:

> I was low and uneasy about––yesterday. Mr. Simeon did me "good, like a medicine;" and his prayer with me took off the weight which lay heavy upon me. He calls me his father: he pours out his prayer for me, as an instrument from whose counsel he has profited; and was as fervent and importunate with God for me, as my son or yourself.[107]

The fruit of Simeon's closeness to God was not only perceptible to others, it inspired them. As with his piety more broadly, men did not just learn from his character, they sought to replicate it. On a summer evening in 1797, Wilberforce wrote in his journal, "Simeon with us—his heart glowing with love of Christ. How full he is of love, and of desire to promote the spiritual benefit of others. Oh! that I might copy him, as he Christ. My path is indeed difficult, and full of enemies. But God in Christ can and will strengthen and uphold us if we trust in him."[108] While it has

---

105. Moule, *Charles Simeon*, 180.
106. Venn, *Life and Letters*, 473.
107. Venn, *Life and Letters*, 481–82.
108. Carus, *Memoirs*, 150.

been established that Wilberforce and Simeon shared a fierce hatred for the slave trade, this quote reveals that it was the Cambridge minister's thriving relationship to God that steeled Wilberforce's perseverance in the abolition movement. A similar effect can be seen in Simeon's first curate Thomason, who marveled, "It is astonishing how free [Simeon] is of all fear of man."[109] Notably, Thomason attributed this fearlessness to Simeon's communion with God.

> What evidences his zeal in the cause of God more perhaps than anything else, is that after labouring and labouring for his young men, that his lectures may be as profitable as possible, he then kneels down and thanks God, that he makes him in any degree useful to his "dear—dear young servants." This should be a great spur to us, that we may cooperate as it were with him, and live in continual dependence upon, and communion with God; that thus, by every effort in our power, aided by the grace and assistance of God, we may at length realize his wishes concerning us.[110]

Not only was this aspect of Simeon's piety attractive to his mentors, peers, and pupils—but it was seen as essential to his usefulness in ministry.

Spiritual Disciplines

The character of Simeon's communion with God was shaped by a staunch commitment to spiritual disciplines. Regular rhythms of prayer and Scripture reading formed the bedrock of his spirituality. Robert Houseman (1759–1838) of Lancaster—whom Simeon claimed as his first convert—gave an arousing testimony of the latter's commitment to prayer and meditation on the word of God.[111] "Never did I see," said Houseman, "such consistency and reality of devotion, such warmth of piety, such zeal, such love. Never did I see one who abounded so much in prayer."[112] Informed by Houseman, Carus described Simeon's daily habits in his personal devotions:

> Mr. Simeon invariably rose every morning . . . at four o'clock; and, after lighting his fire, he devoted the first four hours of the day to private prayer, and the devotional study of the

---

109. Carus, *Memoirs*, 98.
110. Carus, *Memoirs*, 98.
111. Hopkins, *Charles Simeon of Cambridge*, 98–99.
112. Hopkins, *Charles Simeon of Cambridge*, 99.

Scriptures. He would then ring his bell, and calling in his friend with his servant, engage with them in what he termed his family prayer. Here was the secret of his great grace and spiritual strength. Deriving instruction from such a source, and seeking it with such diligence, he was comforted in all his trials, and prepared for every duty.[113]

The sheer amount of time Simeon spent on his devotions is staggering. However, it is perhaps more noteworthy how he employed personal spiritual disciplines to expose others to his own intimate experience of God. For example, a young Samuel Marsden (1765–1838) marveled when he witnessed Simeon in private prayer.[114] Carus recounted the memorable encounter.

> I recollect once Marsden's telling me of a remarkable instance in that dear man of God, Mr. Simeon. Mr. Marsden, you know, was his intimate friend, and had access to him even in his most retired moments. He told me that he called once upon him, and found him so absorbed in the contemplation of the Son of God, and so overpowered with a display of his mercy to his soul, that, full of the animating theme, he was incapable of pronouncing a single word: at length, after an interval, with accents big he exclaimed, "Glory! glory! glory!" The relation of this affected me much, I remember; and I asked myself, "Why I was so much a stranger to it? Why such coldness in my soul? If I love, why am I thus? You see a pattern of Christian zeal and fervency in that man of God."[115]

Simeon radiated with a zeal that aroused all those around him to hunger for God.

Separation from the World

Much of Simeon's pursuit of piety came at the cost of resisting the cares of the world. For Simeon, this did not merely include the world's temptations to sin, but also morally neutral matters that would distract him from

---

113. Carus, *Memoirs*, 67.

114. Samuel Marsden was a Cambridge-educated priest, who ministered with the CMS in Australia and New Zealand. He is remembered for playing a prominent role in bringing the gospel to New Zealand, and his relationship to convicts in Australia. For more on his life, see Marsden, *Rev. Samuel Marsden*.

115. Carus, *Memoirs*, 100.

the pursuit of Christ, and usefulness in his kingdom. For example, practical piety was the only reason he ever shared for his lifelong singleness.

> What has been my language at *all times* and to *all persons?* Has it not been this?—I should hate the University above all places as a married man; but the singular way in which I have been called to my present post, and its almost incalculable importance, forbid the thought of my now leaving it:—therefore I think I shall never marry.... Again—in my present situation I am quite a rich man, and almost as free from care as an angel; but if I were to marry, I should instantly become a poor man (reducing my income one half, while I doubled my expenditure):—therefore I think I shall never marry.[116]

Simeon certainly did not hold an antagonistic view of marriage, as did single ministers like John Berridge. However, he believed the institution would pose an impediment to his service of God in Cambridge.

Withdrawal from the world marked his life from the moment of conversion. In an 1823 letter to Charlotte Sofia Somerset (1771–1854), the Duchess of Beaufort, he declared, "I am a man of some firmness and decision of character; and from the first moment that I set myself to seek the Lord, I gave up myself wholly to Him, and separated myself altogether from the world."[117] Indeed, it was such separation that invited the reproach of Cambridge for so many years. Throughout his life, Simeon underscored the duty of ministers especially to come out of the world. He once remarked at a conversation party that ministers should err on the side of over-separation from worldly activities instead of conformity:

> The Minister must come out from the world, and yet he may be sinning in doing so, if he act from a sense of being holier than the rest, or, as the Scripture phrase is, lest he should smell "the smoke under his nose."—(Isaiah lxv. 5.) A young Minister had better err by too great a departure from the world than run the risk of taking fire into the tinder of his heart by too great a conformity.[118]

Charles Bridges would reflect a similar sentiment in the pastoral theology of *The Christian Ministry*.

---

116. Carus, *Memoirs*, 230.
117. Carus, *Memoirs*, 582.
118. Brown, *Recollections*, 119.

> Accurate and earnest statements of truth, combined with sociable conformity to the world, will give no offence, and bring no conviction. Cowper's line—"If parsons fiddle, why may'nt laymen dance?"—has at least as much truth as wit in it. If we go one step into the world, our flock will take the sanction to go two; the third will be still more easy, and the atmosphere more enticing, till at last it proves that "a bird hastens to the snare, and does not know that it is for his life."[119]

Notably, Simeon tended to refrain from drawing out specific applications on the topic of withdrawal from the world. For example, it is striking that Simeon neglected to comment on any particular practice in his sermon on 1 John 2:15, "Love not the world, neither the things that are in the world. If any man love the world, the love of the Father is not in him." Instead, Simeon warned against Christians cultivating censorious dispositions towards one another, noting that the "prohibition relates to *the heart and the affections*, which are not to be set on the world, or on any thing in it, *in comparison of God*."[120] To Simeon, worldly activities must be avoided so much as they present impediments to Christian joy.

Religious Affections

Due to decreasing strength in ministry, Simeon took a sabbatical in the early months of 1807, following the counsel of several friends. During this period, his physical health not only revived, but he also regained spiritual vigor. Though he was refreshed by visiting friends like Wilberforce, Newton, and Richard Cecil (1748–1810)—it is his reflections on his soul's experience that garner attention, for this is one of the few periods of his life in which he kept a thorough journal. On Easter Sunday, he recorded,

> My mind, on the whole, was comfortable in the recollection of the mercy vouchsafed to me on this day twenty-eight years ago. I felt myself happy and thankful, that the peace which then flowed into my soul, had never been entirely lost; and that I was as much bent as ever on the securing of the prize of my high calling.... At the Lord's table my soul was much refreshed.[121]

---

119. Bridges, *Christian Ministry*, 121.
120. Simeon, *Expository Outlines*, 20:403.
121. Carus, *Memoirs*, 222.

The following Sunday, he remarked, "I felt that the Sabbath was indeed a delight. My soul rejoiced in God my Saviour. . . . At the Lord's table I found God very present with me."[122] The following Thursday, he wrote in his journal, "Felt happy in my soul, and desirous of living more to God. Time is passing, and eternity approaching. O that in my journey which I am to begin tomorrow I may have the presence of God!"[123] These quotes add texture to the portrait of Simeon's piety—not least for his earnest pursuit of the presence of God. On April 16, he provided more commentary on his spiritual state.

> I have been highly favoured of the Lord for several days. Sometimes indeed I have been as dull and stupid as ever; but frequently, and in an unusual degree, my spirit has rejoiced in God my Saviour. Doubtless the elevation of my joy has arisen in part from a flow of animal spirits . . . but if we can "rejoice even with joy unspeakable and glorified," I think it desirable to do so; provided we preserve a becoming jealousy respecting the abuse of our affection in a way of enthusiasm or of pride.[124]

It remains impressive the degree to which Simeon's life revolved around his sense of personal fellowship with the Divine. To borrow Henry Scougal's phrase, he constantly made it his aim to experience the life of God in his soul.[125]

It was such communion with God that Simeon longed to see experienced by others throughout his ministry. In a memorable anecdote from his 1796 preaching circuit in Scotland, Simeon had an intimate conversation with Alexander Stewart, the minister at Moulin, a small village in central Scotland. Stewart confided in Simeon that he had no real personal faith. Simeon's subsequent exhortation completely changed Stewart's life, leading him to later declare, "Ever since the blessed period of Mr Simeon's visit, my thoughts have continued more steadily fixed on divine things; and my communion with God has been much more lively, by many degrees, than I remember to have experienced before."[126] Rejoicing after Stewart's conversion, Simeon wrote to him,

---

122. Carus, *Memoirs*, 223.
123. Carus, *Memoirs*, 224.
124. Carus, *Memoirs*, 225.
125. Scougal, *Life of God*. Scougal's work highly influenced early evangelicals George Whitefield and John Wesley.
126. Hopkins, *Charles Simeon of Cambridge*, 139.

It is our privilege to expect those invisible interpositions, if we commit our way to Him, and every instance that comes to our notice, should encourage us to acknowledge Him in all our ways. I am exceedingly comforted, my dear brother, with the account which you give of your soul. O how desirable is it for all, but especially for ministers, to have their souls deeply and devoutly impressed.[127]

Communion Applied

For Simeon, the priority of communion with God was not a private matter. He consistently promoted such experimental religion to his disciples. He once wrote passionately to a young minister,

> My dear friend, walk close with God: it is the only way to be either safe or happy: live retired—read much—pray much—abound in all offices of love—shun the company that may draw you aside—seek the company of those from whom you may receive edification in your soul—be dying daily to the world—consider yourself as a soldier that is not to be "entangled with the things of this life, in order that you may please Him who hath chosen you to be a soldier." Finally, "be faithful unto death, and Christ will give thee a crown of life."[128]

Another lengthier, and more prescriptive quote properly conveys the tenor of his counsel to young ordinands.

> That I may not be mistaken in reference to a preparation for a Fellowship, I add, set apart a day for fasting and prayer. At the close of that day dedicate, as before God, such a portion of your time to the prosecution of academical studies as you judge right: and then adhere steadily to your plan, dedicating to the service of your God and Saviour the remainder of your time. This will bring a blessing upon your soul, and upon your very studies. You need not be told that, by putting oil to the wheels of a carriage, the labour to the horses is diminished, and the progress of the traveler accelerated in a degree that an ignorant and inexperienced person could never conceive. I trust you have often found the blessed effect of a divine unction: how sweetly and rapidly have you proceeded when in a heavenly frame![129]

127. Carus, *Memoirs*, 135.
128. Carus, *Memoirs*, 190.
129. Carus, *Memoirs*, 492–93.

For Simeon, piety was always eminently practical: nothing fit a minister more for his labors than intimate communion with God.

Conclusion

This chapter has shown how Simeon's personal piety formed an essential element of his pastoral theology. Simeon did not only teach his disciples *how* to shepherd, he showed them *who* and *what* to be as a man of God. Thus, what he prioritized in Christian character inevitably and indelibly effected his followers. For example, when examining the life of Thomas Thomason, one cannot help but be impressed by the place of piety in his life. Simeon himself remarked on it.[130] Yet arguably everything Thomason learned in the realm of piety he derived from his pastoral mentor. Sargent asserted the impact of Simeon's influence on Thomason: "Nor was that all;—for in Mr. Simeon he has before him a living example of an elevated description, ever seeming to suggest this is not your rest, you are not come to the land of which the Lord God has said, 'He will give it you.'"[131]

---

130. Carus, *Memoirs*, 696–99.
131. Sargent, *Rev. T. T. Thomason*, 101.

CHAPTER 5

Parish Pastor

In April of 1783, having assumed his role at Holy Trinity only a few months prior, Simeon preached a message on the responsibility of ministers. The sermon is fascinating on a number of fronts. First, Simeon evidenced a confidence in his role whilst enduring great hostility from his congregation. Second—and more importantly for the purposes of this chapter—he offered a glimpse of a well-formed pastoral philosophy at the young age of twenty-three. He told the congregation,

> It may be asked, perhaps, why do you speak to us about the duties of the Ministry, when we come to hear concerning our own duties? I have done it for your sakes as well as for my own—for your sakes, because by remembering the very nature of my office, and the care incumbent on me for the welfare of your immortal souls, you will consider whatever may appear in my discourses harsh, earnest, or alarming, not as the effects of enthusiasm, but as the rational dictates of a heart impressed with a sense both of the value of the soul and the importance of eternity; and by recollecting the awful consequences of my neglect, you will be more inclined to receive favourably any well-meant admonitions.[1]

Simeon saw himself as a custodian of eternal souls.[2] As a preacher of the gospel, he felt duty-bound to constantly pursue the good of those

1. Moule, *Charles Simeon*, 47.
2. Simeon rarely used the word "vicar" or "rector" to describe his role, without a single recorded use in his sermons. Meanwhile, he frequently used the words "pastor,"

entrusted into his care. Not only did this inform his personal philosophy of ministry, but he viewed it as crucial to convey such priorities to his congregation. Moreover, as will be shown below, he sought to furnish his followers with the same tireless commitment to the good of souls. This chapter will examine Simeon as a parish pastor, highlighting his views and practice in three areas: the pastor's relationship to parishioners, visitation ministry, and congregational life. Though these three areas will present some overlap, together they will provide a fuller picture of Simeon's pastoral theology.

The Pastor and the Parish

Simeon's understanding of the relationship between pastor and parishioner must be discussed first. One of the passages that loomed largest in Simeon's pastoral theology was 1 Thess 2:1–12. In addition to preaching on the text, he extensively commented on it in his conversation parties to draw out lessons for future ordinands. The Pauline passage reads as follows:

> For yourselves, brethren, know our entrance in unto you, that it was not in vain: But even after that we had suffered before, and were shamefully entreated, as ye know, at Philippi, we were bold in our God to speak unto you the gospel of God with much contention. For our exhortation was not of deceit, nor of uncleanness, nor in guile: But as we were allowed of God to be put in trust with the gospel, even so we speak; not as pleasing men, but God, which trieth our hearts. For neither at any time used we flattering words, as ye know, nor a cloke of covetousness; God is witness: Nor of men sought we glory, neither of you, nor yet of others, when we might have been burdensome, as the apostles of Christ. But we were gentle among you, even as a nurse cherisheth her children: So being affectionately desirous of you, we were willing to have imparted unto you, not the gospel of God only, but also our own souls, because ye were dear unto us. For ye remember, brethren, our labour and travail: for labouring night and day, because we would not be chargeable unto any of you, we preached unto you the gospel of God. Ye are witnesses, and God also, how holily and justly and unblameably we behaved ourselves among you that believe: As ye know how we exhorted and comforted and charged every one of you, as

---

"shepherd," and "minister" to describe himself.

a father doth his children, That ye would walk worthy of God, who hath called you unto his kingdom and glory.

A Shepherd to His Sheep

In his sermon on the text, Simeon first highlighted the shepherding aspect of the minister's role. To be a faithful shepherd encompassed a host of responsibilities.

> Ministers are represented in the Scriptures under a great variety of characters. Sometimes they are called shepherds, whose office is to search out the straying sheep, and bring them to the fold of Christ: and, when once brought thither, to watch over them with all imaginable care, "strengthening the diseased, healing the sick, binding up the broken, bringing back again any that have been driven away:" and as to the lambs, they are to "carry them in their bosom, and gently to lead those that are with young (Note: Ezekiel 34:2; Ezekiel 34:4 and Isaiah 40:11)."[3]

Though Simeon almost certainly understood "strengthening" and "healing" to be more a spiritual duty than a physical one, he lived in a time when it was not uncommon for some parish pastors to provide medical care to their people.[4]

A Father to His Family

In addition to the picture of shepherding, the minister was likened to a father. Simeon continued his exposition,

> But [ministers] are designated by a far more exalted character, even that of a father; which comprehends in it everything that is tender and endearing (Note: 1 Corinthians 4:14-15). How much of care and responsibility is involved in this relation, may be judged from the complaint which Moses poured out before

---

3. Simeon, *Expository Outlines*, 18:285.

4. Murray, *J. C. Ryle*, 61. Ryle commented on his first curacy in the early 1840s. "I cured many ague cases by administering first an Emetic of Ipecac and Syrup, and afterwards Tincture of Quinine. I saved many lives in Scarlet fever by supplying them with large quantities of very strong BeefTea, made from concentrated essence, and insisted on their swallowing it, as long as their throats kept open. However, 10 per cent of the population had the Scarlet fever and 10 per cent died, chiefly children."

God, when he was called upon to stand, as it were, in this relation to all the people of Israel (Note: Numbers 11:11–14).[5]

Like the apostle Paul, Simeon viewed it as quite appropriate to relate to his parishioners as a loving, caring father.

A Mother to Her Children

Yet notwithstanding this masculine motif, he more extensively and frequently commented upon the feminine imagery employed by Paul.

> There is however a still more tender image by which God is pleased to represent his own stupendous love to his people, and by which also the duty of ministers is portrayed; I mean that of a mother, nursing her infant offspring (Note: Isaiah 66:10–13). St. Paul, declaring his anxiety for the welfare of his converts, compares his feelings with the pangs of a woman in child-birth (Note: Galatians 4:19); and his delight in them, with that of a mother cherishing in her bosom her new-born infant. The language in our text is exquisitely beautiful and touching. The nurse spoken of, is not an alien, but a nursing-mother: it is not in her arms only, but in her bosom, that she cherishes the child. In all her treatment of it, she is not harsh, as one that is soon wearied in performing offices of love; but gentle. If absent from her infant for a few hours only, she is most affectionately desirous of it, and delights to draw forth to it the breast, even though it be with great pain and inconvenience to herself; and she would impart to it, as it were, her vital strength, yea, her very soul: and all this she does to it because of the tender affection which she bears towards it. The whole creation does not afford a sublimer image than this; yet this fitly represents the conduct of St. Paul towards the Church of Christ, and consequently, the conduct of every faithful minister, in proportion as he resembles St. Paul.[6]

Notably, Simeon did not view Paul and his coworkers (Timothy and Silvanus) as exceptional exemplars. Rather, he viewed their pattern as prescriptive for all pastors. He clarified,

> Every minister indeed is not called to forego in like manner his claims of temporal support; but every minister should be

---

5. Simeon, *Expository Outlines*, 18:285.
6. Simeon, *Expository Outlines*, 18:285–86.

> able to declare to his people, as in the presence of God, "I seek not yours, but you." The only object of a faithful servant of Christ is, to advance the welfare of his people: for this end he will "not count even life itself dear to him," but will "endure all things for the elect's sake, that they may obtain the salvation that is in Christ Jesus with eternal glory (Note: Act 20:24 and 2 Timothy 2:10)." And if he be really called to sacrifice his life in the sacred cause, he will account it rather a ground for congratulation than any cause of sorrow or condolence (Note: Philippians 2:17-18).[7]

As a good shepherd to his sheep, and parent to his children, Simeon viewed the minister's invariable objective to advance the welfare of his flock. Ministers were not to be hired hands who performed their duties devoid of affection for their people. Sacrificial love was built into their very job description.

For Simeon, so much of his care for souls came in the simple display of patience and gentleness. Though not averse to speaking hard truths, he made it his constant aim to win his hearers. In one conversation party, he used a nautical illustration to make the point. "A Minister is bound to probe all such principles to the quick, to be ready always to answer, and to know how to explain. We should not wish to sail as near the wind as we can, but a Minister's duty is to know how near he or others may sail to the wind without being upset."[8] Elsewhere, he promoted the pattern of Moses in leading through gradual change.

> Do not thus undervalue the precious souls entrusted to you. Be gentle among your people, even as a nursing mother cherisheth her children. I know that it is self-denial, yet put a veil over your face; not a permanent one as Moses did, but such as will allow you gradually to open the minds of your people. Seek, as your grand duty, to do what God desires to be done, in such a way as you find allowed and directed in Scripture.[9]

The next chapter will show how he applied this particular emphasis in preaching. In the meantime, his gentle posture toward his flock should be appreciated as a broader principle of his pastoral theology, both in the pulpit and throughout his parish.

---

7. Simeon, *Expository Outlines*, 18:286–87.
8. Brown, *Recollections*, 258.
9. Brown, *Recollections*, 169–70.

Simeon understood it to be a peculiar struggle of young men to emphasize boldness *at the expense* of gentleness. He regularly, therefore, promoted the affection and character commended in 1 Thess 2 in his training of young men. Again, he commented on the text:

> Throughout this whole passage see how St. Paul appeals to his flock, again and again, for their own testimony of what his work and his manners had been among them.... And every Minister should so conduct himself as to have approved himself to the consciences of his flock; not for their mere praise, but that he may be able to appeal to their hearts for the truth of all he says when speaking of his own ministry. "Our entrance in unto you was not in vain." How sweet to look around us, and be able to see this in the altered lives of our flock![10]

It is on this point Simeon made his thoughts on biblical boldness plain.

> "We were bold in our God to speak unto you." Ministers are apt to mistake what boldness is. Souls are committed into your hands, and your faithfulness to God must be shown in striving to save them, St. Paul means not here that boldness which recklessly speaks all out. Where is the humility of such ministrations? St. Paul speaketh of "boldness in God;" indifference to the earthly consequence to yourselves which will result from the world's enmity to God. He means not a rough, coarse, stern manner of undaunted effrontery. You must be cautious and fearful of its effects on the poor sinners who hear you. Our Saviour said, "I have many things to say to you, but ye cannot bear them now." St. Paul fed his flock with milk, not with strong meat, because they needed that discrimination. He gave them the sincere (simple or unmixed) milk of the word, that they might grow thereby. You must not put new wine into old bottles, else you will have to answer to God for the bursting of the bottles. How wrong is the argumentative, or critical, or metaphysical style which one often hears preached among beginners in religion, instead of the simple Gospel of Jesus! Preach as your flock is able to bear it; lead them on by degrees. When they understand and have got firm hold of a principle, then close with them upon that, and be mighty to speak it unto them. Draw forth all that hinges upon that principle, and then be bold in God, and never flinch from any truths, however severe, which flow from that principle. Deliver the whole counsel of God, but choose your times and opportunities, and tell them as they are able to hear it.

10. Brown, *Recollections*, 160.

> An opposite conduct is selfishness, pride, ostentation. Speak the Gospel, so as to win souls, "with much contention" (i.e., earnestness). Be in earnest. Plead as if your own soul hung on it; plead with them as you would with your own children.[11]

Simeon believed that apostolic boldness was not the raw determination to tactlessly say true things. Rather, true boldness—that character which was to mark all ministers—must be accompanied by an earnestness to win the consciences of one's hearers. It was such earnestness that governed all of Simeon's interactions with his flock.

Year after year, Simeon's greatest aim in ministry was the spiritual growth of his people. He commended the rugged pursuit of others' spiritual good as the pastor's highest joy. "If a man be a faithful servant of Christ," he asserted, "the prosperity of his people will be the one aim of all his labours, and the one source of all his joys: both at the present hour, and in the prospect of the eternal world, their welfare will be 'his hope, his joy, his crown of rejoicing.' Is it asked, wherefore they are so dear to him? we answer, He glories in them.'"[12] Playing on Paul's feminine picture in 1 Thess 2, he expounded,

> And O! what a blessed period will that be, when the faithful minister shall present his converts before the throne of God, saying, "Here am I, and the children thou hast given me!" Not even in the presence of the Lord Jesus Christ himself will he forget those with whom, as St. Paul expresses it, he once travailed in birth: "there will they be his joy and crown of rejoicing:" there will they be, as it were, jewels in his crown. Every fresh accession to the Church thus enhances the minister's joy: and in the prospect of this, "he joys according to the joy in harvest, and as men rejoice when they divide the spoil (Note: Isaiah 9:3)."[13]

So intense was Simeon's pleasure in his people that he rejoiced in their progress through whatever means or servant. In the last chapter, the way that Simeon, after a period of sabbatical, celebrated the peculiar growth of many of his parishioners under the preaching of Thomas Thomason was highlighted. On another occasion, he beamed with delight to discover an older woman in his congregation who had been deeply moved by John Berridge's preaching.[14]

11. Brown, *Recollections*, 160–61.
12. Simeon, *Expository Outlines*, 18:300.
13. Simeon, *Expository Outlines*, 18:302.
14. Brown, *Recollections*, 152–53.

Visitation

Like the generation of many evangelical Anglicans who preceded him, Simeon continued the tradition of maintaining a regular visitation schedule with his flock. Newton, Venn, and Berridge modeled ministries in which the fruit reaped in the pulpit grew from the seeds sown through parochial visitation. Readers gain insight into the character of Simeon's personal encounters with his people through an account of a conversation he had with a dying woman in his congregation.

> I once visited a poor dying woman. I asked if she was a sinner. "Yes, a great one." She must repent. "So I do every day." You must believe in Christ. "I do with all my heart." You must pray unceasingly for mercy. "So I do." In short, whatever I advised she told me she did it. At last I said, "My good woman, why did you deceive me? I was sent for to visit a sinner, but you are an angel; don't deceive me any more, for you are certainly an angel; you do everything just as it ought to be done. A sinner would find out his sins in everything he did,—would feel that he did nothing well, but you do everything well: you are an angel." This opened the poor creature's eyes, and was blessed for her good, and made the means of awakening her. I hope she is now in heaven.[15]

Elsewhere, Simeon recounted a visit to a young woman's family that resulted in the latter's conversion.[16] The anecdote serves to underscore Simeon's profound love for souls. Carus wrote of the encounter, "So strong an impression did this event make on Mr. Simeon, that when alluding to it, just thirty years after, he says, 'If my whole life had been spent without any other compensation than this, my labours had been richly recompensed.'"[17]

As much as Simeon enjoyed visitation, the size of his congregation, compounded by his health problems, limited his ability to maintain a regimented visitation schedule with all his parishioners. Simeon acknowledge his limitations once in a conversation party.

> I love these little conversation meetings; they diffuse a spirit of love amongst us. I would I could have them oftener; but I must be glad to do just what I can. I am not now able to speak much,

---

15. Brown, *Recollections*, 192–93.
16. Carus, *Memoirs*, 49–53.
17. Carus, *Memoirs*, 53.

or loud. I need rest, and I shall have it in heaven. These little meetings seem to me somewhat of a foretaste of heaven.[18]

As the eighteenth century drew to a close, something had to be done to accommodate the growing pastoral needs of his bustling congregation. In addition to bringing on curates in the late 1790s, there were two critical means Simeon employed to shepherd his people: the laity and societies.

Elders and Laypeople

Simeon believed in the appointment of elders to help care for his flock. These would be godly layman who could aid him in the parochial needs of the congregation. In fact, Simeon promoted the use of such men as he counseled young ordinands to avoid burning themselves out with home visits.

> If, on entering a parish, your people invite you, I would say, as a general principle, go and see them all once, but not as a habit. Yet it might be unwise to do even this. Every man must be guided by the circumstances of the specific cases. When anything is doubtful, act throughout life against the bent of your inclination. Take God's word for your rule; try yourselves by it; but do not try other persons by your rule.[19]

To preserve longevity in ministry, Simeon advised the swift and judicious recruitment of elders and laypersons for support:

> A Minister is . . . the Pastor, a far higher and more important office. He has more to do in the closet and study than even in the cottage. Let him nominate Elders, laymen, and laywomen, to visit the sick, to pray with them, and read to his people. I do not wholly approve of prayer meetings, nor would have these Elders help in that way, but in visiting his people. Let him meet his Elders, as a body, statedly, and hear from them the state of his parish in its minutest points. But let a Minister be careful to bear in mind that, if this engine of good be not quite under his own control, it will become sectarian, and prove so far injurious to his people.[20]

---

18. Brown, *Recollections*, 159.
19. Brown, *Recollections*, 217.
20. Brown, *Recollections*, 217–18.

Societies

Simeon also used elders and motivated laypeople to form societies or small groups within his parish for the purpose of Christian growth. Brown explains how he organized this part of his ministry.

> It is unnecessary in this work to advert to Mr. Simeon's ministrations among his parishioners, further than mentioning as an illustration his mode of conversational instruction among them, so long as health permitted him to take an active share in ordinary parochial work. He arranged the seriously disposed people in his parish into six societies of men and women, separately, each of which he was accustomed to meet in private every month, that he might be brought into personal intercourse with every individual of his flock who was willing thus to meet him.[21]

Though not without challenges, Simeon himself attested to the utility of societies at a meeting of the Eclectic Society in 1811. On that occasion, those in attendance discussed, "In what way can a minister maintain order and discipline in his church, so as best to answer the ends of God in the original appointment of them?" Simeon shared as follows:

> I have six societies, each of which I meet monthly. There is also a society of twelve, whom I call stewards, who have the management of our funds, and consist of the most serious and wise men in the congregation. By these stewards, who mix with all the members of the societies, I thoroughly know the affairs of each of them.
>
> When persons are discovered to have received an impression under the ministry, he is spoken to on the matter, and deliberation takes place. This plan excites a great solicitude in persons awakened to unite themselves to our societies; and a specific union is formed, and an intimate connexion is established, between me and them.
>
> The stewards know and counteract, as far as is in their power, any danger of error or sin into which the members may seem to fall; if they do not succeed, they bring the case to me.
>
> By these means I have been enabled to preserve my people so much together, that, for twenty-eight years, I have scarcely lost one whom I would not have dismissed.
>
> Some evils attending this system. During long absence, the stewards became rather too much their own masters, and not quite so humble and manageable as they were.

---

21. Brown, *Recollections*, 46–47.

There are about one hundred and twenty persons in these societies.... The ends are two in such societies:—To build up the Church in faith and love; to perpetuate the Church by the accession of new members.[22]

Simeon's experiment with societies demonstrated at least two crucial things about his pastoral theology, (1) he understood the monumental importance of Christians helping others grow in Christlikeness, and (2) he had the humility to recognize his own limitations in personally engaging everyone in his parish in perpetuity. Though Simeon affirmed a sharp distinction between ordained clergy and the laity, he was not afraid to involve his congregation in the work of ministry.

Congregational Life

As a parish pastor, Simeon viewed his responsibility to extend beyond his own personal interactions with the congregation. Indeed, his stewardship also entailed the mobilization of the members of Holy Trinity to serve and edify one another. Readers gain a glimpse of this every-member ministry in his sermon on Heb 10:23–25, where the biblical author writes, "Let us hold fast the profession of our faith without wavering; (for he is faithful that promised;) and let us consider one another to provoke unto love and to good works: not forsaking the assembling of ourselves together, as the manner of some is; but exhorting one another: and so much the more, as ye see the day approaching." From this text, Simeon asserted that parishioners shared a duty to care for one another.

> When once we become united to Christ by faith, we become members of the body, of which he is the Head. To that body we from henceforth have duties, even as the members of our corporeal frame have to the body of which they constitute a part. With that body we are to unite, both in its public and social meetings, and not by withdrawing ourselves from it, to shew an indifference to its welfare. Some there were, even in the Apostle's days, who, through cowardice or worldly mindedness, forsook the assemblies of the Church: and some there are who do so at the present day. But whatever vain excuses they may offer for their conduct, they grossly neglect their duty, which is, to edify, as far as they are able, every member of Christ's mystical body.[23]

22. Pratt, *Evangelical Leaders*, 490.
23. Simeon, *Expository Outlines*, 19:339.

For Simeon, union with Christ meant union with Christ's bride. This meant that the brilliance of the gospel was the fact that God did not merely save individual Christians. Much more, his grace created a new humanity—a biblical community of all those who belong to God. And membership of this community brought with it special privileges and responsibilities.

> We should "consider one another;" we should notice each other's wants and weaknesses, defects and failings, in order to guard each other against the very beginnings of declension in the divine life, and to stimulate one another to exertion in the cause of truth and love. We should mark also one another's abilities and opportunities for serving God, in order that the energies of all may be employed to the best effect. The members of our natural body, if attempting to execute offices for which they are not fitted, can effect little; but, when exerting themselves in their appropriate sphere, they all contribute to the general good. Thus should all the members of the Church seek out for themselves, and assign to each other, such offices as they are best qualified to perform; that, each labouring in his proper vocation, the whole body may be edified, and God's name be glorified.[24]

Elsewhere, Simeon made a similar point from a sermon in Ezekiel.

> Doubtless it is in the first place the duty of *ministers* to follow the steps of this great Shepherd, because his flock is more immediately committed to their care. But it is also the duty of every one in his place and station to exert himself to the utmost to enlarge and edify the flock of Christ. And, if we were more diligent in our respective spheres, how many might be reduced from their wanderings, or strengthened in their difficulties, or comforted in their troubles! We know not how useful a word in season might prove. "Let us then, as the elect of God, put on bowels of mercies," and shew our relation to Christ by our conformity to his image.[25]

Simeon manifested his priority of an every-member ministry in a variety of spheres of church life. Central to his role as a parish pastor was the furnishing of a mature laity, equipped for the work of ministry.

---

24. Simeon, *Expository Outlines*, 19:339.
25. Simeon, *Expository Outlines*, 9:424.

Congregational Singing

Simeon sought throughout his tenure to improve the singing of Holy Trinity. In Anglican circles, it was not uncommon for church music in those days to either be virtually non-existent or chiefly the domain of a trained choir. The dawn of the long eighteenth century brought with it a revolution of hymn singing. The popularity of hymns grew especially in Dissenting circles, though not without controversy. The Particular Baptist Benjamin Keach (1640–1704) introduced hymns to his congregation as early as 1673, forming the basis of a decades-long conflict. Keach sparred with fellow Baptist Isaac Marlow (1645–1710) on the topic throughout the 1690s.[26] Ultimately, hymn-singing won the day among Dissenters.[27] Throughout the Eighteenth Century—aided by Isaac Watts and the Wesleys—hymns became a hallmark of Methodist revivals. In 1779, the year of Simeon's conversion, John Newton published *Olney Hymns* with the help of William Cowper, a work that would revolutionize singing in conformist and Nonconformist circles.[28] Despite the popularity of *Olney Hymns*, a number of factors inhibited the spread of hymns throughout the established church. Bruce Hindmarsh explains,

> Hymns won their way first among Dissenters (though not among all) before becoming one of the distinctive marks of Methodism, borrowing much along the way from immigrant Moravians. Associated thus with irregularity (Dissent), enthusiasm (Methodism), and non-Englishness (Moravians), hymns were tolerated only slowly within the Established Church and not given official recognition until a consistory court at York settled a controversy over the use of hymns which arose in a Sheffield church early in the nineteenth century.[29]

For Simeon, if wisely introduced, hymns were an aid to the life of a church.

Simeon believed that singing must encompass the entire congregation. He published a selection of hymns in 1795 titled *A Collection of Psalms and Hymns from various Authors, chiefly designed for the use of Publick Worship*.[30] While some hymnals were introduced for private or

---

26. Keach, *Breach Repaired*. See also Marlow, *Brief Discourse Concerning Singing*.
27. Haykin and Robinson, "Particular Baptist Debates," 285–308.
28. Newton and Cowper, *Olney Hymns*.
29. Hindmarsh, *John Newton*, 263.
30. Spinks, "Book of Common Prayer," 267.

societal use, Simeon made clear the purpose of his collection. Singing was to be congregational. Thus, whether in his choice of songs or the instruments he employed, he endeavored to accentuate the voices of his people. He once commented, "I put up the organ and gallery of Trinity Church at my own expense. But even an organ in church is open to abuse. When half the service is engrossed by the organ, and when congregational singing is put away, then it is very bad."[31] Simeon, like the apostle Paul, understood congregational singing to be a critical way of causing God's word to dwell richly in his people (Col 3:16). A well-placed hymn had the ability to reinforce the sermon in a marvelous way. Simeon used the following memorable illustration:

> A screw is the most powerful of mechanical forces. The screw, as it turns round and round again and again, is forced deeper and deeper, and gains such ahold, that it is impossible to withdraw if by force from the wood in which it is inserted. So with the truth you would teach your hearers: if you urge it again and again, round and round, deeper and deeper, Satan will never be able to pull it out again from their hearts. In my sermons the application is always another turn of the screw, *and where I can, the very hymn which I select for the singing is a turn of the screw*. This is a valuable rule for you to adhere to.[32]

Such an effect was not lost on Henry Martyn, who attested to his sense of God's presence during the congregational singing of Holy Trinity.[33] Evidently, Martyn sensed such presence regularly.

Though Simeon supported the use of hymns, he did not view them as was worth the cost of controversy. He once chided a young minister who, upon hastily introducing hymns to his congregation, so upset his people that they complained to their presiding bishop. His thorough rebuke reflected his pastoral instincts.

> Circumstanced as you are, I feel no hesitation in saying that you should avoid everything that can give offence, except the faithful preaching of "Christ crucified." Why should you stand out about the hymns? You are very injudicious in this. You should consider that when a storm is raised you are not the only sufferer. Pray study to maintain peace, though you make some sacrifices for it. . . . I do intreat you to recede from

---

31. Brown, *Recollections*, 222.
32. Brown, *Recollections*, 197 (emphasis added).
33. Hopkins, *Charles Simeon of Cambridge*, 41.

> everything that will excite needless offence. You are not aware, that, whilst you are afraid of being thought to act from the fear of man, you are actually under its influence: only it is the religious that you fear, instead of the irreligious. I beg you not to attend to such advisers. Study the character of St. Paul. See how he, "though free from all, became the servant of all." ... This, in few words, is my advice: first, Preach faithfully; but speak the truth *in love*: second, Do all the good you can in visiting your parish, but don't exercise any pastoral function out of it: third, Put aside Hymns, which are quite unnecessary.[34]

Therefore to Simeon, though hymns were a useful aid to his congregation's life, their immediate employ was not necessary for all ministers—at least not at the expense of a church's unity.[35] Hymns were not as much the issue as the sheer biblical mandate for congregational singing.

Some of Simeon's success in rallying the congregation's voice in song might be attributable to his public exhortations on the topic, for it is clear that singing was not always a strength of Holy Trinity. In a sermon on 2 Chr 5, he chided his people,

> It is much to be regretted that, in our worshipping assemblies, the greater part of the congregation never join in this part of the service [the singing]; they seem to think that they are not interested in it, and that it may well be left to those few who may have studied music as a science but would it not appear absurd in the highest degree, if the prayers also were left to a few select persons, and the bulk of the congregation were to sit still, as though they had no need to join in the devotions?[36]

At the same time, despite the importance of congregational edification, the chief end of Christian singing was the glory of God. Simeon continued,

> The singing of psalms and hymns without any sense of joy and gratitude, is a hypocritical service, and wholly unacceptable to God: we may indeed please the congregation, and establish our own reputation for skill; but these are very unworthy motives to be influenced by, when we are solemnly addressing the Most High God: persons actuated by such considerations sing to their own praise and glory, rather than to God's; and therefore they

---

34. Carus, *Memoirs*, 385.
35. Carus, *Memoirs*, 386.
36. Simeon, *Expository Outlines*, 5:58.

must rest satisfied with *their* reward, i.e. the reward they seek after; for it is certain that they will never receive any testimony of God's approbation. Let me therefore remind you all, that the end of singing is to thank and praise the Lord; and that, whenever we join in psalms and hymns, we must be especially careful that we "make melody in our hearts to the Lord."[37]

Simeon thus concluded his exhortation, "Yes, my Brethren, let me hope that many of you will unite your endeavours: . . . let not one be silent; and while we are united in singing the high praise of our God, may God himself come down in the midst of us, and fill the house with his glory!"[38]

Women and Children

In the cultivation of Holy Trinity's robust congregational life, Simeon did not neglect the women of his parish. Indeed, they were invaluable to him. Not only did he seek to care for their souls, he also marshalled them for the work of ministry. The inclusion of women in his conversation parties has already been highlighted. He also served the wives of ministers through hosting retreats. Though he did not believe women were to formally serve in the pastoral office, these gestures were rather progressive for his day. Simeon believed spiritual and pastoral authority in the church was the domain of men. But this did not mean women were completely barred from any type of teaching. He once remarked in a conversation party,

> The woman was not to usurp the authority or place of the man,—his headship in the Church. Circumstances must regulate how far this bears on the present state of society and of the Church. I do not know all the circumstances under which Mrs. Stephens, for instance, now gives addresses or ministrations, and therefore cannot pronounce a judgement. If she merely teaches children, or the parents of those children who come in upon their own request, I should not say she is doing wrong. There is no harm in women teaching children, or instructing the poor, provided it be done in such a way as to accord with their place and sex, and so as not to assume to themselves the man's place.[39]

---

37. Simeon, *Expository Outlines*, 5:59.
38. Simeon, *Expository Outlines*, 5:65.
39. Brown, *Recollections*, 92.

Notably, Simeon upheld male headship in the church and family while welcoming the gifts of women in various contexts. He believed both men and women had respective gifts to be used in the parish and society.[40] It has also been mentioned how Simeon employed laywomen in the informal ministry of Holy Trinity "to visit the sick, to pray with them, and read to his people."[41]

Simeon viewed godly women as great assets to be valued in the local church. Though he remained single his entire life, he always bore a special appreciation for ministers' wives. This can be seen in his extensive commentary on 1 Thess 2, where he did not limit its application to pastors.

> The remarks flowing from this passage are more obviously addressed to young Ministers, or intending Ministers. But you who are Ministers' wives are not less deeply interested—Ministresses, half-Ministers, often the more important and useful half in your husbands' parishes. How vast is the duty which rests with you, how important your means of promoting the cause of God, without going beyond your own proper province and work! Therefore, you also ought to get the spirit of this passage into your hearts and minds.[42]

Clearly, the cultivation of competent, committed laywomen played a significant role in Simeon's parish ministry.

In addition to serving the women of his parish, Simeon took great interest in his congregation's children. He carved out time in the evenings to teach Bible lessons to local boys and girls. Toward the end of his ministry, he attested, "I used in years back to have an evening school, and the children would come to me puffing and heated from running after work was done, that they might not be too late; for they used to love it very much, and their proficiency was delightful."[43]

Simeon found ministry to children to be an extraordinary means of reaching adults. For example, at one point in his tenure, he assigned children Scripture to read at home. He shared the following anecdote:

> I used to set the children three chapters to read at home, and then went out to examine them. One of the boys received as a prize a book respecting Daniel in the lions' den, and showed

---

40. Brown, *Recollections*, 150.
41. Brown, *Recollections*, 217.
42. Brown, *Recollections*, 165.
43. Brown, *Recollections*, 152.

it to his mother. She read it, and said, "Here was a man who chose rather to be thrown to lions than give up praying three times a-day, and here am I, with the wrath of God lying against me for my sins, and have never yet prayed even once a-day." This simple reflection was made the means of changing her character, and for twenty years she has been one of the most useful persons on the face of the earth. How does teaching children prove a bridge of access to their parents![44]

The Poor

Part of a parish pastor's duties included a ministry to the poor. However, Simeon did not reduce the impoverished in his community to a mere outlet for ministry. Rather, he highly esteemed the "pious poor" of his parish.[45] Simeon believed the poor were often more poised to respond to the ministry of the word because they lacked the self-sufficiency of the wealthy.

> *Learning is good.* It enlarges the mind, but is often abused, and, when abused, makes men harder to be turned to God. The immoral man is easier turned to God than the self-sufficient one, of general decency of life. The one allows that he is disobeying God, but persists in his sin; the other persists in his own ways and faults, and says he is only doing what he ought to do. Learning often fosters pride, yet we find pride in the illiterate. Learning opens men's minds to conviction on every subject but religion. All men fancy they know enough of religion by intuition, and refuse to be taught. The grace of God only can convert any soul.[46]

Simeon also attested to the power of God's power to redeem the destitute from their circumstances. "There is a proverb, 'The heart of the poor shall give learning to the wise.' Teach the head through the heart. Do not wait to instruct your people's minds before you begin to preach the truth and Gospel to them. The Gospel is the best means of enlarging the mind—the best means of civilizing."[47]

---

44. Brown, *Recollections*, 116.
45. Brown, *Recollections*, 156.
46. Brown, *Recollections*, 206.
47. Brown, *Recollections*, 206.

Thus, over the course of his long ministry, Simeon developed a deep affection for his parishioners who came from meager means. He relayed two memorable encounters of indigent members of his parish.

> I visited a poor and godly woman who had . . . been bedridden for seven years, and was a dreadful sufferer in body. When she was apparently in the agonies of death, I said to her, "How sweet will heaven be after this!" She replied quickly, "Certainly, Sir, it will be very sweet, but in some respects this situation is preferable; for in heaven all is fixed, but now I know that this affliction which I am bearing is working out for me a far more exceeding weight of glory." There was another poor woman with whom I was talking about the spiritual pleasure she said she had derived from sitting to hear a certain service and sermon; she described it thus, "O, Sir, it was like sitting in heavenly places in Christ Jesus."[48]

Congregational Prayer

An eminent part of Holy Trinity's congregational life came in its commitment to prayer. This was manifested in the ministries of societies and visitation circuits. But this emphasis was not without explicit instruction for Simeon. Early in his ministry, he urged his people,

> Let me beseech you, in St Paul's words, to "pray for me, and for all" ministers, that we may be replenished with the truth of the Gospel, and enabled to declare the whole counsel of God, so that the ignorant may be instructed, the wavering confirmed, the feeble comforted, and the strong established, and that both we who sow in preaching God's Word, and you who reap in hearing it, may rejoice together for ever and ever.[49]

It is noteworthy that Simeon charged his congregation to be concerned for needs beyond their parish, alerting them to the concerns of Henry Martyn. Sargent recorded how, "From Mr. Simeon [Martyn] learnt, to his exceeding comfort, that his flock at Cambridge intended, on the day of his departure, as far as it could be ascertained, to give themselves to fasting and prayer."[50]

---

48. Brown, *Recollections*, 156–57.
49. Moule, *Charles Simeon*, 47.
50. Sargent, *Rev. Henry Martyn*, 91–92.

The Parishioners and Their Pastor

As pastors were to cultivate a particular posture to their people, so were people to their pastor. Based on passages like 1 Tim 3 and 1 Thess 2, Simeon believed that if ministers bore the responsibility to engage with their people as fathers to children, then parishioners bore the reciprocal obligation to submit to their pastor.

> A husband and wife, a parent and child, a magistrate and subject, have each their appropriate duties; and so have also a minister and his people: and as the minister's duties are fitly represented by those of a mother, so those of the people may justly be considered as analogous to those of an affectionate and obedient child.[51]

Affection and obedience represented the twin virtues that governed the church member's relationship with his pastor. For Simeon, this meant at least four duties.

First, parishioners were called to love their pastor. Expounding again from 1 Thess, he averred,

> In this very epistle [1 Thessalonians], wherein St. Paul testifies such unbounded love to his converts, he tells them what they also ought to feel towards those who ministered unto them: "We beseech you, brethren, to know them who labour among you, and are over you in the Lord, and admonish you; and to esteem them very highly in love for their work's sake (Note: 1 Thessalonians 5:12–13)." We speak not here of that partiality, which renders men unwilling; to receive the Gospel from any one besides their own favourite minister;—*that* is a reprehensible attachment, leading to an idolatrous regard to some, and a contemptuous disregard of others: but a grateful sense of the obligations conferred by those who labour in the word and doctrine, ought to be cultivated and expressed by all (Note: 1 Timothy 5:17). Indeed it can scarcely be carried to too great an extent: it should not stop short of any sacrifice, not even of the surrender of life itself, if by such means their labours may be preserved for the Church of Christ (Note: Romans 16:3–4).[52]

---

51. Simeon, *Expository Outlines*, 18:287.
52. Simeon, *Expository Outlines*, 18:287–88.

Pastors were not dictators who demanded submission—they were good parents who gained the hearts of their children. Thus, affection befitted the people's posture.

Second, Simeon called on church members to give attention to their pastor's instruction. On this point, Simeon expressed the highest esteem for his office.

> No one can doubt whether this be the duty of a child towards his parent (Note: See Deuteronomy 27:16): and it is equally the duty of a people towards their spiritual parent. A minister is sent especially from God himself to impart unto them the knowledge of the Gospel. Though he is only an earthen vessel, he has the treasures of salvation committed to him for the benefit of others; and, as a faithful steward, he is to dispense them to all according to their several necessities. He is to them in the place of God himself. He is to them in God's stead, when he is proclaiming to them, in his name, the word of reconciliation. His word, as far as it agrees with the inspired volume, is the word, not of man, but of God: and they who despise it, despise not man, but God.[53]

With all blood-earnestness, Simeon—soberly reflecting on Paul's view of the ministry of the Word—viewed defiance of a preacher's instruction akin to defying God himself. As shall be shown in the next chapter, Simeon's view of preaching could lead to no other conclusion. He understood true preaching to be God's word ministered through God's man to God's people. Thus, any rejection of right preaching was a rejection of God's will.

Third, parishioners were called to submit to pastoral authority. On this point, Simeon sought to evade the pitfalls of authoritarianism and anarchy. "This in the Church of Rome is carried to an absurd and impious extent: but in the reformed Churches, and especially in our own, it is almost entirely set aside; and a minister who claims the measure of authority which God has given him for the edification of his Church, is considered as a usurper."[54] The solution to authoritative abuses in the church was not the abolition of authority. Neither should people default to distrusting authority. Rather, Christians were to bless God for and submit to godly ministers. Speaking on the relevance of authoritative roles, Simeon continued,

---

53. Simeon, *Expository Outlines*, 18:288.
54. Simeon, *Expository Outlines*, 18:288.

> But what would be the consequence, if the parent had no authority in his own family? What but confusion must ensue, if all his children thought themselves at liberty to follow their own inclinations, without any direction or restraint from him? True, a minister is "not a lord over God's heritage:" his authority relates only to things pertaining to the welfare of his Church; but in these his judgment should be a rule of conduct to those committed to him. This is the command of God himself respecting it: "Obey them that have the rule over you, and submit yourselves: for they watch for your souls, as they that must give account; that they may do it with joy, and not with grief: for that is unprofitable for you (Note: Hebrews 13:17)."

Fourth, Simeon called on men and women to cooperate with their ministers in every good work. In doing so, he acknowledged his limitations and reinforced his commitment to an every-member ministry.

> A minister cannot do everything. Moses had seventy elders given to him, as assistants in his great work: and such should our people be in the Church of God. They can aid in instructing the rising generation: they may do incalculable good, in searching out the wants and necessities of the poor, and in administering, not to the temporal benefit only of their neighbours, but also to the benefit of their souls. Women, as well as men, have much in their power: and, without the aid of their people, it is little, comparatively, that any ministers can effect. The Apostles themselves were greatly indebted in this respect to their people; and to this even St. Paul ascribed, in some degree at least, the efficiency of his labours (Note: Romans 16:1–2; Romans 16:6; Romans 16:9; Romans 16:12). What if, in a large family, the children cannot supply the place of their father? can they do nothing to second his endeavours, and to promote the welfare of the whole? Thus then should even the weakest amongst our people labour, according to their ability, to promote to the uttermost the advancement of the Redeemer's kingdom, and the glory of his great name. The richer part should contribute of their abundance to help forward every pious and benevolent plan; and the poorer afford their aid also in any way that may best comport with their sphere, and be best suited to their several capacities.[55]

It has been shown thus far the nature of Simeon's approach to his parish pastorate. The great apostle of Cambridge understood ministry to be deeply relational: shepherd to sheep—father to family—mother

---

55. Simeon, *Expository Outlines*, 18:289.

to children. This dynamic led him to foster a commitment to visitation and a life of equipping the saints for the work of ministry. This chapter will conclude by highlighting his influence in this area on some prominent pupils.

Influence

Invariably, Simeon's teaching and practice in the realm of parish life impacted his followers. In fact, John Sargent believed that Simeon's pastoral care was on brightest display in his care for future ordinands. He wrote, "Mr. Simeon's exertions, especially, in behalf of those who were intended for ministry, were great and incessant. The sight or even the anticipation of spiritual progress in any one who, in after life, 'was to teach and premonish the Lord's family,' was to him an overflowing recompense for all his labors."[56]

William Carus, Simeon's celebrated biographer and immediate successor at Holy Trinity Church, clearly modeled his ministry after his predecessor. As seen throughout this project, Carus's reverence for his vicar's pastoral patience can be seen in page after page of his memoirs. Yet Carus did not merely write appreciatively of his mentor. He preached what Simeon practiced. In a sermon titled *The Personal Duties of the Minister*, Carus expounded Paul's instruction to Timothy, "Take heed unto thyself" (1 Tim 4:16):

> He must take heed therefore, that in his statements of truth he exhibits *truly* the whole truth; making nothing too prominent through *partiality*, and concealing nothing through *prejudice*; "not shunning to declare all the counsel of God," "keeping back nothing that is profitable," but distributing to every one according to his capacity and need; thus administering milk to babes, yet not refusing "strong meat" to men. All this requires especial wisdom from above, and divine guidance.[57]

Carus was not the only curate to promote a Simeon-like posture toward his people. Both Thomas Thomason and Henry Martyn learned longsuffering through Simeon's constant guidance.[58]

---

56. Sargent, *Life of the Rev. T. T. Thomason*, 52.
57. Carus, *Personal Duties*, 11.
58. Brown, *Recollections*, 96.

Thomason, for his part, felt an immediate attraction to Simeon not merely for the power of his pulpit, but for the warmth of his pastoral care. In a letter from his early Cambridge days, he reflected, "Mr. Simeon watches over us as a shepherd over his sheep. . . . His Christian love and zeal prompt him to notice us."[59] But Thomason, like Carus, not only admired the quality of Simeon's parish practice, he emulated it in his subsequent pastorate. Simeon himself raved to John Sargent about the character of Thomason's ministry. In an 1832 letter, Simeon said,

> Were I to compare him [Thomason] with anything, it would be with the light, in which a great diversity of rays are joined, but no one more conspicuous than another. Towards God, he was distinguished by a simplicity of mind and purpose; and towards man, by a placidity of manner and deportment. I never saw anything of self blended with his actions. He seemed to have one end and aim in all that he did: and what he did was never by an effort, so much as by a habit. . . . In this respect there was an extraordinary resemblance between him and Mrs. Thomason. Each executed a great deal in every day; but throughout the whole day, though there was much business, there was no bustle, no parade. Each lived only for the Lord, and to glorify Him seemed to be the one business of their lives.[60]

Simeon went on to show how the Thomasons' self-forgetfulness bred a sacrificial devotedness to their people.

> The parishes in which they were able to exert their influence seemed as their own family: schools of industry, as well as other schools, were established by them; the poor and the sick were visited and relieved; and all that Christian love could devise was planned, and executed with the tenderest assiduity, and most unwearied constancy. . . . [Mr. Thomason] was a father amongst his children, or a pastor amongst his flock. In his addresses there was an unrivalled simplicity, and a divine unction, which left a savour that is not forgotten to this hour.[61]

In terms of pastoral influence, such commitment to parishioners is traceable to none other than Simeon.

The evident influence of Simeon on Charles Bridges was seen in chapter 2. Indeed, the fingerprints of Simeon's pastoral theology are traceable

---

59. Sargent, *Rev. T. T. Thomason*, 52.
60. Carus, *Memoirs*, 697.
61. Carus, *Memoirs*, 697–98.

throughout Bridges's *The Christian Ministry*. In terms of congregational care, Thomas Chalmers praised Bridges for the state of his parish.

> He took me to his church and a few of his cottages, and I never witnessed such closeness and efficiency of pastoral work as he exemplified in his addresses to the mothers of families. He makes a real business both of the Christianity of his own soul and the Christianity of his family and parish, watching over the souls of all as one who must give an account.[62]

Such a commendation is unsurprising, for the evangelical character of Bridges's shepherding was an unmistakable hallmark of Simeon's ministry during the former's Cambridge years.

Chapter 2 also surveyed the legacy of John Bird Sumner. Like Simeon, Sumner prioritized preaching, modesty in his life, and visitation of his flock.[63] Particularly, his shared emphasis on lay-visitation has already been highlighted.[64] Nigel Scotland asserts, "Like his associate Charles Simeon, he [Sumner] valued preaching and regarded visiting and the education of the poor as of paramount importance."[65] Indeed, this set Sumner in distinction from his peers: "He did not, unlike some of his colleagues on the bench, indulge in an opulent or lavish mode of existence. His time in Chester was marked by a gracious, but modest lifestyle."[66] Given the massive footprint Sumner left on Victorian Anglicanism, the breadth of Simeon's pastoral influence was truly staggering.

Conclusion

This chapter has emphasized the interpersonal character of Simeon's parish ministry. Simeon—first and fundamentally—was a pastor. Indeed, care for souls formed the blazing center of his pastoral theology. Thus, he cultivated a posture of patience and warmth toward his people. From his own labors in personal visitation, to his use of a robust laity, he fostered an every-member ministry that equipped ordinary Christians to watch over one another. Countless followers went on to exhibit this emphasis. Indeed, Sargent spoke for many when he described Thomason's appraisal

---

62. Hanna, *Writings of Thomas Chalmers*, 396–97.
63. Scotland, *John Bird Sumner*, 98.
64. Sumner, *Charge Delivered*, 23.
65. Scotland, *John Bird Sumner*, 62.
66. Scotland, *John Bird Sumner*, 62.

of Simeon's familial devotion to his flock, "In him, Mr. Thomason found the fidelity of a devoted pastor; the affection of a father and a friend. Of these benefits he thankfully availed himself: and the grateful remembrance of them to his dying hour was indelible."[67]

---

67. Sargent, *Rev. T. T. Thomason*, 52.

CHAPTER 6

Preaching Paragon

IT HAS BEEN DEMONSTRATED thus far that Simeon exercised a significant impact on pre-Victorian evangelicalism. This was never lost on Simeon himself. He often appraised the strategic nature of the station to which he had been called. The intellectual center of Cambridge granted him extensive opportunities to lastingly influence a vast array of young men. Each day afforded him the ability to exemplify the ideals of an evangelical ministry. He once reflected at a conversation party,

> Trinity Church holds about nine hundred, without the children, and it is filled. But many of those who hear me are legions in themselves, because they are going forth to preach, or else to fill stations of influence in society. In that view, I look upon my position here as the highest and most important in the kingdom, nor would I exchange it for any other. If you have dukes and nobles to hear you, they seldom attend to what you say. Not so the congregations at Cambridge.[1]

This book has shown how pastoral theology was the greatest realm of Simeon's impact. Moreover, it has been argued that Simeon's Anglicanism, piety, and parochial ministry formed significant elements of that pastoral theology. Nevertheless, it was Simeon's pulpit that exerted the greatest influence on his followers, for preaching not only represented his greatest means of mentorship, but it also was the part of his pastoral theology most thoroughly replicated by his disciples. This chapter will

1. Brown, *Recollections*, 176.

present Simeon's philosophy of proclamation. Before examining this philosophy, Simeon must be situated in the context of his day.

The Popular Perspective of Pastoral Ministry

To rightly evaluate Simeon's philosophy of ministry, we must understand the religious climate of his country. Throughout the long eighteenth century, many parishioners in the established church held a low view of the clergy. In Georgian England, clergymen were often the younger sons of the gentry. As younger sons almost never received an inheritance, many fathers guided them toward the ministry in order for them to retain independence in a respectable career. In fact, this was true in the case of Charles, who was the fourth and youngest son of Richard Simeon. Though Richard played a role in his son's ordination, he would never share his son's evangelical convictions or a meaningful devotion to the established church.[2] For Richard, the clergy was one of several suitable career paths for his youngest son. This broader dynamic often failed to produce ministers with a distinctly high view of their profession. Clerical ministry was more a matter of convenience rather than calling.

Jane Austen satirically criticized this low view of the clergy in her novels. She did so with portrayals of characters like Mr. Collins—a bumbling vicar who had more interest in superficial matters than the spiritual good of his parish.[3] She also channeled a popular sentiment toward ministers through the character Mary Crawford in *Mansfield Park*. Chastising a young man interested in Christian ministry, Mary said, "What is to be done in the church? Men love to distinguish themselves . . . but not in the church. A clergyman is nothing."[4] She continued,

> One does not see much of [the] influence and importance [of ministers] in society, and how can it be acquired where they are so seldom seen themselves? How can two sermons a week, even supposing them worth hearing . . . govern the conduct and fashion the manners of a large congregation for the rest of the week? One scarcely sees a clergyman out of his pulpit.[5]

---

2. Hopkins, *Charles Simeon of Cambridge*, 37.
3. Austen, *Pride and Prejudice*.
4. Austen, *Mansfield Park*, 81.
5. Austen, *Mansfield Park*, 82.

Readers can grasp Mary's poor view of both pastoral ministry and preaching in particular. Such a sentiment was common in Simeon's day. In fact, it was such low standards and expectations that gave way to the common phenomenon of men experiencing evangelical conversions while in ministry. Even some of the great leading lights of early evangelicalism like John and Charles Wesley were converted after embarking upon their careers in the established church.[6] In light of this, students of Simeon's life must appreciate that his project of raising up faithful preachers in the Church of England ran against a current of ministerial apathy. Simeon's approach to preaching, among other disciplines, brought to vivid display the contrast between his followers and the common parish priest of the day. As a pastor to pastors, Simeon made every effort to reclaim a high view of the preaching office. As previously stated, this chapter will present Simeon's philosophy of proclamation—which formed the pinnacle of his pastoral theology—by examining his view of three essential features of preaching: the preacher himself, his preaching, and his hearers.

The Preacher

In order to discern Simeon's thinking about preachers and preaching, the best place to go is Simeon himself. As the vicar of Holy Trinity for over half a century, Simeon preached over twenty-five hundred sermons. These words are preserved in twenty-one volumes covering the entire Bible. A survey of Simeon's commentary on the most prominent biblical texts on preaching yields a consistent philosophy. While Simeon's expositions are instructive, he did not limit his views to the pulpit. In addition to his sermons, as shown throughout this project, Simeon mentored countless future ministers through weekly conversation parties. From the comfort of his sitting room, Simeon sagely instructed up to sixty men at a time. Such men went on to shake England with the evangelical preaching they learned at the feet of their esteemed mentor.

The Preacher as Ambassador of God

To Simeon, the preacher was first and foremost an ambassador of God. This divine designation pointed not to the intrinsic character of the

---

6. Green, *John Wesley*.

preacher, but to the sovereign nature of the One who sent him. He declared,

> "The word" is that which every minister must "preach." He is not at liberty to amuse the people with the fancies and conceits of men, but must declare simply the mind and will of God. He is sent of God for that very end. He is an ambassador from God to man, authorized to declare on what terms God will be reconciled to his rebellious subjects.[7]

The preacher was to be a herald of a king, a royal ambassador with the express charge to faithfully convey the message of his master. Accordingly, Simeon viewed it as entirely inappropriate for a minister to proclaim his own will from the pulpit. The work of an ambassador ruled out all personal musing, performance, and speculation.

The Preacher as Equipped by God

Yet, in order to faithfully execute the mission of an ambassador, a preacher must be equipped for the work of ministry. In 2 Tim 3:16–17, the apostle Paul remarked on the sufficiency of Scripture: "All scripture is given by inspiration of God, and is profitable for doctrine, for reproof, for correction, for instruction in righteousness: that the man of God may be perfect, thoroughly furnished unto all good works." Though Simeon could apply Paul's broader point to all believers, he understood the phrase "man of God" to refer to ministers of the gospel. "We cannot conceive of any good work," said Simeon, "which a person instructed out of the Holy Scriptures is not fitted to perform. Take him as 'a man of God,' discharging the ministerial office: he may learn from the Scriptures how to demean himself in the Church of God so wisely and so profitably, that nothing shall be wanting to the edification of his flock."[8] Whether in public ministry or his private walk with God, the principal preparation of the preacher proceeded from the Word of God.

Chapter 4 has covered the place of piety in Simeon's pastoral theology. This is an essential discussion, for he understood the preacher's public ministry flowed from one's private life. Those familiar with Simeon attested that this conviction was formed not merely from his reflection on Scripture, but from his own experiential communion with God. Simeon

---

7. Simeon, *Expository Outlines*, 19:76–77.
8. Simeon, *Expository Outlines*, 19:74.

the preacher cannot be comprehended apart from Simeon the man. He was the same man whom Samuel Marsden observed in the 1790s "was contemplating God oblivious to everything around him till he finally burst out with the words 'Glory! Glory! Glory!'"[9] The man who weekly ascended the pulpit of Holy Trinity was the one who left Wilberforce undone by his total devotion to God. Wilberforce recorded in his journal, "Simeon with us—his heart glowing with love of Christ. How full he is of love, and of desire to promote the spiritual benefit of others. Oh! that I might copy him as he Christ."[10] To misapprehend the relationship between piety and preaching in Simeon's pastoral theology would be to render the latter utterly futile. For he believed that in order to be owned by God in the pulpit, the preacher must be fixed on Christ in private. He must possess a "secret walk with God."[11]

The Preaching

Without a doubt, Simeon's preaching ministry was his most profound contribution to the evangelicalism of his day. In his concerted efforts to mentor young men, he sought to win them to an evangelical brand of preaching. He influenced preachers through two major channels. First, as an offshoot to his famous conversation parties, Simeon also hosted sermon classes for gownsmen (Cambridge students) called to preach.[12] These smaller gatherings were by invite only. In each session, Simeon offered a text for consideration, charging men to produce a sermon outline for the text. After they presented their outlines, Simeon provided them feedback on their content. Thus, Simeon slowly transmitted his particular style of evangelical preaching to an entire generation of Anglican ministers.

Of course, the second channel for influencing preachers was the pulpit of Holy Trinity Church. From this post, Simeon inspired countless prospective preachers. To this day, his sermons at Holy Trinity remain his greatest written legacy. The twenty-one volumes of *Horae Homileticae* (also known as *Expository Outlines of the Whole Bible*) capture well Simeon's method of expositional preaching. These sermon skeletons have served preachers for generations, even a young Charles Spurgeon

---

9. Hopkins, *Charles Simeon of Cambridge*, 100.
10. Hopkins, *Charles Simeon of Cambridge*, 166.
11. Simeon, *Expository Outlines*, 19:74.
12. Brown, *Recollections*, 51–53.

(1834–1892), who read Simeon's sermons as a teenager.[13] As shown earlier, Simeon understood the gravity of his unique sphere of influence, often grappling with the immensity of his Cambridge platform. When he mounted the pulpit of Trinity Church, he assumed the role of a general addressing his soldiers. Each sermon was a model to ministers, and marshalled them to go forth with the same gospel.[14]

In his introduction to his sermon volumes, Simeon asserted that true preaching must ultimately possess three chief aims: to humble the sinner, exalt the Savior, and promote holiness.[15] And these three aims stemmed from the presupposition that "the great argument of Scripture, is the glory of God's own name."[16] For over five decades, Simeon gave himself to this type of proclamation in the pulpit of Holy Trinity. Though he has left an expansive amount of material on the topic, Simeon's written legacy presents a distinct philosophy of preaching. This philosophy will now be considered in five parts: power, content, method, style, and manner.

The Power of Preaching

Simeon understood preaching to be more than forceful oratory. A sermon was a divine message: God's word, through God's man, to God's people. To faithfully preach the Bible was to convey the words and will of the Almighty. Simeon believed that in such preaching, the Spirit of God was pleased to reveal truth to human beings. In fact, without the power of God's Spirit, the preaching of Scripture was rendered impotent. Commenting on 1 Tim 3, he declared, "Plain as the Scriptures are, they are yet 'a sealed book' to all whose eyes have not been enlightened by the Spirit of God. The natural man, how learned soever he may be, cannot enter into their spiritual import, because he has not a spiritual discernment."[17] Simeon shrewdly noted that even the twelve disciples—who were trained by Jesus for three years during his earthly

---

13. Spurgeon, *Lost Sermons*, 258; and 295.
14. Brown, *Recollections*, 176.
15. Simeon, *Expository Outlines*, 1:xxi.
16. Pratt, *Evangelical Leaders*, 329. Strikingly, Simeon made this assertion in the context of a discussion with leading evangelicals on the looming prospect of war with the French. The anecdote presents an illuminating insight into Simeon's pastoral instincts. Even a discussion of national security was cause to assert the glory of God.
17. Simeon, *Expository Outlines*, 19:74.

ministry—needed their minds opened by him in order to understand the Scriptures. Hence Simeon proclaimed:

> So do ye need the teachings of God's Spirit, without which you will be in darkness to the latest hour of your lives. Pray then to him, as David did; "Open thou mine eyes, that I may behold wondrous things out of thy law!" Then shall you "be guided into all truth;" and find the Scriptures fully adequate to all the gracious ends for which they have been revealed.[18]

The salient point here is that Simeon understood that the true power of preaching was not to be found in force of personality, but in the sovereign work of God's Spirit. Only God's power—moving through his word—could save men and women. In order for the preaching moment to be effectual, God must anoint it and create new life. Speaking on the power of God's word in preaching, he asserted, "It is 'the sword of the Spirit' also. It is, in short, that instrument whereby the Sacred Three accomplish all their mysterious purposes in converting and saving a ruined world."[19] Simeon's confidence rested in God's Triune activity through his word. He believed sermons were to be demonstrations of God's power: "But then it must be wielded by an almighty arm: it must 'come in demonstration of the Spirit and of power' or else it will fail of producing any permanent effect. None but He who moved upon the chaos, and formed it into order and beauty, can new create the soul."[20] Despite Simeon's extensive commentary on sermon preparation, he heartily believed that unless God's Spirit accompanied his preaching, his task was absolutely hopeless.

The Content of Preaching

For Simeon, Scripture had to form the content of preaching. Readers ought to appreciate Simeon's emphasis on this point in light of his evangelical conversion in 1779. The power of God's word loomed large in Simeon's thought due to the inexplicable nature of his conversion experience. Despite the lifeless presentation of the liturgy during his early years at Cambridge, it was the biblical language of Anglican worship that haunted Simeon's conscience in the weeks leading up to taking the Lord's

---

18. Simeon, *Expository Outlines*, 19:74.
19. Simeon, *Expository Outlines*, 18:277.
20. Simeon, *Expository Outlines*, 18:277.

Supper. As already cited, Simeon often meditated on his conversion experience, understanding deeply and personally what it was to experience God's power and presence through his word.[21] Thus, he earnestly maintained that a sermon must center on that same word. This philosophy was at odds with the prevailing approach to preaching in his day. Gary Jenkins notes that in the long eighteenth century,

> a style of preaching developed that was strongly moralistic in tone, that emphasized reason rather than revelation, and ethics rather than doctrine. The Tillotsonian "Gospel of Moral Rectitude" dominated the English pulpit for much of the eighteenth century, leading Sydney Smith to observe that anyone "taking up an English sermon, expects to find it a tedious essay, full of common-place morality."[22]

As an evangelical, Simeon's view of the Bible was never unclear. He was the epitome of the hallmarks famously asserted by Bebbington: biblicism, crucicentrism, conversionism, and activism.[23] These four qualities form the connective tissue that united the evangelical movement, especially during the long eighteenth century. Simeon was no innovator here. He understood the Bible to be the word of God; therefore, it had an authoritative bearing upon all people. He accepted what today is known as the verbal plenary inspiration of Scripture, a view that preserves Scripture as both the words of man and God.[24] Commenting on biblical authorship, he said,

> In what they wrote indeed, they expressed themselves, each in his own peculiar style, as any other writer would have done: but in *the matter* of what they wrote, they were inspired of God; and in *the manner* of expressing it they were preserved by that same Spirit from any error or mistake. So that of the whole Scriptures, both of the Old and New Testament, we may affirm, that God is the Author of them, and that every part of them has been "given by inspiration from him."[25]

Simeon affirmed the apostle Peter's teaching that the Bible—both Old and New Testaments—were written by holy men who were "moved

---

21. Carus, *Memoirs*, 9.
22. Jenkins, *Tale of Two Preachers*, 12.
23. Bebbington, *Evangelicalism in Modern Britain*, 3.
24. Stott, *Authority of the Bible*.
25. Simeon, *Expository Outlines*, 19:74.

by the Holy Ghost" (1 Pet 1:21). Such a view of Scripture rendered the whole Bible as profitable for preaching. Though some Christian preachers may be inclined to diminish the importance of the Old Testament, Simeon made every effort to present the whole counsel of God to the people of Holy Trinity. Of his twenty-one volumes, ten of them cover the Old Testament.

Ever the earnest evangelical, Simeon believed Jesus Christ to be the hermeneutical key to Scripture. All of the old covenant pointed to God's cosmic reconciliation to his people through the atonement of his Son. Though Jesus is not named in the Old Testament, he is the great theme of a unified Scripture. Expounding 2 Tim 3:16–17, Simeon contended,

> To anyone who reads the writings of Moses and the Prophets with humility and prayer, there was every needful instruction both in relation to faith and practice. The whole Mosaic dispensation taught [Timothy] this great lesson, that he must be saved by a vicarious sacrifice; and all the prophets directed his views to that great sacrifice, which should, in due time, be offered by our Lord Jesus Christ.[26]

Simeon sought to ensure his sermons were not governed by any political, personal, or philosophical agenda. For over half a century, he made it his task to deliver God's word to God's people. And Christ was the great key to interpreting God's word for God's people.

The Method of Preaching

Upon assuming the role of vicar of Holy Trinity in 1782, Simeon lacked preaching models. Though his orbit included men like John Newton, Henry Venn, and John Berridge, none of these ministers influenced Simeon toward the method of preaching that would mark his ministry. It is fair to suggest that his foremost preaching mentor was Jean Claude (1619–1687), a French Calvinist Divine who had written a short work on preaching titled *An Essay on the Composition of a Sermon*.[27] In the 1780s, the work was zealously circulated by the Cambridge Baptist Robert Robinson, who added notes to the treatise.[28] Claude's *Essay* lent flesh

---

26. Simeon, *Expository Outlines*, 19:71.
27. Claude, *Composition of a Sermon*.
28. Though Simeon appears to have used Robinson's translation, he forsook Robinson's notes for use of his own. See Simeon, *Expository Outlines*, 21:291.

to the bones of Simeon's emerging preaching philosophy in the former's emphasis that preachers must proclaim the "entire sense of the whole text."[29] Simeon found Claude to confirm his own developing thought.[30] As a result, he swiftly republished the essay in 1792 with his own notes, along with one hundred of his sermons. This work constituted the first edition of Simeon's twenty-one volume magnum opus *Horae Homileticae*, which, having been completed in 1832, comprised over 2,500 of his sermon outlines.[31]

In addition to Claude, it is worth highlighting another significant resource that influenced Simeon: John Brown's (1722–1787) *Self-interpreting Bible*.[32] Brown was a Scottish Presbyterian whose work appeared first in the 1770s in Edinburgh and was reprinted many times in both Scotland and America. Carus recounts how important the book was to Simeon.

> The copy of the Scriptures, which became the favourite companion of his devotional hours from this period, was a quarto volume of Brown's *Self-interpreting Bible*; which to the end of his life he was continually enriching with valuable notes of his own. So much did he price this commentary, that in 1787, Jan. 19, he wrote to the author at Haddington, "Your Self-interpreting Bible, seems to stand in lieu of all other comments; and I am daily receiving so much edification and instruction from it, that I would wish it in the hands of all serious ministers. I have conceived a thought of purchasing a few to give to those godly ministers. . . . I take the liberty therefore of asking whether you, (whose heart seems to be much set upon forwarding the cause

---

29. Hopkins, *Charles Simeon of Cambridge*, 58.

30. Hopkins explains Claude's influence on Simeon. "What [Claude] had to say appealed to Simeon's methodical mind, and was in tune with his own ideas. For example, of sermons that did not give 'the entire sense of the whole text' Claude commented, in Robinson's translation, 'Preachments of this kind are extremely disgustful.' . . . [Simeon] so valued his explanation of how sermon composition should be carried out that he had it bound up with his own works as an epilogue occupying over a hundred pages." Hopkins also cites Claude's use of introduction, explanation, and application in sermon composition as another point of influence on Simeon. See Hopkins, *Charles Simeon of Cambridge*, 58.

31. Simeon's *Expository Outlines* (*Horae Homileticae*) reads like an expository commentary. Each sermon ranges from about one thousand to two thousand words. Though they were not complete sermon manuscripts, they were very detailed outlines written in the form of multi-paragraph essays.

32. Brown, *Self-interpreting Bible*. Though Simeon made great use of Brown's Bible, he never indicated precisely what he found so instructive.

of Christ), could procure me forty at the booksellers' price for *that purpose alone*; and to inform me whether there will be a new edition soon.[33]

Despite these literary influences, the development of Simeon's preaching remains noteworthy for its originality. Throughout the long eighteenth century, Anglican ministers frequently used the sermons of others in their pulpits. Hennell comments,

> After the Restoration the Homilies seem to have been abandoned, but the practice of reading other men's compositions persisted. As late as 1806 a typical conscientious country clergyman was portrayed as one who "preaches regularly" and "takes the pains of writing out the best sermons he can find." It was from this practice that Simeon sought to wean his students.[34]

Through years of practice, Simeon honed his craft—developing a method of preaching entirely his own. Through promoting this method, he broke the tradition of the borrowed sermon.[35] By his death in 1836, countless pulpits across the globe were filled with evangelical preachers formed in the mold of their mentor. On the issue of preaching method, Simeon taught his followers in every sermon to be expositional, textual, proportional, and doctrinal.

Expositional Preaching

Though Simeon refrained from covering every verse of Scripture in his preaching ministry, he left no book of the Bible without commentary. He championed the practice of expounding whole books of the Bible, a method today known as expository preaching. He believed this practice to best preserve doctrine as it was presented in Scripture. He bristled at the thought of any preaching model that downplayed doctrinal or practical parts of the Bible.

> There are some who bring forward the doctrinal part of Scripture exclusively, and leave the practical part entirely out of sight: there are others who insist only on the practical parts, and leave out the doctrinal. There are some also to whom many of the doctrines contained in the sacred volume are perfectly hateful;

33. Carus, *Memoirs*, 68.
34. Hennell, "Simeon and the Ministry," 141.
35. Hennell, "Simeon and the Ministry," 143.

and who never in all their lives so much as mentioned the doctrines of predestination and election, but to explain them away, and to abuse the persons who maintained them.³⁶

To Simeon, an intellectually honest preacher would be unable to avoid certain doctrines if he is determined to preach through the entire Bible.

> But by expounding whole books of Scripture, every doctrine must be noticed in its turn, and the connexion between them and our practice must be pointed out. True it is, that this mode of preaching would not altogether exclude false doctrine: but it would render the establishment of errors more difficult, because the hearers would be able to judge, in some good measure, how far the true and legitimate sense of Scripture was given, and how far it was perverted. The benefit of this therefore cannot be too highly appreciated.³⁷

Only faithful expositional preaching could rightly display the doctrinal system of the Bible.

Yet Simeon maintained an aversion to preaching that was constrained by systematic theology: warmly embracing a type of biblicism that endeavored to let every text of Scripture speak for itself. Because of this, Simeon reserved his most provocative comments for High Calvinists and Arminians alike.³⁸ He once said to his students, "Calvinists and Arminians—Both of them are right in all they affirm, and wrong in all they deny."³⁹ Simeon's emphasis on theological moderation lent itself to critiquing Calvinism more than Arminianism, probably due to the fact that he was usually identified as a Calvinist. Simeon himself had inherited a moderate brand of Calvinism from his early mentors. He likened himself to John Newton, who famously described his approach to Reformed doctrine, saying, "I am more of a Calvinist than anything else; but I use my Calvinism in my writings and my preaching as I use this sugar. . . . I do not give it alone, and whole; but mixed and diluted."⁴⁰ Reflecting on his own ministry, Simeon would echo the exact

---

36. Simeon, *Expository Outlines*, 4:291.

37. Simeon, *Expository Outlines*, 4:291.

38. At times, Simeon referred to his High Calvinist brethren as "Ultra Evangelicals," viewing them as a threat to the reputation of the larger evangelical movement. See Carter, *Anglican Evangelicals*, 106.

39. Brown, *Recollections*, 267.

40. Cecil, *Life of John Newton*, 129–30.

same sentiment in his conversation parties, even employing Newton's illustration.[41] As a moderate Calvinist, Simeon aimed to be self-critical of his own broader theological camp. This impulse was most prominently on display in his well-known exchange with the Arminian John Wesley.[42] There, Simeon—owning the title of a Calvinist—irenically vied for doctrinal unity and common cause with the evangelical giant. For Simeon, his project was a ceaseless effort to raise a generation of committed, gospel-loving ministers that organically rooted their preaching solely in divine revelation. Therefore, faithful exposition of whole books of the Bible was the silver bullet for balanced preaching.

Textual Preaching

As an expositional preacher, Simeon was a biblicist, which meant that he sought to shape his mind by the truth and nomenclature of Scripture. The sermon text was not to be a springboard for the preacher's own ideas: rather he was duty-bound to determine authorial intent. Preachers were to be tethered to their text, endeavoring to expound the Bible in simple submission to the natural interpretation of the Bible. He argued that his invariable assignment was "to bring out of Scripture what is there, and not to thrust in what I think might be there. I have a great jealousy on this head; never to speak more or less than I believe to be the mind of the Spirit in the passage I am expounding."[43] Simeon held himself and his followers to this standard of interpreting the Bible along the lines of authorial intent.

Simeon's biblicist preaching model provided preachers with boundaries in their exposition. As noted earlier, he believed Christ to be the unifying theme of the Old and New Testaments. Yet he steered away from inserting Christ into texts unless he felt he had sure warrant to do so. Hugh Evan Hopkins writes of Simeon's disapproval of speculative exegesis, "He would not allow men to misinterpret the Scriptures by making them 'refer to Christ and his salvation when no such object appears to have been in the contemplation of the inspired writer.' . . . Yet, when there was clear justification for it, no one could more movingly proclaim Christ

---

41. Brown, *Recollections*, 278.
42. Hopkins, *Charles Simeon of Cambridge*, 174–75.
43. Moule, *Charles Simeon*, 77.

as the key to all the Scriptures."[44] The sermon was not to be a setting for speculation. The pulpit was not the place for theories. Preachers were to forcefully proclaim only those truths which were eminently plain in Scripture. Elsewhere, he cautioned his students against an over-zealous preoccupation with biblical typology. "In studying Scripture, we may, if we choose, and for our own edification, carry the analogy of types a little beyond the Apostles. But in preaching we must not do so, for we thus make the auditory, of course, judges. It is well for us only to tell them what we know is the declaration of God in His word, that they may receive it as the word of God."[45] Because Simeon comprehended the minister's task as that of a herald, he felt at no liberty to wander from his mission. Rather, he deeply sensed the gravity of his duty. "I want to teach, not to amuse. I will never say, *this is so*, unless I am certain in my own mind that it is the real meaning. I do not wish to preach a text unless I can prove from Scripture what I preach. Divine truth is too awful to be trifled with."[46]

Proportional Preaching

Along with his commitment to expositional and textual preaching, Simeon commended the benefits of proportional preaching. He felt that through the scrupulous application of his method, he was able to attain a balance in his preaching. Commenting on Acts 20, he decried the liabilities of preaching in rigid conformity to a theological system. "Nor must there be any bias in our minds towards any one part of the system above another; to doctrines above duties, or to duties above doctrines: every truth that is revealed in the Scripture must be brought forth in its place, and have that measure of prominence in our statements which it bears in the sacred volume."[47] Preachers ought to proclaim certain doctrines in proportion to their representation in Scripture, drawing out the themes that the biblical authors emphasize. He continued, "On points of dubious aspect we may express ourselves with doubt; but on all the great leading features of redemption we should express no more doubt than on the most self-evident truth that can be subjected to our view. In delivering these truths, also, we should 'speak as the oracles of

---

44. Hopkins, *Charles Simeon of Cambridge*, 178.
45. Brown, *Recollections*, 180.
46. Brown, *Recollections*, 376.
47. Simeon, *Expository Outlines*, 14:514.

God' even as 'Ambassadors from God, in whose place we stand,' and whose word we deliver."[48]

Doctrinal Preaching

Simeon's unceasing charge to young ministers was to "be Bible Christians, and not system Christians."[49] With such an emphasis on proportional biblicism, readers should not conclude that Simeon completely disparaged systematic thinking. Rather, he insisted that any theological system must be shaped by the nomenclature of the Bible. The following quote accurately conveys Simeon's affirmation of the systematic nature of Scripture:

> There is such a perfect unity in the system of revelation, that you cannot overthrow one part, without overturning the whole. Let the divinity of our Lord and Saviour be denied, and you entirely destroy the doctrine of the atonement also. Let the influences of the Holy Spirit be denied, and the transformation of the soul into the Divine image must fall with it. Let the merit of good works be maintained, and the whole covenant of grace is annihilated. There are indeed matters of less moment, which are less clearly revealed, and respecting which persons of equal piety may differ: but in every thing which is of fundamental importance, we find in the Scriptures the most abundant means of discovering truth, and of refuting error.[50]

Much of Simeon's critique of systematic preaching was the tone or manner of such preaching. Too often, preachers presented heads of doctrine in such angular categories that they betrayed the natural language of the Bible. Though Simeon would oppose the extremities he often perceived present in Calvinism and Arminianism, he inherited from Newton and Venn their moderate evangelical Calvinism.

Style and Preparation

As for style and preparation, Simeon had a tremendous amount of insight. His advice varied depending on the topic and recipient of the advice.

48. Simeon, *Expository Outlines*, 14:514.
49. Brown, *Recollections*, 269.
50. Simeon, *Expository Outlines*, 19:73.

Though Simeon's technique changed slightly over the years, it was his general practice to preach from an extended annotated outline, which he referred to as a "skeleton." Even late into his ministry, Simeon rehearsed his sermon aloud several times to ensure smoothness of delivery and maximization of effect.[51] This seemingly extemporaneous manner of preaching was rarely seen in his day.[52] Most Anglican ministers in the long eighteenth century glued themselves to their manuscripts. Simeon took great umbrage at the cold, dull delivery of such preachers. At the same time, Simeon exhorted preachers not to preach extemporaneously until they were several years into ministry. In fact, he advised men to preach from manuscripts for their first three to four hundred sermons.[53] Yet they were to do so vigorously, filled with the earnestness of their task. Abner Brown reflected upon the effect Simeon's style had on his hearers.

> Simeon's sermons, as delivered by himself, were always sui generis (of its own kind). The correctness of the diction, the frequent eloquence of the style, the honest sincerity, the thoughtful originality, that characterized them, soon compelled even a stranger to forget the peculiarities of manner or gesture, and to listen with deep, often with breathless, attention, as to an ambassador from God, delivering a powerful and loving message to each hearer individually.[54]

Simeon painstakingly ensured that any efforts in improving his style were to the benefit of his hearers. For the congregants, his style—combined with hours of preparation for each sermon—only served to reinforce the sobriety of his divine assignment. Brown continued, "Whether in the pulpit or in the room, his speaking eye, his affection, impressive tone, his animated gesture, even when exaggerated and mistaken, compelled attention and commanded respect."[55]

Simeon's conversation parties and sermon lectures were not without practical instruction. He regularly offered counsel on granular details of enunciation, tone, and voice. Though some of his advice is now dated by the technological limitations of the day, his insights reflect a concerted effort that his disciples master all facets of spoken communication. For

---

51. Carus, *Memoirs*, 63.
52. Brown, *Recollections*, 26.
53. Brown, *Recollections*, 178.
54. Brown, *Recollections*, 10.
55. Brown, *Recollections*, 11.

example, in challenging his students to project in their sermons, he shared his own practice at Holy Trinity. "I preach usually to the small door in the west gallery of Trinity Church: it is a good central spot for me to direct my countenance to; it is a fair average of the more distant parts of the congregation. When I perceive that the door distinctly hears me, then I know that all the congregation may."[56] Elsewhere, with great particularity, he exhorted his students to only use their "natural voice" when preaching—to increase volume without elevating their tone.[57] He even educated ordinands on emphasis and enunciation. He once said,

> Beware of laying emphasis upon every word, or with great frequency. Rather mark importance by the management of time than of stress, except in special cases. Just as it is in music. Group a sentence together by a rapid enunciation, and mark the emphasis by pauses between the more emphatic parts.... Speaking is music: how tame would mere isochronous music be! There are pauses in Handel's works which not even an angel could fill up with notes. You cannot think between the strokes of St. Paul's clock; your attention is absorbed and kept up by the pauses.[58]

As noted below, though most of Simeon's sermon philosophy revolved around content and manner, he was not indifferent to the mundane subtleties of his craft.

Originality

Simeon fervently advocated that preachers preserve originality in their style. Men were not to adopt the exact style of another preacher. Instead, he appealed for preachers to utilize their own God-given personalities. "Every honest Minister," said Simeon, "has his own peculiar turn of idea and mode of preaching; let him study it as well as he can, and improve and correct it; but not try to take up a style or manner which is not his own, for that would injure his usefulness and make him artificial."[59] To Simeon, the preacher must have a significant degree of self-understanding, both to discern his weaknesses and maximize his strengths. Simeon

---

56. Brown, *Recollections*, 186.
57. Brown, *Recollections*, 187.
58. Brown, *Recollections*, 188.
59. Brown, *Recollections*, 131.

would have longed for the modern ability to record one's own sermons. He once lamented his inability to hear his own preaching. "How difficult for a Minister to know his own faults of style or manner, or mode of thinking! There is one Preacher whom I would give twenty pounds any day to hear, even for a single sermon, but I grieve that it is impossible. I cannot ever hear Charles Simeon preach."[60]

Simplicity

In his example and counsel to ordinands, Simeon lobbied for simplicity in preaching. He once asserted, "My aim in the style of preaching is to do it so plainly and simply, that all may understand, and be ready to say, 'I could have made as good a sermon myself.'"[61] Simeon never desired to be novel in content. In the same conversation party, he asserted his own rules for preaching.

> I do not seek out new and remarkable views. But such a practice I abhor. It is not preaching God's truth, but self. Always take the plain straightforward meaning of a passage, and strive to find out what was the mind of God as clearly revealed in the text. I want to get the marrow out of every passage, and make a valuable commentary for the use of the Church.[62]

This practical end of helping the church led Simeon to preach with as much clarity as possible. He aimed to be understood by all of his hearers: "Leaving others to do the drudgery and break the bones, I seek only to get the richness and nutriment of the passage."[63] This meant that Simeon endeavored for his style to not distract his hearers from the message itself. He would have agreed with James Denney (1856–1917), who famously quipped, "No man can give at once the impression that he himself is clever and that Christ is mighty to save."[64]

Simeon believed true preaching was not an academic exercise, but life for the soul. Thus, the goal of the sermon was not to explain the words of the text, but the *meaning* of the text. He explained,

---

60. Brown, *Recollections*, 131.
61. Brown, *Recollections*, 177.
62. Brown, *Recollections*, 176.
63. Brown, *Recollections*, 177.
64. Denney, *Studies in Theology*, 161.

> Preach not your text, but the subject of the text. Take the subject of the text; illustrate it by the words of the text, but preach always the subject of it. Let your sermon come naturally out of your text, "totus, tersus, atque rotundus, (whole, clean, and round)" like the kernel out of a hazelnut; and not piecemeal, and, after much trouble to your hearers, like the kernel out of a walnut.... A sermon should be like a telescope: each successive division of it should be as an additional lens to bring the subject of your text nearer, and make it more distinct.[65]

In proclaiming the subject or meaning of the text, Simeon viewed illustration as a valuable tool in the hands of a skilled minister. He asserted,

> General information, too, is important; it enables a Preacher to bring out things new and old. The new things have been often told, and are yet new; the old are not stale, for they are put into new clothing. Illustration is a most important instrument in a Preacher's hand, and prevails with all, especially the illiterate. We must lead our people's minds onwards, and not keep them to be always babes. This is an error with some very excellent men.[66]

Central to the preacher's task was the advancing understanding of his hearers.

Simeon's priority on simplicity would lead him to opt for plain language. At times, this would lead him to avoid elaborate and flowery words. He once advised his students in one of his conversation parties,

> I always reject imagery when it occurs to my mind in preaching. I want to keep my people's attention off the Preacher, off the manner, and to rivet it upon the truth which I have to tell. Other minds may have different ways of bringing out truth, and producing effects; but I think you, who are looking forward to the ministry, will thank me hereafter for cautioning you strongly against the use of imagery and a flowering style. Get at the heart with the truth, not at the feelings by brilliancy.[67]

The pursuit of simplicity led Simeon to instruct his disciples to begin their ministries by gravitating to easier texts before moving to more complex ones. He said, "The usual run of obvious and excellent texts in the Bible

---

65. Brown, *Recollections*, 183.
66. Brown, *Recollections*, 194.
67. Brown, *Recollections*, 181.

is about five hundred, and I should advise Ministers to preach generally from these, before they enter upon any which are less so."[68]

Simeon's desire to be understood by his hearers came in sharp display in his critique of the Puritan Richard Baxter (1615–1691). Though he generally commended Baxter's doctrine, he advised his students against Baxter's tedious method of preaching.

> Baxter, in one of his works goes on, 'Sixty-Fifthly,' as if any person could remember the sixty-four preceding heads. Yet, by attending to his simple distinction, you may have a hundred and fifty heads in your sermon without either confusion or obscurity. Only do not *name* the minute subdivisions of your sermons; it will confuse your hearers, especially if they have been a little inattentive.[69]

Simeon's sermons managed to be both detail-oriented and digestible to his entire congregation, both town and gown. He appealed to the illiterate members of his parish, while at the same time, stimulated the minds of the Cambridge elite.

The brilliance of Simeon's simplicity stemmed from a desire to awaken within his hearers an appetite for God's word. He feared that much preaching in his day discouraged the average Christian from studying the Bible on his or her own.[70] Yet he believed that simple explanations would render most parts of the Bible readily comprehensible to people in the pews. This meant that preachers had a duty to not obscure God's word with lofty speech. He believed Scripture "must be declared *plainly, without disguise; fully, without concealment; firmly, without doubt; authoritatively, without fear.* It is not to be wrapt up in polished language, for the sake of pleasing a fastidious ear; but to be opened in the simplest terms."[71] Ultimately, as shall be shown later, Simeon believed the preacher's language should be selected with the aim to help the congregation commune with God.

---

68. Brown, *Recollections*, 177.
69. Brown, *Recollections*, 183.
70. Simeon, *Expository Outlines*, 4:291.
71. Simeon, *Expository Outlines*, 14:514.

Manner

If Simeon merely tentatively held some of his views on style and preparation, he maintained an intense commitment to a specific manner of preaching. Every preacher's demeanor should be distinguished by certain qualities. In his own preaching and counsel to young ministers, he regularly returned to the same traits: power, authority, earnestness, and love.

Power

As ambassadors of the Almighty, the words of preachers were to be accompanied by God's power. By virtue of their office and task, ministers were to pursue and possess a Spirit-anointed power from God. Like the Puritans who formerly preached from Simeon's pulpit, he commended ministers to pursue unction in their sermons. Referring to preachers, he said, "We have the very same message to deliver as that which was committed to the apostle Paul. And, though we cannot hope, like him, to have our word confirmed with miracles, we may hope that it shall be accompanied with power from on high, to the conviction and consolation of those who hear us."[72] Simeon believed preachers were to exhibit a dependence on the Spirit's power in their preaching. This meant that they were "to waive [sic] the use of all rhetorical ornaments, and of artificial statements that savour of human wisdom; and to look to the influences of the Holy Spirit to render our word effectual for the good of men. The same holy watchfulness should be found in us respecting the honour of God in the work of man's salvation."[73] Simeon understood the preacher's rhetorical gifts to hold the same place as persuasion in evangelism. Though he understood the skilled use of speech and wisdom to be commendable in preaching and evangelism, both acts should be accompanied by a clear display of dependence on God's Spirit to yield results.

> Were our talents ever so great, we ought to deem the exercise of them, in dispensing the Gospel, a matter of extreme care and jealousy. I mean not that they are to be laid aside; for they may be employed to good purpose: but they are not to be employed for the purpose of display, or to exalt our own wisdom: they must be improved only for the purpose of unfolding more clearly the great mysteries of the Gospel, and of rendering them

---

72. Simeon, *Expository Outlines*, 16:56.
73. Simeon, *Expository Outlines*, 16:56.

> more intelligible to the meanest capacity. The object which we should ever keep in view should be, to have our word accompanied with a divine unction to the souls of men, and to see faith wrought in their hearts with a divine power.[74]

Simeon desired that his preaching be attended by God's presence. This dependence upon God to accompany his preaching governed Simeon's assessment of himself in the pulpit. Brown recounted an anecdote in which a minister spoke with Simeon after one of his sermons. "A Clergyman once meeting him in the country said,—'I had the pleasure of hearing you at such a place from such a text.' But Mr. Simeon shook his head mournfully, exclaiming, 'Did you hear that sermon? Sad, sad! Poor, poor! You should have heard me preach from that text at L——. Oh it was grand.'"[75] Lest anyone perceive from this reply a sense of pride, Brown continued, "Those who knew Mr. Simeon intimately would at once comprehend his meaning to be, that on the one occasion he had preached under a load of spiritual deadness and weakness; but on the other, with the comforting sense of God's presence, and blessing, and sustaining strength."[76] Here, readers can appreciate that Simeon's high view of preaching failed to elevate his view of himself. Rather, it served to diminish the preacher's gifts while heightening his reliance upon God in the preaching moment.

Authority

Along with power came authority. Just as the preacher's power came from God, Simeon believed preaching to possess a delegated authority from Christ. Due to this divine fiat, preachers had no right to proclaim their own words. In Simeon's mind, he sharply distinguished between the word of man and the Word of God.

> The word of man, though true, has little weight, in comparison of the word of God: "*that* is quick and powerful, and sharper than a two-edged sword." It is inconceivable what an advantage a preacher has, when he can say, "Thus saith the Lord:" then every doctrine demands the obedience of faith, and every precept the obedience of righteousness. When told that the word

---

74. Simeon, *Expository Outlines*, 16:56.
75. Brown, *Recollections*, 37.
76. Brown, *Recollections*, 37.

which is delivered to them will judge them in the last day, the people will not dare to trifle with it, as they will with the declarations of fallible men.[77]

Because Simeon believed Scripture to be the only basis for true preaching, the task entailed a right to proclaim God's word in a tone of authority. It was their divine prerogative to speak as the oracles of God (1 Pet 4:11). He contended that much of the failure of preaching in his day was due to a misunderstanding of authority. "Were this matter more attentively considered, we have no doubt but that more frequent appeals would be made to Scripture in our public harangues; and that the obsolete method of expounding Scripture would have at least some measure of that attention which it deserves."[78]

To Simeon, if preachers truly endeavored to preach with power and authority, it would facilitate communion between the congregation and God. The task of preaching was to mediate the presence of God in such a way that the hearers meaningfully engaged with the Almighty. In this way, preachers were merely instruments through which believers could behold their God. He most forcefully made this point in his sermons on the ministry of Ezra the priest. In Neh 8, the people of God—after years of rebellion and neglect of Scripture—recommit themselves to God's word. After Ezra had opened up the word of the Lord, it says in Neh 8:6, "And Ezra blessed the Lord, the great God. And all the people answered, Amen, Amen, with lifting up their hands; and they bowed their heads, and worshipped the Lord with their faces to the ground." Commenting on this text, Simeon proclaimed,

> This was a deportment which became sinners in the presence of their God: they did not look to the creature, but to God, whose voice they heard, and whose authority they acknowledged, in every word that was spoken. What a contrast does this form with the manner in which the word of God is heard amongst us! How rarely do we find persons duly impressed with a sense of their obligation to God for giving them a revelation of his will! How rarely do men at this day look through the preacher unto God, and hear God speaking to them by the voice of his servants![79]

He expressed a similar sentiment in an exposition of 1 Thess 2.

---

77. Simeon, *Expository Outlines*, 4:291.
78. Simeon, *Expository Outlines*, 4:291.
79. Simeon, *Expository Outlines*, 4:292.

> Whenever you come up to the house of God, come with prepared hearts, as Israel did to Mount Sinai at the giving of the law. Look through the minister to God himself. Sit at his feet, as Mary at the feet of Jesus. Seek not to be *pleased*, but *edified*. Do not indulge a critical and captious spirit; but "receive with meekness the engrafted word;" and then you shall find it both able and effectual to save your souls (Note: James 1:21). If it be a precept or an exhortation, a promise or a threatening, receive it as if it were addressed to you by an audible voice from heaven: so shall it descend on your souls as dew or rain, that fail not to accomplish the ends for which they are sent.[80]

In every sermon, Simeon maintained the astonishing conviction that preaching brokered fellowship with God. Each address was an occasion for God's people to engage in doxology. Thus, Simeon lamented the common paltry view of preaching that reduced sermons to dry theological treatises. Such a view rendered communion with the Divine unimaginable. Instead, he made it his soul's ambition for his people to behold God through his preaching.

Earnestness and Love

For all of his emphasis on power and authority, one might expect Simeon's manner in preaching to strike a domineering tone. However, he laid great stress on the need for preaching to be earnest and loving in its mode of expression. In his own ministry, Simeon's passion captured the attention of everyone who heard him, even the smallest child.[81] This passion stemmed from both an awareness of his own infirmities and the needs of his people. Yet such gravity was always to be accompanied with gladness. Hence, he charged his students to be happy preachers. Using himself as an example, he expressed, "I am happy. . . . I always preach happily, and also vigorously, when I can feel humbled in the dust for my own utter worthlessness, when I can feel that I am the worst of sinners."[82] He viewed preaching to be most effective when born out of a posture of humility.

A fuller view of Simeon's pastoral theology presents a shepherd intimately connected to his sheep. As a dedicated parishioner, he insisted on the need for preachers to proclaim God's truth with sensitivity to the needs

---

80. Simeon, *Expository Outlines*, 18:299.
81. Brown, *Recollections*, 8.
82. Brown, *Recollections*, 332.

of God's people. Such an emphasis was doubly significant given the savage tactics of Simeon's congregation for the first several years of his ministry. It was not until decades into his pastorate at Holy Trinity that Simeon even had the freedom to preach with desired regularity in his pulpit. One might expect the pastor of such a stiff-necked people to preach with little regard or affection for his hearers. However, Simeon made every effort to seek the good of the souls entrusted into his care. Preachers needed to do more than say true things. Rather, they needed a judicious impulse to speak in such a manner as to have an effect upon their people. He recognized this to be a peculiar challenge to young ministers.

> *Young Ministers say, they must acquit their consciences, and speak faithfully, whether people will hear or forbear.*—My young friends, you have a higher duty than to tell out God's whole truth at once, and commend yourselves to God as faithful. You have to win souls; and if your addresses make them shut their ears, what are you doing but saying, 'I will preach the whole truth, even if sure that I shall send them to hell by it?' Is not that essentially selfish in you? Milk will nourish a babe; beef will choke it: which does the mother give? Do not thus undervalue the precious souls entrusted to you. Be gentle among your people, even as a nursing mother cherisheth her children.[83]

Though he rarely shied away from tough doctrines, Simeon endeavored to explain difficult truths only when he believed his people were ready. In doing so, he attempted to follow the pattern of Jesus. Simeon asserted to his disciples,

> You must speak the truth with fidelity, yet so as your hearers can bear it. Our Lord did so. His first sermon was a quotation from Isaiah 1; but look at the passage: our Lord read only a part of it. He said, "The Spirit of the Lord hath anointed me to preach the Gospel to the poor, etc., to proclaim the acceptable year of the Lord;" but there He stopped and closed the book; He did not read the rest of the clause, "and the day of vengeance of our God." He would not alarm them in His first sermon; they could not bear it.[84]

For Simeon, it was not optional for a preacher to leave a congregation in doubt of his love for them. This meant that the task of preaching involved more than speaking truth; a preacher must strike an affectionate

83. Brown, *Recollections*, 169.
84. Brown, *Recollections*, 188–89.

tone. As highlighted earlier, in one of his conversation parties, Simeon chastised a young Henry Martyn for preaching callously on the topic of hell. His critique centered not on the topic of hell, but on Martyn's lack of love and gentleness.[85] Elsewhere he averred, "Love should be the spring of all actions, and especially of a Minister's. If a man's heart be full of love, he will rarely offend. He may have severe things to say, but he will say them in love."[86]

Beyond tone, preaching was to flow from knowledge of people and their needs. Just as Scripture had several aims—namely, to reprove, correct and instruct—preachers must exercise wisdom in discerning the pressing needs of their people. Simeon said, "If there be errors in the Church, he must 'reprove' them, and establish the truth in opposition to them. If there be any sins committed, he must 'rebuke' them; and, if need be, with sharpness and severity too, 'that the name of God and his doctrine be not blasphemed.'"[87] To Simeon, the preacher's burden was to discern when to lift up drooping hands and strengthen weak knees, and when to rebuke and correct wandering sheep. Such wisdom necessitated that preachers know their people's circumstances. It also necessitated that preachers appreciate the ability of their people. He charged his students: "Deliver the whole counsel of God, but choose your times and opportunities, and tell them as they are able to hear it."[88]

Before moving away from Simeon's thoughts on earnestness, it is worth highlighting again his exposition of 1 Thess 2, particularly verses 7 and 8. There the apostle Paul writes, "We were gentle among you, even as a nurse [nursing mother] cherisheth her children; so being affectionately desirous of you, we were willing to have imparted to you, not the Gospel only, but also our own souls, because ye were dear unto us." Commenting on this text, Simeon remarked,

> [Paul] did not draw out of his mind for his sermons such things as might acquire for him reputation as a clever Preacher, or a learned defender of the faith—acquire him a great name. His character is sweetly pourtrayed in verses 7 and 8, which contain a pattern for all Ministers. How different from the usual views of even good men on ministerial character.[89]

---

85. Brown, *Recollections*, 96.
86. Brown, *Recollections*, 188.
87. Simeon, *Expository Outlines*, 19:77.
88. Brown, *Recollections*, 161.
89. Brown, *Recollections*, 163.

Simeon continued to expound the apostle's illustration.

> Follow up the image: how gentle is a mother—fearful of causing pain, watchful, tender, kind; living only for her children; cautious and earnest, not only to avoid injuring, but to prevent others from injuring; delighting in her little ones; placing them as her chief joy; depriving and denying herself for their sakes; not trying to be thought a good mother, but with her whole heart and soul being one; cherishing her dear ones; willing, not only to give such things as are prepared for her infant, but drawing out her own breast to give it nourishment.[90]

In applying the illustration, Simeon laid profound stress on the minister's preaching. His proclamation was to be infused with earnestness for the souls of his hearers.

> A Minister should put his "own soul" into his sermon. Why does not a mother give meat and strong food to her babe? She knows it is not good for it, and she gives it her own breast. Let a Minister act in the same spirit. A nursing mother never forgets her babe; has a regard to it in all she eats for her own nourishment; is cautious to abstain from what makes her breast less nourishing to her babe, from all that might distress or injure the little one. So let a Minister have an eye to his people in all the spiritual food he takes, the books he reads, the views he allows to enter his mind; in all he does, even as a private individual, lest the tone of his thoughts should become prejudicial to his flock, his sermons less nutritive for them, or stronger than they can bear. "Affectionately desirous," St. Paul saith. A mother, if separated for a few hours from her child, longs for it, is desirous of it, yearns over it; nor does she at any time so fondly love it as while imparting nourishment to it. Be it so with the Minister also. His separation from Sunday to weekday, from weekday to Sunday, should make him yearn over his people until he is again imparting to them spiritual food. With the nursing mother all this is so, because her babe is dear to her; be it so likewise with you Ministers, because your people are dear to you.[91]

With Christ and the apostles as his models—and weathered by his decades at Holy Trinity—Simeon found earnestness and love to be indispensable elements of evangelical preaching.

---

90. Brown, *Recollections*, 163.
91. Brown, *Recollections*, 163–64.

In all of his counsel on the tone and manner of preaching, Simeon at times would acknowledge the profound difficulty of preaching. He once lamented to his students,

> It is not an easy thing to preach.—It is easy for a Minister to prate in a pulpit, and even to speak much good matter; but to preach is not easy,—to carry his congregation on his shoulders as it were to heaven; to weep over them, pray for them, deliver the truth with a weeping, praying heart; and if a Minister has grace to do so now and then, he ought to be very thankful.[92]

Simeon advised that when preachers seek to convict their hearers of sin, they conduct themselves as surgeons, not as butchers.[93] And if preachers were met with continued hostility, they must persevere.

> [The preacher] must be content to give "line upon line, precept upon precept, here a little and there a little." And if, in return for all his kindness, he meet with nothing but reproach and persecution, he must still persist in using his best efforts, if by any means he may at last be made useful even to one. Confident that his "doctrine" is right, he must labour to inculcate it on all; and leave to God the issue, whether it be to blind and harden men, or to convert and save their souls.[94]

The Hearers

Though Simeon may have viewed the sermon as a monologue, he certainly believed the congregation to have an integral role in preaching. Simeon perceived the preacher and hearers to both have duties in the preaching moment. As ministers held the solemn duty to preach the Word in season and out of season, it was incumbent upon the people of God to meaningfully receive God's word. In one sermon, he soberly warned his people concerning this responsibility. "You shall all, ere long, stand at the judgment-seat of Christ, and 'give an account of yourselves to God;' and receive at his hands according to what you have done in the body, whether it be good or evil. It becomes YOU, then, to 'receive with meekness every word' that is delivered, as it becomes *me* also to 'speak even as the oracles

---

92. Brown, *Recollections*, 106.
93. Brown, *Recollections*, 199.
94. Simeon, *Expository Outlines*, 4:77–78.

of God.'"⁹⁵ Simeon recognized that preachers and hearers alike were to appraise their roles in the preaching event with the same seriousness. As preachers proclaimed God's word as God's mouthpiece, the hearer's aim was to hear God speak. As the herald conveyed the message of the king, so the subjects submitted to their sovereign.

Simeon also acknowledged that God extended special promises to his people in the context of gathered worship. In light of this, the reception of the preached word was to be met with expectation. Hearers were to marry that expectation with prayer.

> If the mighty working of God's power be requisite, even of the same power that raised Jesus Christ from the dead, we should implore his presence before we go up to his house; we should be lifting up our hearts in ejaculatory prayer while we are hearing his word; and, after the seed has been sown, we should water it with our prayers and tears.⁹⁶

Simeon believed that the failure of so many preachers in the ministry of the word was the prayerlessness of their people. Hence, he charged his hearers, "Let us then abound more in the great duty of prayer; and God will pour out his Spirit upon us: He will give us that unction of the Holy One that shall teach us all things; and make his word to be 'the power of God to the salvation of our souls.'"⁹⁷ With all expectation and prayer, Simeon's view of preaching envisioned a people determined to behold God through his called ambassadors.

Influence

Simeon's monumental influence on evangelical preaching—as an element of his larger pastoral theology—remains, without a doubt, his greatest area of impact on the Christian world. Though his preaching philosophy is most easily perceived in the immediate generation that followed him, his legacy in this area endures to this generation. John Stott and J. I. Packer (1926-1920)—two leading lights of the evangelical movement in the twentieth century—explicitly traced their roots as preachers back to Simeon. In 1986, Stott published a collection of Simeon sermons, offering an introduction at the beginning of the volume in

---

95. Simeon, *Expository Outlines*, 4:79.
96. Simeon, *Expository Outlines*, 18:279.
97. Simeon, *Expository Outlines*, 18:280.

tribute to his ministerial hero. "Charles Simeon was one of the greatest and most persuasive preachers the Church of England has ever known."[98] Stott maintained a special connection to Simeon throughout his whole life. He reflected, "On many occasions I have had the privilege of preaching from his pulpit in Holy Trinity Church, Cambridge, and standing where he stood, have prayed for a measure of his outstanding faithfulness."[99] Similar praise was expressed by Packer, who in an essay on Simeon's preaching, asserted that the Cambridge minister "is one of the towering evangelical preachers in the history of Anglican preaching. He stands as an inspiration to many contemporary evangelical preachers first of all because of his exemplary life as a preacher and mentor of preachers."[100] These evangelical giants were not alone in their esteem of Simeon. Today, The Charles Simeon Trust—a preaching workshop ministry founded in 2001—trains thousands of preachers throughout the globe—making it their mission "to promote the growth of the gospel of Jesus Christ throughout the world by training up the next generation of Biblical expositors."[101] This chapter will conclude by highlighting the influence Simeon exerted on the preaching of the first generation of ministers that followed him.

William Carus

Though the legacy of William Carus has not been thoroughly discussed in this project, his preaching is a noteworthy example of Simeon's tutelage. Having served as Simeon's final curate, Carus is mostly remembered for his preservation of his mentor's memoirs. Nevertheless, as the man trusted to shepherd Holy Trinity in the wake the great "Apostle of Cambridge," his preaching was impressive in his own right. Doubtless, what made Carus a suitable heir to Simeon's pulpit was his application of his mentor's teaching. We see such application in a sermon Carus preached on 1 Tim 4:16—a text in which Paul charges his protégé Timothy to "take heed unto thyself." In expounding the text, Carus—faithful to Simeon's instruction to bring forth the meaning of the text—delivered

---

98. Stott, *Evangelical Preaching*, xxvii.
99. Stott, *Evangelical Preaching*, xxvii.
100. Packer, "Expository Preaching," 140.
101. "Brief History." The Charles Simeon Trust models itself after the Proclamation Trust, a ministry founded by Dick Lucas (b. 1925), an Anglican evangelical and another notable admirer of Simeon.

a clear outline based on the authorial intent of passage. He said, "These three points then, viz. 1) our *spirit*, 2) our *knowledge*, and 3) our *conduct*, will require to be especially considered, in reviewing the nature of this personal overview."[102] In the simplicity of Simeon, Carus followed the pattern of his mentor.

John Sumner

Archbishop John Sumner also inherited Simeon's preaching philosophy. It was shown in chapter 2 how massive an impact Sumner made on the Church of England. Doubtless, this included the furtherance of an evangelical brand of preaching throughout the land. On this point, Nigel Scotland has asserted the inseparable link between Sumner and Simeon.

> If the Societies to which Sumner gave his energies revealed his Clapham coattails, his preaching and pastoral work did so even more. As a young Cambridge undergraduate John Bird's commitment to the evangelical faith intensified and deepened under Simeon's ministry. He left University convinced of the supreme importance of good, straightforward well illustrated biblical preaching. Simeon had published his *Horae Homileticae* in 21 volumes and his outlines became the model used by many of the younger generations of clergy who followed him. Sumner was to do likewise and throughout his life he produced practical expositions of most of the books of the New Testament. These were written both for private devotional reading and also to aid busy and over-burdened parish clergy with their Sunday sermons.[103]

E. R. Moore has also noted the resemblance between the preaching of Sumner and that of Simeon, arguing that the former "can thus be seen to mirror those of his mentor, and at the same time prove how fruitful were those labours of Simeon in his rooms at Cambridge."[104]

Francis Close

Yet another example of Simeon's preaching legacy can be seen in the ministry of Francis Close. Hennell writes of the monumental impression the

---

102. Carus, *Personal Duties*, 6.
103. Scotland, *John Bird Sumner*, 103.
104. Scotland, *John Bird Sumner*, 103.

former had on the latter, "At the heart of Close's power at Cheltenham was his preaching. He was Simeon's most literal pupil. He constructed his sermons on the basis of the sermon skeletons he had learned to use at Cambridge; they were always Bible expositions. He spoke naturally as Simeon had always taught him to speak."[105] In 1861, the Dean of Carlisle published a volume of eighty sermon outlines titled *On the Composition of a Sermon* in the model of *Horae Homileticae*. Though Close emerged as one of Simeon's most dedicated disciples, he failed to mention Simeon in the work. Despite this, Simeon's influence on Close's preaching was undeniable.[106] Following Simeon's funeral, in a sermon at Cheltenham, Close memorialized his mentor by underscoring his earnestness.

> Never shall I forget one remarkable instance which I myself witnessed, of his affectionate concern for the souls entrusted to him. He was preaching upon those striking words: "All day long I have stretched forth my hands unto a disobedient and gainsaying people (Rom. 10:20, 21)." And after having urged all his hearers to accept the proffered mercy, he reminded them that there were those present to whom he had preached Christ for more than thirty years, but they continued indifferent to a Saviour's love; and pursuing this train of expostulation for some time, he at length became quite overpowered by his feeling, and he sank down in the pulpit and burst into a flood of tears, and few who were present could refrain from weeping with him.[107]

As the disciple arguably most like Simeon, Close sought to exhibit such earnestness in his own pulpit ministry.

Perhaps the most fascinating point of influence that Simeon had was on Close's preaching was in the realm of typology. The two exhibited the same exact care and caution when it came to identifying and tracing types of Christ in their sermons. For example, in a sermon on Gen 37, Simeon—with trepidation—identified Joseph as a type of Christ in the unfolding biblical narrative.

> We are not expressly told in Scripture that the events of Joseph's life were intended to prefigure those which should afterwards be accomplished in the Messiah: but the humiliation and exaltation of each, together with the means whereby both the one and the other were effected, are so much alike, that we can scarcely view

---

105. Hennell, *Sons of the Prophets*, 108.
106. Hopkins, *Charles Simeon of Cambridge*, 62.
107. Close, *Occasional Sermons*, 187.

> them in any other light than as a typical prophecy fulfilled in the Antitype. It is not however our intention to prosecute the history of Joseph in this view: we shall rather notice some of the most striking particulars as tending to elucidate the passions by which mankind in general are actuated, and the changes to which they are exposed.[108]

Simeon's constitutional reluctance to identify Joseph as a type of Christ exemplified a hesitance to fancifully interpret Scripture. As noted earlier, Simeon resisted any impulse to speculate in the pulpit. In another sermon on the narrative of Joseph's life, Simeon declared,

> Peculiar care is to be used in unfolding the types, lest, by indulging our own imagination, we bring the very truth of God itself into contempt. Where the Scriptures themselves have marked the typical reference, we may proceed without fear; but when once they cease to guide us, we should not venture one step but with fear and trembling. This observation is peculiarly applicable to the subject before us. It does not appear that Joseph is anywhere declared to be a type of Christ, notwithstanding the circumstances wherein they resemble each other are as numerous and remarkable, as in almost any other instance whatever. We forbear therefore to assert any thing on this subject with confidence; while, in compliance with the opinion of the most judicious commentators, and indeed with the almost irresistible conviction of our own mind, we proceed to trace the resemblance of Joseph to Christ.[109]

These quotes are doubly fascinating when compared to Close's exposition of the Joseph story, where we see a similar carefulness in interpreting the unfolding narrative of salvation-history. Close wrote,

> The character and history of Joseph do in so many particulars accord with those of the Lord Jesus Christ, that all the commentators have without hesitation considered the former as typical of the latter. Yet it is remarkable that Joseph is never referred to in the New Testament as a typical person, nor is there any direct allusion to his story as emblematic of the Messiah: it cannot therefore be properly asserted that Joseph was a type of Christ; while at the same time there can be no impropriety in viewing his interesting life and exemplary conduct as illustrative of the character and history of the Redeemer. The language

---

108. Simeon, *Expository Outlines*, 1:260.
109. Simeon, *Expository Outlines*, 1:309.

of the dying patriarch in the text could not have been more apposite, had the spirit of prophecy here expressly signified the sufferings of Christ, and the glory which should follow: nor is the silence of the New Testament sufficient to prove that no such allusion was intended.[110]

Like Simeon, Close resisted overzealous typology, and—as a preacher of Christ—avoided "beelines" to the cross, opting to interpret passages naturally.[111] In their approach to typology, Simeon and Close also resembled each other in their expositions of the narratives of Zerubbabel in Zechariah, as well Eliakim in Isaiah. Through the important post of Cheltenham, and countless others, Simeon's preaching style infused a panoply of parishes.

Charles Bridges

Simeon's preaching was also immortalized in the works of Charles Bridges. As highlighted in chapter 2, *The Christian Ministry* went through nine editions within the first twenty years of its original publishing. There, Bridges instructed preachers on how to make use of Simeon's recorded sermons.

> Mr. Simeon's well-known and most useful work, may be said to give precisely that measure of help which is required—encouragement to inexperienced diligence, and at the same time a fair scope for the exercise of personal talent. The care and thought requisite to produce from his volume a complete and well-proportioned discourse, are fully equal to the labour of an original composition—so skillfully are the breaks contrived to exercise the judgment in suitably filling the vacuum, and in the accurate arrangement of the scriptural matter. Perhaps the highest commendation of the work is that a mere copyist would exhibit the Skeletons like the bones in the prophetic vision: very dry. Whereas a thoughtful mind would find ample and profitable employment in clothing them with solid matter, in the form of symmetry and strength.[112]

---

110. Close, *Nine Sermons*, 123–24.

111. Drummond, *Prince of Preachers*, 223. Drummond, along with many since, attributed the phrase of making "a beeline to the cross" to Charles Spurgeon. To this day, there exists no record of Spurgeon ever using the phrase.

112. Bridges, *Christian Ministry*, 199.

Bridges understood the genius of Simeon's skeleton manuscripts to allow thoughtful preachers to retain a degree of originality. Meanwhile, a plagiarist would find them unprofitable. In illustrating a good use of Simeon's *Horae Homileticae*, Bridges highlighted the work of Henry Martyn.

> We might take an illustration—Mr. Martyn's Sermon on Psalm 9.17; which fills up Mr. Simeon's Skeleton on that text. It was worked out (as we incidentally learn from his Life) under circumstances of particular disadvantage and mental agitation. But the life that is infused throughout, the variety of its enlargements, the accuracy of the proportions of its several parts, the skill with which the breaks are completed, and the warm and strong colouring given to the whole—all combine to give it the power and effect of an original and talented composition.[113]

Notably, we see a disciple of Simeon tracing the influence of his mentor in a fellow disciple.

Henry Martyn

Simeon's preaching arguably impacted Henry Martyn more than any other. Early in his journals, he recorded the great impressions that the pulpit of Holy Trinity made on him. "At Mr. Simeon's church this evening," said Martyn, "His sermon was very impressive, on Revelation 3:2. Thanks to God, that though my graces are declining, and my corruptions increasing, I am not unwilling to be reclaimed. For with all this evil in my heart, I would not, could not, choose any other than God for my portion."[114] Simeon's preaching endowed Martyn with a sense of satisfaction in God. Elsewhere, Martyn reflected on Simeon's preaching on Christ's command to love in John 15. He wrote, "I saw my utter want of such love as he described it: so disinterested, sympathizing, beneficent, and self-denying. Resolved to make the acquisition of it the daily subject of my future endeavours."[115] In yet another instance, he mulled over a Simeon sermon: this time on a text from 2 Chr. Martyn attested that the message "discovered to me my corruption and vileness more than any sermon I had ever heard. . . . Oh, that I had a more piercing sense of the Divine presence! How much sin in the purest services! If I were sitting in heavenly places

---

113. Bridges, *Christian Ministry*, 199.
114. Sargent, *Rev. Henry Martyn*, 37.
115. Sargent, *Rev. Henry Martyn*, 40.

with Christ, or rather with my thoughts habitually there, how would every duty, but especially this of social prayer, become easy."[116] In this series of quotes, one can perceive how Simeon's sermons produced both repentance and resolve. Throughout his tenure at Trinity, Simeon's preaching blended a realistic understanding of the challenges of the Christian life, while at the same time upholding the ideals of faithful discipleship. Such preaching rarely broke bruised reeds. Rather, he emboldened sensitive men like Martyn to advance in the faith.

Conclusion

As demonstrated in this work, Simeon's brand of preaching ultimately spread across the Church of England. By the 1830s, High Anglicans faced a formidable foe in the evangelical wing of their denomination. Simeon experienced the pleasure of watching his influence spread well beyond Cambridge, reaching the corners of the globe through men like Henry Martyn and Thomas Thomason. In fact, he once expressed to his congregation that he viewed his ministry as the pouring of salt into stagnant waters, diffusing life into dry land all over the world.[117] Thomas Chalmers of Glasgow repeated a similar sentiment to Simeon in a letter. With high esteem for the vicar of Holy Trinity, he addressed Simeon: "It is my earnest prayer . . . that salt through your means may long continue to be thrown into such a copious and emanating fountain as your university, and that days of glory and of holiness may speedily come upon the Church of England."[118]

At the center of Simeon's influence was a specific view of preaching: a view that esteemed preachers as ambassadors of God, preaching as the word of God, and congregations as the people of God. Preaching was God's word through God's man to God's people. Preachers were not commissioned to amuse men or speak their own thoughts. They were to be heralds of an almighty sovereign. "If they preach what is founded on the Scriptures," he said, "their word, so far as it is agreeable to the mind of God, is to be considered as God's."[119] As such, Simeon believed preaching to have an entirely unique character in its power, content, method, style,

---

116. Sargent, *Rev. Henry Martyn*, 42.
117. Hopkins, *Charles Simeon of Cambridge*, 118.
118. Hopkins, *Charles Simeon of Cambridge*, 118.
119. Jenkins, *Tale of Two Preachers*, 8.

and manner. Such a view necessitated an elevated view of the hearers of true preaching. More than communication, preaching was communion—an event in which needy people prayerfully, expectantly, and joyfully beheld God through the instrument of the preacher.

CHAPTER 7

Conclusion

AFTER HALF A CENTURY in his role at Holy Trinity, Simeon claimed to a crowded conversation party of university students, "When I came to Cambridge as an undergraduate, I was the only one that held the sentiments we now all entertain."[1] This was a tremendous assertion. Though the evangelical wing of the Church of England never prevailed as a dominant influence in the denomination, it did experience seismic growth over Simeon's lifetime. Peter Virgin traces the progress of evangelicalism in Cambridge from the 1770s to the 1830s.

> In the 1770s, of the twelve pulpits in the town, only one was occupied by an Evangelical—capacious Samuel Ogden, incumbent of the Round Church—but by 1836, the year of the death of their acknowledged Cambridge leader, Charles Simeon, six were at their disposal, while a seventh, Great St Mary's, was shared between an 'orthodox' vicar and an Evangelical curate.[2]

That the vicar of Holy Trinity played an enormous part in the advance of evangelicalism is inarguable. A best estimate shows he likely trained over 1,100 pastors over the course of his life.[3] Yet the degree of Simeon's profound influence has not been the central assertion of this

---

1. Brown, *Recollections*, 258. Simeon likely meant this assertion seriously, not literally. It is estimated that by Simeon's death, a third of Anglican churches were evangelical. See also Prime, *Charles Simeon*, 239.
2. Virgin, *Age of Negligence*, 22.
3. Jenkins, *Tale of Two Preachers*, 4.

book. Rather, it has shown that the driving force behind Charles Simeon's storied ministry was a robust pastoral theology. I have endeavored to prove that Simeon possessed a well-orbed view of the pastorate that included distinct approaches to churchmanship, personal piety, local parish ministry, and preaching. In an age when the vast majority of England's ministers were educated in Cambridge and Oxford, Simeon assiduously invested in future ordinands.[4] His gospel convictions rallied a host of ministers to faithfulness, stretching far beyond the borders of England.

This study has emphasized Simeon's uniqueness as an evangelical leader in distinction from some of his peers. While Whitefield, the Wesleys, and (to a lesser degree) Newton led *outward-facing* ministries, Simeon had a different strategy for impacting global Christianity. By staying local and exemplifying an extraordinary commitment to ordinary ministry, he marshalled a multitude of ministers ready to follow his model. Thus, he indelibly marked the Church of England and the world. Though Simeon could have pursued a higher station than his post at Holy Trinity, he chose to stay local. He even criticized the vaunted Thomas Chalmers for leaving his parish for a career in the academy.[5] On the other hand, Simeon—in order to reach people *outside* his parish—molded pastors. And in order to train pastors, he cared for the people *within* his parish.

Summary of Findings

In an effort to explain Simeon's pastoral theology, several aspects of his ministry have been underscored. I have highlighted Simeon as an influencer of influencers—a devotee to his denomination—an upholder of evangelical piety—a local pastor of parishioners—and a distinguished preacher of the gospel.

---

4. Simeon's influence is even more intriguing when juxtaposed to John Henry Newman and the Oxford Movement. Leonard Elliott Binns notes, "The work [Simeon] did for the Church has seldom been fully recognized. He had not about him the wistful air which drew men to follow John Henry Newman, nor is his career such as to excite romantic admiration, but there is little doubt that Bishop Charles Wordsworth [who was not an evangelical] was right when he asserted that Simeon's was a more powerful influence even than Newman's when judged merely by the number of young men whom he attracted to himself." See Binns, *Evangelical Movement*, 88. Simeon and Newman—though separated by a generation or two—were widely perceived as respective leaders of their divergent movements. See Nockles, "Church Parties," 351.

5. Brown, *Recollections*, 199. Simeon said, "I once approved of Dr. Chalmers removing to St. Andrew's, because I supposed that the Professor's Chair gave him a seat in the General Assembly; but otherwise I think he did wrong to leave his parish."

Ministerial Mentor

In chapter 2, it was observed how Simeon—notwithstanding his great originality—had the benefit of a handful of mentors. From John Berridge, he learned the value of singleness and the power of preaching.[6] From John Thornton, he acquired a heart for humility.[7] And from Henry Venn, he inherited a pastoral warmth that he zealously passed on to Victorian evangelicals.[8] Through a variety of means, Simeon's position in Cambridge allowed him to double as both ministerial mentor and minister-maker.[9] Accordingly, the parade of pastors who followed him included future bishops, missionaries, and ordinary clergymen. Pupils like Henry Martyn bolstered a burgeoning missionary movement. John Sumner the Simeonite—having been promoted to England's most prestigious diocese—prevented impediments to the evangelical cause in the established church. And if Charles Bridges was not shaped in the evangelical nursery of Cambridge, his *Christian Ministry* would not have had such an impact.[10]

Archetypal Anglican

Chapter 3 explored Simeon's relationship to the Church of England, revealing him to be one of her most loyal subjects. He embodied the spirit of evangelicalism in Anglican mode. Thus, he is well-regarded as the most influential of Anglican evangelicals, "who in many respects was the shaper, if not the founder, of the movement within the Church of England."[11] Over the course of Simeon's life, he saw the status of evangelicalism in the established church move from that of a barely tolerated radical fringe to a thriving, forceful influence. It was shown how Simeon followed Venn not only in his warmth as an evangelical, but also in his zeal as a churchman. This in many ways gave way to the longevity

---

6. Smyth, *Simeon and Church Order*, 269–70.

7. Carus, *Memoirs*, 74.

8. Brown, *Recollections*, 139.

9. Brown, *Recollections*, 203. In one of his later conversation parties, Simeon shared an example of how one of his followers had succeeded the esteemed John William Fletcher of Madeley. Such Simeonite successions were routine throughout his ministry, and for years after.

10. Bridges, *Christian Ministry*, back cover blurb.

11. Bray, *Anglicanism*, 28.

of Simeon's influence in Anglican circles. His life bore witness that his views were not merely consistent with the forms and doctrine of the established church, but were her greatest source of health.[12] From his love affair with the liturgy to his concern over Dissent, Simeon evinced a stalwart commitment to the Anglican Way.[13]

Personal Piety

Chapter 4 played a crucial role in this project, for, it was not Simeon's great gifts that granted him such massive influence, but it was his great likeness to Christ.[14] His character won the hearts of his followers, spurring them to greater devotion to God and service in his kingdom. Young ministers did not just learn from Simeon, they longed to be like him. Five particular aspects of his piety were highlighted: (1) the evangelical character of his spirituality, (2) the place of suffering in his ministry, (3) the priority of generosity and social concern in his life, (4) his humility and contentment, and (5) his communion with God. At the center of Simeon's ministry, was a thriving friendship with the Lord. And Simeon's devotion to God bred a love and concern for his fellow man. It was his personal piety which came to blazing display in his relentless support of the missionary cause.

Chapter 4 also definitively proved his disgust for the slave trade, though heretofore, it has been erroneously asserted that Simeon was totally silent on the topic.[15] In reality, he used the platform of his pulpit on various occasions to vehemently condemn the barbarous practice, evidencing a thirst for justice that reflected God's character. As Simeon modeled a ministry of faithfulness, he did not only teach his disciples *how* to shepherd, he showed them *who* and *what* to be as a man of God.

---

12. Simeon's example, along with others in the long eighteenth century gave fuel to the polemical writings of J. C. Ryle on this topic. See Ryle, *Last Century*, 39, 103, 128–29, 258.

13. Brown, *Recollections*, 60.

14. Robert Murray M'Cheyne famously averred, "It is not great talents God bless so much as great likeness to Jesus." See Bonar, *Rev. Robert Murray M'Cheyne*, 282.

15. Hopkins, *Charles Simeon of Cambridge*, 198–99.

Parish Pastor

Chapter 5 surveyed Simeon's local parish ministry, highlighting his commitment to pastoral visitation and congregational life. To Simeon, ministry was not merely a professional domain, it was personal. He gave his life to the good of souls. Leaning into the lessons of 1 Thess 2, he understood the role of the pastor was that of a shepherd to sheep, a father to family, and a mother to children. In his effort to advance the welfare of his flock, Simeon laid particular stress on the place of gentleness in ministry. In all their teaching and exhortations, ministers were to tenderly nurture the faith of their people. "Milk will nourish a babe," he declared, "beef will choke it: which does the mother give? Do not thus undervalue the precious souls entrusted to you. Be gentle among your people, even as a nursing mother cherisheth her children."[16] Central to the parish life of Holy Trinity was an earnest commitment to congregational activity. From his own efforts in personal visitation, to his rallying of a robust laity, he fostered an every-member ministry that equipped ordinary Christians to watch over one another.

Preaching Paragon

The pulpit of Holy Trinity was undoubtedly the greatest means by which Simeon influenced his followers. Chapter 6 showed how his preaching not only represented his greatest means of mentorship, but it also was the part of his pastoral theology most thoroughly replicated by his disciples. Two centuries on—the spirit of the apostle of Cambridge lives on organically and institutionally. For example, every year, the Charles Simeon Trust hosts dozens of preaching workshops and classes for thousands of expositors across the globe.[17] That Simeon forwarded a particular brand of exegesis that emphasized authorial intent has been asserted by many resources on Simeon. Yet this thesis has sought to deepen the broader understanding of Simeon's preaching by highlighting his understanding of the ontology of biblical proclamation. A sermon was a divine message: God's word, through God's man, to God's people. To faithfully preach the Bible was to convey the words and will

---

16. Brown, *Recollections*, 169.
17. "Brief History."

of the Almighty. Thus, the task of hearers in the preaching moment was to look "through the preacher unto God."[18]

Further Areas of Research

Additional areas of future research on Simeon abound. In the spirit of this study, further examination of his views on biblical theology demand closer attention. Is there a unifying theme to Simeon's preaching, and thus, the Scriptures themselves? How did Simeon distinguish between the responsible teaching of Christological typology and speculative exegesis? In terms of systematic theology, has Simeon's antagonistic rhetoric toward Calvinism been overstated? If according to Simeon, the Bible did in fact have a system, what was the nature of that system?[19] In terms of pastoral practice, how did Simeon's use of lay-societies compare to evangelical Anglicans before and after his ministry? In light of these important questions, I hope to see significant attention given to Simeon scholarship in the days ahead.

A Final Word

As an heir to the Reformed tradition, I find myself in constant debt to evangelical Anglicans of the eighteenth and nineteenth centuries. And as a young pastor, I have sensed a constant need for mentors, both dead and living. I have discovered a well of pastoral wisdom at the feet of men like Richard Sibbes, John Newton, Charles Bridges, J. C. Ryle, and of course, Charles Simeon. In addition to his exemplary exegesis, Simeon was an especially bright and shining model of pastoral faithfulness. My hope is that this project on his pastoral theology will cast a spotlight on the zealous, warm, evangelical character of his ministry. I desire that pastors recognize not only the truth of his theology, but also the beauty of his character.

Simeon viewed a man's calling to ministry as "the entire surrender of the heart and soul to God, to be for His glory and service."[20] Simeon exhibited this soul-surrender throughout his entire pastorate. All that he imbibed from the generation prior, and everything he gleaned from the

---

18. Simeon, *Expository Outlines*, 4:292.
19. Brown, *Recollections*, 212.
20. Brown, *Recollections*, 207.

furnace of tribulation, he earnestly entrusted to faithful men who were able to teach others (2 Tim 2:2). As an evangelical exemplar, he steeled an army of zealous churchmen, who in the following decades, preserved his theology in unbroken succession. In his piety, he furnished his followers with a hunger for God and heart for his people. In his shepherding, he showed a generation of ordinands how to care for souls. In his sermons, he modeled a method of proclamation that shook the nation. Simeon tirelessly gave his life to prepare pastors to pastor. From his quarters, he coached them—in his classroom, he trained them—from his pulpit, he roused them—in his parish, he watched over them. Showing sheep how to shepherd was the unifying mission of his life: and in doing so, he bestowed upon his beloved Church of England a great supply of noble sons.

Bibliography

Primary Sources

"Act of Uniformity 1662." National Archives of the United Kingdom. https://www.legislation.gov.uk/aep/Cha2/14/4/data.pdf.

Austen, Jane. *Jane Austen's Letters*. Edited by Deirdre Le Faye. Oxford: Oxford University Press, 2011.

———. *Mansfield Park*. London: Chapman and Hall, 1870.

———. *Pride and Prejudice*. New York: Scribner's Sons, 1918.

Bonar, Andrew. *The Memoir and Remains of the Rev. Robert Murray M'Cheyne*. Carlisle, PA: Banner of Truth Trust, 2019.

Braithwaite, Joseph Bevan. *Memoirs of Joseph Gurney*. Madison, WI: Fletcher and Alexander, 1854.

Bridges, Charles. *The Christian Ministry: With an Inquiry into the Causes of Its Inefficiency*. Carlisle, PA: Banner of Truth Trust, 1959.

———. *An Exposition of the Book of Ecclesiastes*. New York: Robert Carter & Brothers, 1860.

"A Brief History." Charles Simeon Trust. 2025. https://simeontrust.org/about/a-brief-history/.

———. *Psalm 119: An Exposition*. Carlisle, PA: Banner of Truth Trust, 1974.

Brontë, Patrick. *The Maid of Killarney: or, Albion and Flora: a Modern Tale in Which Are Interwoven Some Cursory Remarks on Religion and Politics*. London: Baldwin, Cradock and Joy, 1818.

Brown, Abner. *Recollections of the Conversation Parties of the Rev. Charles Simeon, M. A., Senior Fellow of King's College, and Perpetual Curate of Trinity Church, Cambridge*. London: Hamilton, Adams, 1863.

Brown, John. *The Self-Interpreting Bible: Containing the Old and New Testaments, to Which Are Annexed an Extensive Introduction*. Edinburgh: Thomas Ireland, 1831.

Bull, Josiah. *Memorials of the Rev. William Bull, of Newport Pagnell*. Oxford: Oxford University Press, 1865.

Butler, Perry. "From the Early Eighteenth Century to the Present Day." In *The Study of Anglicanism*, edited by Stephen Sykes et al., 30-54. Minneapolis: Fortress, 2004.

Butler, Samuel. *The Way of All Flesh*. New York: E. P. Dutton, 1917.

Cadogan, William. *The Life of the Rev. William Romaine.* London: T. Bensley, 1796.
Carus, William, ed. *Memoirs of the Life of the Rev. Charles Simeon, M.A., Late Senior Fellow of King's College and Minister of Trinity Church, Cambridge.* London: J. Hatchard & Sons, 1847.
———. *The Personal Duties of the Minister: A Sermon Preached in the Parish Church of St Michael, Cambridge, on Thursday, July 24, 1845, at the Visitation of the Venerable the Archdeacon of Ely.* Cambridge: Cambridge University Press, 1845.
Chalmers, Thomas. *The Right Ecclesiastical Economy of a Large Town.* Edinburgh: John Anderson, 1835.
"The Churchman's Confession." *Eclectic Review* 2 (March 1806) 237.
Claude, Jean. *An Essay on the Composition of a Sermon.* Translated by Robert Robinson. Cambridge: Francis Hodson, 1779.
Close, Francis. *Apology for the Evangelical Party, Being a Reply to the Pamphlet of the Rev. W. Gresley, A.M., on "The Real Danger of the Church."* London: J. Hatchard, 1846.
———. *Nine Sermons Illustrative of Some of the Typical Persons of the Old Testament.* London: Hatchard, Hamilton, Adams, Lee, Wight, Lovesey, Davies, 1836.
———. *Occasional Sermons, Preached in the Parish Church of Cheltenham.* London: Seeley, Burnside, and Seeley, 1844.
Cowper, William. "There Is a Fountain." In *Trinity Hymnal,* 188. Philadelphia: Great Commission, 1961.
Denney, James. *Studies in Theology: Lectures Delivered in Chicago Theological Seminary by the Rev. James Denney, D.D.* London: Hodder & Stoughton, 1896.
Dickens, Charles. *The Pickwick Papers.* New York: Penguin, 1999.
Dyer, George. *Memoirs of the Life and Writings of Robert Robinson.* London: G. G. and J. Robinson, 1796.
Eliot, George. *Janet's Repentance: Scenes of Clerical Life.* New York: Norman L. Munro, 1883.
Fitzgerald, John. *The Quiet Worker for Good: A Familiar Sketch of the Late John Charlesworth.* London: Dalton & Lucy, 1865.
Flower, Benjamin. *National Sins Considered, in Two Letters to the Rev. Thomas Robinson, Vicar of St. Mary's, Leicester, on His Serious Exhortation to the Inhabitants of Great Britain, with Reference to the Fast: To Which Are Added a Letter From the Rev. Robert Hall, to the Rev. Charles Simeon; and Reflections on War, by the Late Rev. W. Law.* Cambridge: Benjamin Flower, 1796.
Haldane, Robert. *The Authenticity and Inspiration of the Holy Scriptures.* Edinburgh: William Whyte, 1845.
Hanna, William. *Memoirs of the Life and Writings of Thomas Chalmers.* 3 vols. New York: Harper & Brothers, 1850.
———. *Memoirs of the Life and Writings of Thomas Chalmers, D.D., LL.D.* 3 vols. New York: Harper & Brothers, 1851.
Jowett, Benjamin, et al. *Essays and Reviews.* London: John W. Parker, 1860.
Keach, Benjamin. *The Breach Repaired in God's Worship: or, Singing of Psalms, Hymns, and Spiritual Songs, Proved to Be an Holy Ordinance of Jesus Christ.* London: John Hancock, 1691.
Knight, William. *Memoir of Henry Venn.* London: Seeley, Jackson, and Haliday, 1882.
"The Late Dean of Carlisle." *Marlborough Express.* December 20, 1882. https://paperspast.natlib.govt.nz/newspapers/MEX18821220.2.26.

London Gazette, November 25, 1856, 3919.
Marlow, Isaac. *A Brief Discourse Concerning Singing in the Publick Worship of God in the Gospel-Church*. London, 1690.
Marsh, Catherine. *The Life of the Rev. William Marsh, D.D.* New York: Robert Carter & Brothers, 1868.
Members of the University of Oxford. *Tracts for Our Times*. London: J. H. Parker, Oxford, 1840.
———. *Tracts for the Times*. Vol. 1. New York: Charles Henry, 1839.
Morley, John. *The Life of William Ewart Gladstone*. Vol. 1. New York: Macmillan, 1903.
Moule, Handley C. G. *Charles Simeon*. London: Methuen, 1892.
Newman, John Henry. *An Essay on the Development of Christian Doctrine*. 6th ed. Notre Dame: University of Notre Dame Press, 2015.
———. *Lectures on the Prophetical Office of the Church*. London: J. H. Parker, Oxford, 1837.
———. *Newman on Worship, Reverence, and Ritual*. Edited by Peter A. Kwasniewski. New York: Os Justi, 2019.
———. *Parochial and Plain Sermons*. 1839. San Francisco: Ignatius, 1997.
———. *Parochial and Plain Sermons*. 4 vols. London: Longmans, Green, 1891.
Newton, John. *Apologia: Four Letters to a Minister of an Independent Church by a Minister of the Church of England*. London: J. Buckland and J. Johnson, 1784.
———. *Twenty-Five Letters Hitherto Unpublished, of the Rev. John Newton*. Edited by Robert Jones. Edinburgh, 1847.
———. *Wise Counsel: John Newton's Letters to John Ryland Jr*. Edited by Grant Gordon. Carlisle, PA: Banner of Truth Trust, 2009.
Newton, John, and William Cowper. *Olney Hymns*. London: Hamilton, Adams and Co, 1877.
———. *The Works of Rev. John Newton*. 4 vols. New York: Robert Carter, 1844.
Noble, John. *A Memoir of the Rev. Robert Turlington Noble*. Cambridge: Harvard University, 1867.
Pratt, Josiah. *The Thought of the Evangelical Leaders: Notes of the Discussions of the Eclectic Society London During the Years 1798-1814*. Edited by John H. Pratt. Carlisle, PA: Banner of Truth Trust, 1978.
Preston, Matthew Morris. *Memoranda of the Rev. Charles Simeon, M.A.* London: Richard Watts, 1840.
"Review of Biddulph's Essays on the Liturgy." *Christian Observer* 2 (1803) 558–61.
Rhea, Sarah J. *Life of Henry Martyn, Missionary to India and Persia, 1781 to 1812*. Chicago: Woman's Presbyterian Board of Missions of the Northwest, 1888.
Romaine, William. *The Life, Walk, and Triumph of Faith*. London: Routledge, 1871.
Ryle, J. C. *Christian Leaders of the 18th Century*. Carlisle, PA: Banner of Truth Trust, 2015.
———. *The Christian Leaders of the Last Century; or, England a Hundred Years Ago*. London: Nelson, 1869.
———. *Home Truths, Seventh Series*. London: William Hunt, 1859.
———. *Old Paths: Being Plain Statements on Some of the Weightier Matters of Christianity*. Carlisle, PA: Banner of Truth Trust, 2015.
Sargent, John. *The Life of the Rev. T. T. Thomason, M. A.* London: R. B. Seeley and W. Burnside, 1833.

———. *A Memoir of The Rev. Henry Martyn, B. D. Fellow of St. John's College, Cambridge; and Chaplain to the Hon. East India Company*. London: Seeley, Burnside, and Seeley, 1844.

Scougal, Henry. *The Life of God in the Soul of Man: or the Nature and Excellency of the Christian Religion*. London: Charles Smith & William Jacob, 1677.

Sidney, Edwin. *The Life of the Rev. Rowland Hill, A. M.* New York: D. Appleton, 1835.

Simeon, Charles. *Evangelical Religion: A Sermon Preached Before the University of Cambridge*. Cambridge: Pitt, 1837.

———. *Expository Outlines on the Whole Bible*. 21 vols. Grand Rapids: Zondervan, 1956.

Smith, George. *Henry Martyn: Saint and Scholar*. London: Religious Tract Society, 1892.

Spurgeon, Charles H. *The Autobiography of Charles H. Spurgeon, Compiled from His Letters, Diaries, and Records by His Wife and Private Secretary*. 4 vols. Cincinnati: Curtis & Jennings, 1900.

———. *Commenting and Commentaries: Two Lectures Addressed to the Students of the Pastors' College, Metropolitan Tabernacle, Together with a Catalogue of Biblical Commentaries and Expositions*. London: Passmore and Alabaster, 1876.

———. *Lectures to My Students*. Carol Stream, IL: Tyndale House, 2010.

———. *The Lost Sermons of C. H. Spurgeon: His Earliest Outlines and Sermons Between 1851 and 1854*. Edited by Christian George. Vol. 1. Nashville: B&H Academic, 2016.

Stock, Eugene. *History of the Church Missionary Society*. 3 vols. London: Church Missionary Society, 1899.

Sumner, J. B. *Apostolic Preaching Considered*. 8th ed. London: Hatchard, 1839.

———. *A Charge Delivered to the Clergy of the Diocese of Chester at the Primary Visitation in August and September 1829*. London: Hatchard, 1829.

Toplady, Augustus. "Rock of Ages." In *Trinity Hymnal*, 223. Philadelphia: Great Commission, 1961.

———. *Works*. 5 vols. London: Walter Row, 1794.

Trevelyan, G. O. *Life and Letters of Lord Macaulay*. 2 vols. London: Longmans, Green, 1876.

Venn, Henry. *The Complete Duty of Man: Or a System of Doctrinal and Practical Christianity*. Glasgow: William Collins, 1829.

———. *The Life and Letters of the Late Rev. Henry Venn, M. A.* New York: Protestant Episcopal Society for the Promotion of Evangelical Knowledge, 1855.

Venn, John. *Annals of a Clerical Family: Being Some Account of the Family and Descendants of William Venn, Vicar of Otterton, Devon, 1600–1621*. London: Macmillan, 1904.

———. *The Life and a Selection from the Letters of the Late Rev. Henry Venn, M.A.* London: John Hatchard, 1834.

Wesley, Charles. "Arise, My Soul, Arise." In *Trinity Hymnal*, 223. Philadelphia: Great Commission, 1961.

———. "Christ the Lord Is Risen Today." In *Trinity Hymnal*, 205. Philadelphia: Great Commission, 1961.

Wesley, John. *Free Grace: A Sermon Preach'd at Bristol*. 4th ed. London, 1754.

———. *The Letters of the Rev. John Wesley, A. M.* 6 vols. Edited by J. Telford. London: Epworth, 1931.

———. *The Works of the Rev. John Wesley, A. M.* London: Epworth, 1967.

Whitefield, George. *A Letter from the Reverend Mr. George Whitefield, to the Reverend Mr. John Wesley, in Answer to His Sermon, Entitled Free Grace*. Boston: G. Rogers, 1740.

Whittingham, Richard. *The Whole Works of the Rev. John Berridge, A.M.: Late Fellow of Claire-Hall, Cambridge, Vicar or Everton, Bedfordshire, And Chaplain to the Early of Buchan with a Memoir of His Life*. London: Ebenezer Palmer, 1864.

Williamson, John. *A Brief Memoir of the Rev. Charles Simeon, M. A.* Oxford: Oxford University Press, 1848.

Wilson, Thomas. *A Short and Plain Instruction and Preparation for the Better Understanding of the Lord's Supper*. London: Routledge, 1859.

Secondary Sources

Aitken, Jonathan. *John Newton: From Disgrace to Amazing Grace*. Wheaton, IL: Crossway, 2007.

Atherstone, Andrew. *Charles Simeon on the Excellency of the Liturgy*. Chippenham, UK: Joint Liturgical Studies, 2011.

———, ed. *The Heart of Faith: Following Christ in the Church of England*. Cambridge: Lutterworth, 2008.

Atherstone, Andrew, and David C. Jones. *Making Evangelical History: Faith, Scholarship and the Evangelical Past*. New York: Routledge, 2019.

Atkins, Gareth. *Converting Britannia: Evangelicals and British Public Life, 1770–1840*. Woodbridge, UK: Boydell, 2019.

Balleine, G. R. *A History of the Evangelical Party in the Church of England*. London: Longmans, Green, 1908.

Bebbington, David. *Evangelicalism in Modern Britain: A History from the 1730s to the 1980s*. New York: Routledge, 1989.

———. *William Ewart Gladstone: Faith and Politics in Victorian Britain*. Grand Rapids: Eerdmans, 1993.

Beeke, Joel R., and Randall J. Pederson. *Meet the Puritans: With a Guide to Modern Reprints*. Grand Rapids: Reformation Heritage, 2006.

———. *Reformed Preaching: Proclaiming God's Word from the Heart of the Preacher to the Heart of His People*. Wheaton, IL: Crossway, 2018.

Bennett, Clinton. "Martyn, Henry." In *Biographical Dictionary of Christian Missions*, edited by Gerald H. Anderson, 438–39. New York: Macmillan Reference USA, 1998.

Benson, Arthur C. *Fasti Etonenses: Biographical History of Eton Selected from the Lives of Celebrated Etonians*. London: Eton R. Ingalton Drake, 1899.

Binns, Leonard Elliott. *The Evangelical Movement in the English Church*. Garden City, NY: Doubleday, 1928.

Booty, John, et al., eds. *The Study of Anglicanism*. Minneapolis: Fortress, 2004.

Bray, Gerald. *Anglicanism: A Reformed Catholic Tradition*. Bellingham, WA: Lexham, 2021.

"Bridges, Charles." Cambridge Alumni Database. https://venn.lib.cam.ac.uk/cgi-bin/search-2018.pl?sur=&suro=w&fir=&firo=c&cit=&cito=c&c=all&z=all&tex=BRGS812C&sye=&eye=&col=all&maxcount=50.

Brown, Ford K. *Fathers of the Victorians: The Age of Wilberforce*. Cambridge: Cambridge University Press, 1961.

Brown, Stewart J., et al., eds. *The Oxford Handbook of the Oxford Movement*. Oxford: Oxford University Press, 2017.

Carter, Grayson. *Anglican Evangelicals: Protestant Secessions from the Via Media, c. 1800–1850*. Eugene, OR: Wipf & Stock, 2001.

Cecil, Richard. *The Life of John Newton*. Fearn, Scotland: Christian Focus, 2000.

Chadwick, Owen. *The Victorian Church: Part One, 1829–1859*. London: SCM, 1971.

Chalmers, Thomas. *The Expulsive Power of a New Affection*. Minneapolis: Curiosmith, 2012.

"Charles Simeon." Britannica. https://www.britannica.com/biography/Charles-Simeon.

Chester, Tim. *Stott on the Christian Life: Between Two Worlds*. Wheaton, IL: Crossway, 2020.

The Church of England. *The Book of Common Prayer and Administration of the Sacraments and Other Rites and Ceremonies of the Church According to the Use of the Church of England*. Cambridge: Cambridge University Press, 1964.

Collins, Irene. *Jane Austen and the Clergy*. New York: Hambledon & London, 1994.

Cook, Faith. *Our Hymn Writers and Their Hymns*. Durham: Evangelical, 2015.

Davies, George C. B. *The First Evangelical Bishop: Some Aspects of the Life of Henry Ryder*. London: Tyndale Press, 1958.

Drummond, Lewis. *Spurgeon: The Prince of Preachers*. Grand Rapids: Kregel, 1992.

Dudley-Smith, Timothy. *John Stott: The Making of a Leader*. Leicester: Inter-Varsity Press, 1999.

Elliot-Binns, L. E. *The Early Evangelicals*. London: Lutterworth, 1953.

Green, Dudley. *Patrick Brontë: Father of Genius*. Stroud, UK: NonSuch, 2010.

Green, Vivian H. H. *John Wesley*. Lanham, MD: University Press of America, 1987.

Gregory, Jeremy, ed. *The Oxford History of Anglicanism, Volume 2: Establishment and Empire, 1662–1829*. Oxford: Oxford University Press, 2017.

Gribben, Crawford. *John Owen and English Puritanism: Experiences of Defeat*. Oxford: Oxford University Press, 2016.

Hague, William. *William Wilberforce: The Life of the Great Anti-Slave Trade Campaigner*. New York: Harper, 2008.

Harding, Alan. *Selina, Countess of Huntingdon*. Eugene, OR: Wipf & Stock, 2007.

Hardwick, Joseph. "Australia and New Zealand." In *The Oxford History of Anglicanism: Vol. 2: Establishment and Empire, 1662–1829*, edited by Jeremy Gregory, 236–252. Oxford: Oxford University Press.

Harris, Khim. *Evangelicals and Education: Evangelical Anglicans and Middle-Class Education in Nineteenth Century England*. Eugene, OR: Wipf & Stock, 2007.

Haydon, Colin, et al., eds. *The Church of England c. 1689–c. 1833: From Toleration to Tractarianism*. Cambridge: Cambridge University Press, 1993.

Haykin, Michael A. G., ed. *The Armies of the Lamb: The Spirituality of Andrew Fuller*. Classics of Reformed Spirituality. Dundas, ON: Joshua, 2001.

Haykin, Michael, and Jeffrey Robinson. "Particular Baptist Debates About Communion and Hymn-Singing." In *Drawn into Controversie: Reformed Theological Diversity and Debates within Seventeenth-Century British Puritanism*, edited by Michael A. G. Haykin and Mark Jones, 285–308. Göttingen: Vandenhoeck & Ruprecht.

Haykin, Michael, and Kenneth Stewart, eds. *The Emergence of Evangelicalism: Exploring Historical Continuities*. Leicester: Apollos, 2008.

Hempton, David. *Methodism: Empire of the Spirit.* New Haven: Yale University Press, 2005.
Hennell, Michael. "Simeon and the Ministry." In *Charles Simeon (1759-1836): Essays Written in Commemoration of His Bi-Centenary by Members of the Evangelical Fellowship of Theological Literature,* edited by Michael Hennell and Arthur Pollard, 139-58. London: SPCK, 1964.
———. *Sons of the Prophets: Evangelical Leaders of the Victorian Church.* London: SPCK, 1979.
Hennell, Michael Murray. *John Venn and the Clapham Sect.* London: Lutterworth, 2003.
Hennell, Michael, and Arthur Pollard, eds. *Charles Simeon (1759-1836): Essays Written in Commemoration of His Bi-Centenary by Members of the Evangelical Fellowship of Theological Literature.* London: SPCK, 1964.
Hindmarsh, D. Bruce. *John Newton and the English Evangelical Tradition.* Oxford: Oxford University Press, 1996.
———. *The Life and Spirituality of John Newton.* Vancouver: Regent College, 2003.
———. *The Spirit of Early Evangelicalism: True Religion in a Modern World.* Oxford: Oxford University Press.
Hopkins, Hugh E. *Charles Simeon of Cambridge.* London: Hodder & Stoughton, 1977.
Hylson-Smith, Kenneth. *Evangelicals in the Church of England, 1734-1984.* Edinburgh: T&T Clark, 1988.
Introvigne, Massimo. *The Plymouth Brethren.* Oxford: Oxford University Press, 2018.
Jenkins, Gary. *A Tale of Two Preachers: Preaching in the Simeon-Stott Tradition.* Cambridge: Grove, 2012.
Ker, Ian. *John Henry Newman.* Oxford: Oxford University Press, 2009.
Klein, Milton. *An Amazing Grace: John Thornton and the Clapham Sect.* New Orleans: University Press of the South, 2004.
Liddon, Henry Parry. *Life of Edward Bouverie Pusey–Doctor of Divinity Canon of Christ Church: Regius Professor of Hebrew in the University of Oxford.* 4 vols. London: Longmans, Green, 1894.
Livingston, James C. *Modern Christian Thought: The Enlightenment and the Nineteenth Century.* Minneapolis: Fortress, 2006.
Loane, Marcus. *Cambridge and the Evangelical Succession.* Fearn, Scotland: Christian Focus, 2007.
———. *John Stott: A Portrait by His Friends.* Edited by Chris Wright. Downers Grove, IL: InterVarsity Press, 2011.
"Location: Parish (Church): Cambridge Holy Trinity." Clergy of the Church of England Database. https://theclergydatabase.org.uk/jsp/locations/DisplayLocation.jsp?locKey=870.
Marsden, J. B. *Memoirs of the Life and Labours of the Rev. Samuel Marsden of Paramatta.* Cambridge: Cambridge University Press, 1858.
Milner, Mary. *Life of Isaac Milner.* New York: Kessington, 2010.
Murray, Iain. "The Controversy Between Whitefield and Wesley–1740." In *The Recurrence of Synergism after the Reformation,* edited by John Hendryx, 48-50. Monergism, 2018.
———. *The Forgotten Spurgeon.* Carlisle, PA: Banner of Truth Trust, 1966.
———. *J. C. Ryle: Prepared to Stand Alone.* Carlisle, PA: Banner of Truth Trust, 2016.
Nockles, Peter. "Church Parties in the Pre-Tractarian Church of England 1750-1833: The 'Orthodox'—Some Problems of Definition and Identity." In *The Church of England c. 1689-c. 1833: From Toleration to Tractarianism,* edited by Colin Haydon et al., 334-59. Cambridge: Cambridge University Press, 1993.

Noll, Mark. *The Rise of Evangelicalism: The Age of Edwards, Whitefield, and the Wesleys.* Leicester: Inter-Varsity Press, 2004.

"Our Story." Church Mission Society. https://churchmissionsociety.org/about/our-story/.

Packer, J. I. "Expository Preaching: Charles Simeon and Ourselves." In *Preach the Word: Essays on Preaching, in Honor of R. Kent Hughes*, edited by Leland Ryken and Todd A. Wilson, 140–54. Wheaton, IL: Crossway, 2007.

———. *A Quest for Godliness: The Puritan Vision of the Christian Life.* Wheaton, IL: Crossway, 2010.

Parsons, K. A. C., ed. *Church Book: St Andrew's Street Baptist Church, Cambridge 1720–1832.* Baptist Historical Society, 1991.

Pearson, Hugh. *The Life and Correspondence of the Reverend Christian Frederick Swartz.* New York: Saxton & Miles, 1842.

Pibworth, R. Nigel. *The Gospel Pedlar: The Story of John Berridge and the Eighteenth-Century Revival.* Welwyn Garden City, UK: Evangelical, 1987.

Piper, John. *Brothers, We Are Not Professionals: A Plea to Pastors for Radical Ministry.* Nashville: Broadman & Holman, 2002.

———. *The Roots of Endurance: Invincible Perseverance in the Lives of John Newton, Charles Simeon, and William Wilberforce.* Wheaton, IL: Crossway, 2002.

Pollard, Arthur. "The Influence and Significance of Simeon's Work." In *Charles Simeon (1759–1836): Essays Written in Commemoration of His Bi-Centenary by Members of the Evangelical Fellowship of Theological Literature*, edited by Michael Hennell and Arthur Pollard, 159–84. London: SPCK, 1964.

———. *Let Wisdom Judge: University Addresses and Sermon Outlines by Charles Simeon.* Leicester: Inter-Varsity Press, 1959.

Prime, Derek. *Charles Simeon: An Ordinary Pastor of Extraordinary Influence. History Today.* Leominster, UK: Day One, 2011.

Prior, Karen Swallow. *Fierce Convictions: The Extraordinary Life of Hannah More: Poet, Reformer, Abolitionist.* Nashville: Nelson, 2014.

Russell, George W. E. *A Short History of the Evangelical Movement.* London: Mowbrays, 1915.

Scotland, Nigel A. D. *Evangelical Anglicans in a Revolutionary Age.* Exeter: Paternoster, 2004.

———. "John Bird Sumner, 1780–1862: Claphamite Evangelical Pastor and Prelate." In *Bulletin of John Rylands Library* 74 (1992) 57–74.

———. *John Bird Sumner: Evangelical Archbishop.* Leominster, UK: Gracewing, 1995.

———. *The Life and Work of John Bird Sumner.* Leominster, UK: Gracewing, 1995.

Seymour, Aaron Crossley Hobart. *The Life and Times of Selina Countess of Huntingdon.* Vol. 1. London: William Edward Painter, 1839.

Slinn, Sara. *The Education of the Anglican Clergy—1780–1839.* Martlesham, UK: Boydell, 2017.

Spinks, Bryan D. "The Book of Common Prayer, Liturgy, and Worship." In *The Oxford History of Anglicanism: Vol. 2: Establishment and Empire, 1662–1829*, edited by Jeremy Gregory, 253–69. Oxford: Oxford University Press, 2017.

Toon, Peter, and Michael Smout. *John Charles Ryle: Evangelical Bishop.* Chicago: J. Clarke, 1976.

Smyth, Charles. *Simeon and Church Order: A Study of the Origins of the Evangelical Revival in Cambridge in the Eighteenth Century.* Cambridge: Cambridge University Press, 1940.

Stott, John. *The Authority of the Bible.* Downers Grove, IL: InterVarsity, 1974.

———. *Between Two Worlds: The Challenge of Preaching Today.* Grand Rapids: Eerdmans, 2017.

———. *Evangelical Preaching: An Anthology of Sermons by Charles Simeon.* Portland, OR: Multnomah, 1986.

Stunt, Timothy C. F. *The Elusive Quest of the Spiritual Malcontent.* Eugene, OR: Wipf & Stock, 2015.

Thomas, Philip H. E. "Doctrine of the Church." In *The Study of Anglicanism*, edited by Stephen Sykes et al., 249–61. Minneapolis: Fortress, 2004.

Van Dixhoorn, Chad. *Creeds, Confessions, and Catechisms: A Reader's Edition.* Wheaton, IL: Crossway, 2022.

Virgin, Peter. *The Church in an Age of Negligence: Ecclesiastical Structure and Problems of Church Reform 1700–1840.* Cambridge: James Clarke, 1989.

Walsh, John, and Stephen Taylor. "Introduction: The Church and Anglicanism in the 'Long' Eighteenth Century." In *The Church of England c. 1689–c. 1833: From Toleration to Tractarianism*, edited by Colin Haydon et al., 1–66. Cambridge: Cambridge University Press, 1993.

Webster, Douglas. "Simeon's Pastoral Theology." In *Charles Simeon (1759–1836): Essays Written in Commemoration of His Bi-Centenary by Members of the Evangelical Fellowship of Theological Literature*, edited by Michael Hennell and Arthur Pollard, 73–119. London: SPCK, 1964.

Winstanley, Denys Arthur. *Early Victorian Cambridge.* Cambridge: Cambridge University Library, 1955.

Yates, Nigel. *Eighteenth-Century Britain: Religion and Politics, 1714–1815.* Harlow, UK: Pearson, 2008.

Dissertations and Theses

Balda, Wesley D. "'Spheres of Influence': Simeon's Trust and Its Implications for Evangelical Patronage." PhD diss., Cambridge University, 1973.

Becht, Barbara. "Charles Simeon: Evangelical or Churchman? Simeon's Contribution to the Baptismal Controversy in the Early Nineteenth Century." MA thesis, Durham University, 1995.

Bennett, John C. "Charles Simeon and the Evangelical Anglican Missionary Movement: A Study of Voluntaryism and Church-Mission Tensions." PhD diss., University of Edinburgh, 1992.

Moore, E. R. "John Bird Sumner: Bishop of Chester 1828–48." MA thesis, University of Manchester, 1976.

www.ingramcontent.com/pod-product-compliance
Lightning Source LLC
Chambersburg PA
CBHW070324230426
43663CB00011B/2210